BRIDGESCAPES

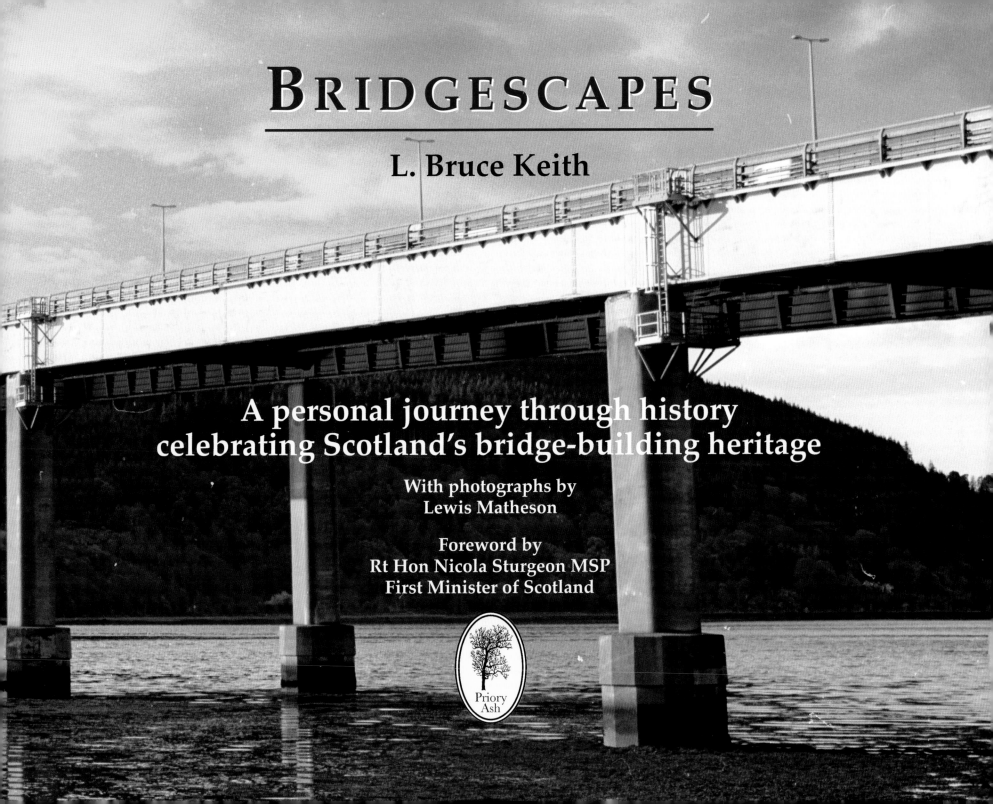

BRIDGESCAPES

L. Bruce Keith

A personal journey through history
celebrating Scotland's bridge-building heritage

With photographs by
Lewis Matheson

Foreword by
Rt Hon Nicola Sturgeon MSP
First Minister of Scotland

Priory
Ash

This book is dedicated to Debbie and Lauren,
and to the Scottish bridge engineers, past and present,
whose structural legacy stands as testimony to their innovation,
and to the thousands of skilled workers whose toil is embedded in our heritage.

© Dunnottar Productions Limited

First published in 2017

British Library Cataloguing in Publication Data

A catalogue record for this book is available
from the British Library.

ISBN 978 0 9566387 3 1

Published by
Dunnottar Productions Limited
Orchard House
322 Thorpe Road
Longthorpe
Peterborough PE3 6LX

In association with
Priory Ash Publishing
2 Denford Ash Cottages
Denford
Kettering
Northamptonshire NN14 4EW

Printed and bound in the Czech Republic

ACKNOWLEDGEMENTS

Producing this book has been a protracted project. I've had a lifelong interest in bridges and started researching the subject in earnest about 15 years ago, but this was an extracurricular activity until I retired in 2014.

The book revolves around images, as they capture the beauty of these structures within the landscape, so my greatest thanks go to Lewis Matheson for his invaluable contribution.

Along the way I've been fortunate to meet several acknowledged experts in this field, most notably Professor Roland Paxton; Peter Cross-Rudkin; Mike Chrimes and Carol Morgan at the Institution of Civil Engineers; Alastair Cullen-Wallace; Iain Murray, Don Fraser, Michael Martin and David Watt at the Queensferry Crossing project; architectural historians at the Royal Commission on the Ancient and Historical Monuments of Scotland (RCAHMS) in Edinburgh; Linda Burke at the Mitchell Library in Glasgow, the National Library of New Zealand in Wellington and Jordana King at the Ottawa Public Library; Professor Gordon Masterton and Karen Dinardo at the Institution of Engineers and Shipbuilders in Scotland; Dr Emily Goetsch and Lorna Black at the National Library of Scotland; Fintan Ryan and Laura Graham at the National Galleries of Scotland; and the Burns Museum, all of whom gave me welcome advice and encouragement.

I also acknowledge the expertise and enthusiasm of local history societies, such as the Montrose Basin Heritage Society, who produce valuable source material.

Special thanks are due to Mike Lowson for his editorial skills and invaluable advice, Carol Scales, the late Tam Dalyell, Colin Shearer, Iain Matheson, Jane Morris, Deborah Keith and Lauren Keith, Will Adams and Michael Sanders of Priory Ash, and a host of friends and acquaintances who have provided support and advice as Lewis and I tried to produce this celebration of our national civil engineering heritage.

I alone take responsibility for any errors which appear.

L. Bruce Keith
Peterborough
2017

CONTENTS

FOREWORD

by Rt Hon Nicola Sturgeon MSP, First Minister of Scotland

Growing up in Ayrshire meant that from early childhood I was aware of the rich legacy of engineering and transport heritage on my doorstep.

My home town of Dreghorn was the birthplace of John Boyd Dunlop, who developed the pneumatic tyre. The oldest surviving public railway viaduct in the world, Laigh Milton, crosses the River Irvine, and in 1816 became one of the first structures to carry a steam engine. The viaduct was authentically restored in the 1990s, open to the public to use as a footbridge while marvelling at the engineering prowess of yesteryear and how the Kilmarnock to Troon Railway paved the way for Scotland's impressive track record in endeavour and innovation.

John Miller's massive viaduct at Ballochmyle was the largest masonry railway arch in the world when it was opened in 1848, and the 23 arches of his Kilmarnock Viaduct from 1850 still dominate the regenerated townscape.

During my childhood in the 1970s, Scottish bridge engineering flourished. The Kingston Bridge, carrying five lanes of traffic in each direction across the Clyde in the heart of Glasgow, opened in 1970, and the following year witnessed the completion of the longest box-girder and cable-stayed bridge in the world, the Erskine Bridge. There were

impressive new bridges at Bonar in the north, at Ballachulish in the west and at Galafoot in the Borders. The 1980s and '90s brought the Kessock, Cromarty and Dornoch bridges in Inverness and the far north-east, while in the north-west who could fail to marvel at the elegance and setting of the Kylesku Bridge, and for the first time since the Ice Age Skye was linked to mainland Scotland with the completion of the Skye Bridge.

The new Millennium has continued that pedigree of bridge engineering excellence. Glasgow proudly boasts both a 'Squinty' and a 'Squiggly' Bridge, as well as the Port Eglinton Viaduct, a key component of the improved transport links and urban regeneration in the city. There's world-class infrastructure evidenced at the Clackmannanshire Bridge, and here, as at the Forthside Pedestrian Bridge in Stirling and the award-winning footbridge at Bracklinn Falls, we see innovations pioneered in the design and construction techniques and the use of both traditional native-grown timber and sustainably recycled materials. In 2015 UNESCO designated the Forth Rail Bridge, the Victorian icon that was the largest civil engineering structure in the world in the 19th century, a World Heritage Site – there is no other country of Scotland's size that has not one, but six, such designations.

Our bridge heritage is interwoven with our industrial, commercial, social and cultural pedigree, which this book seeks to demonstrate through Scotland's history and personal anecdote.

Scotland has earned and sustained a worldwide reputation for civil and bridge engineering, manifested in the legacy of its skills and endeavours not only at home and throughout the UK, but across the globe. This book celebrates the contributions that Thomas Telford, the Rennies, Sir William Arrol and numerous others whose bridges made and, in many cases, continue to make, on every continent. That heritage is not only physical. The very foundations of the civil engineering profession were cast by Scots – not only the Institution of Civil Engineers, but also the American Society of Civil Engineers. Neither is the legacy that solely of engineering brains – we must also honour the countless thousands of Scots whose brawn – sheer endeavour, fortitude

Nicola Sturgeon, First Minister of Scotland, at Bute House, Edinburgh. *The Scottish Government*

and labour – created the structural heritage that they built, the economies they forged and the communities they spawned, and frequently in hostile terrain and harsh environments.

I am especially proud in 2017 to witness the construction of the latest in the long history of Scottish bridges, and, as First Minister, to officiate at its opening. The Queensferry Crossing heralds a new generation of bridge-building in Scotland. It is already in the record books on several counts, including being the longest three-tower cable-stayed bridge in the world. Moreover, it is elegant and it is majestic. It does that while being wholly functional, built to serve Scotland's economy and people, and those who visit, just as bridges have done for centuries past, but in a fashion that displays its 21st-century pedigree.

While revisiting past glories brings a well-placed sense of national pride, it is an important element of this book that it also acknowledges the home-grown skills and talents of today's professional bridge engineers and the contribution many, including Iain Murray, Don Fraser and Michael Martin, have made and continue to make to Scotland's bridge-building heritage both here and internationally.

Rt Hon Nicola Sturgeon MSP
First Minister of Scotland
Bute House,
Edinburgh
June 2017

INTRODUCTION

This book is not intended for 'anoraks'. It isn't a chronicle of every last engineering fact. Instead, it's a celebration of design, ingenuity, intuition and endeavour, in Scotland and beyond. It celebrates the contribution bridges make to Scotland's heritage and legacy and, by so doing, encourages those journeying throughout the country to value them for just that. In appreciating these structures, we gain a better understanding of Scotland's history, its landscape and its people.

It might also help those who suffer from 'gephyrophobia', an anxiety disorder brought about by the fear of crossing bridges. If you have dealt with your fear by avoiding journeys that take you over bridges, this book aims to show you what you've been missing!

But it's much more than just a book about bridges. Woven into the history is a journey – a highly personal journey that has taken me from childhood on the shores of Loch Ness to opposite sides of the world in North America and Australia. It is one of discovery, of family and friends, of professional experiences, and of personal agonies when a life-changing car crash threatened to end my life's journey permanently and very prematurely.

Thankfully, I survived to continue my fascination with the stunning achievements of those Scots who saw every unbridged river, road, ravine or rough moorland as a challenge to be met.

It is also a journey full of warmth and laughter with the close friends and acquaintances I have gained in my personal life and throughout my professional career, and the many remarkable characters I have met along the way.

Writing his excellent *Bridges of Britain* in 1954, Eric de Maré observed that '… any work which helps people to become more aware of their environment must be of some value.'

With this book I hope to create a sense of the significance of bridges in Scottish history, and the contribution they make to the landscape heritage.

A number of the photographs are by Lewis Matheson, a talented young Scottish photographer specially commissioned for the book. He has also sourced archived evidence that illustrates bridge-building's evolution. Together these elements demonstrate bridges' visual quality in their individual design but, more particularly, how that has made a dramatic and, almost without exception, enhancing impact on their environs and surrounding landscape.

We're delighted, for example, to have sourced a photograph from 1871 when the photographer commissioned to capture on celluloid the opening of the Boatford Bridge, a 175-foot-span timber suspension bridge over the River Esk at Langholm, got the scoop of his life. As he clicked the shutter, one of the iron chains broke and the bridge collapsed, sending 30 children and 60 adults tumbling 'into the river amidst a mass of broken timber'. Aside from the drenching, the severest injury was sustained by an 86-year-old man who broke two ribs. Undaunted, the bridge was replaced in 1873.

Our bridge heritage manifests itself not only at home. Scotland's contribution to the development of new technologies and advances in knowledge and understanding in a wide range of disciplines extends well beyond her own shores. The Scottish Enlightenment in the 18th and 19th centuries yielded Scots who made a huge progressive contribution in the fields of medicine (James Simpson), world exploration (Mungo Park and David Livingstone), philosophy (David Hume), and economics (Adam Smith).

Not least among these were celebrated Scottish civil and bridge engineers such as Thomas Telford, the Mylnes and both John Rennies, whose Scottish bridges occur repeatedly throughout the book and whose influence beyond these shores are described in their own chapter.

I am actually writing this Introduction as I cross the magnificent Forth Rail Bridge, opened in 1890, on a ScotRail train heading to Edinburgh. To my right, I can see the Forth Road Bridge, a marvel of its time when it opened in 1964, and beyond that, a little way upriver, is the awe-inspiring new Queensferry Crossing, opened in 2017. I doubt there is anywhere on the planet with three more impressive and iconic bridges so close to each other.

If things had been different, perhaps my lifelong passions might instead have involved football or astronomy, wildflowers or aviation, rock music or stamp collecting. There are those who have waxed long and lyrical about each of those subjects, and many more besides, but I am proud that it is our bridges and the people who designed and built them that have held my interest for as long as I can remember.

Scotland has often led the way when it comes to amazing bridges. I hope you enjoy this journey through their history with me.

Disaster at Boatford Bridge, from *Echoes from the Borders Hills* by J. P. Hyslop (1912). *Courtesy of the National Library of Scotland*

1. WHY BRIDGES?

From keystones to a key moment

On many occasions during my formative years I had a crick in my young neck caused by standing in a pair of wellies in some Highland burn, gazing upwards at the voussoirs and keystone of an arched bridge, as my father, James Forbes Keith, Bridge Engineer for Inverness-shire County Council, inspected the masonry for tell-tale cracks of unwanted structural movement.

His job took him all over that vast county, including the Western Isles, inspecting the rich legacy of bridges, many dating from General Wade's extensive road- and bridge-building activity in the early 18th century

So convinced was I that this was the natural way for a three-year-old to behave that, on a day trip to Edinburgh Zoo in 1958 during a visit to my grandparents in Forfar and Dundee, I disappeared from my parents' side at the polar bear enclosure to be found, after some searching, inspecting the small hump-back bridges formed as part of the network of paths linking the animal enclosures.

Although I was born in Nigeria, where my father was working at the time, I was brought up in Dores. This makes me sound like a hothouse plant ('brought up indoors'), but we lived there, in Torr Gardens, in a two-storey council house with a view over Loch Ness from my bedroom window.

Before my sister, Sheelagh, was born in 1959, my mother and I used to accompany Dad on bridge inspection sojourns, sometimes for up to three days, to Skye and the Outer Isles. The Kyle of Lochalsh Hotel was a frequent rest spot before catching the ferry to Kyleakin. In those days the thought of a bridge across to Skye would have been a distant pipe dream.

In 1960 my parents bought our first family home, a large bungalow in Balloch, 5 miles east of Inverness. Set in about half an acre of garden, it enjoyed panoramic views over the Moray Firth and the Black Isle, stretching to Ben Wyvis, a Munro of 3,432 feet that dominates Easter Ross.

From those early days, I've had a yearning for adventure and exploring, but it has to be said that I've always been slightly accident-prone. Careering down the hill into Balloch on my first two-wheeler bike, I managed to be catapulted over the handlebars, resulting in my being unconscious for four days.

When I regained consciousness, I found myself in Inverness Infirmary, somewhat confused, and spent the next 10 days working on an escape plan. I made it halfway across the adjacent Infirmary Bridge, crossing the River Ness, before

Growing up outdoors in Dores (*right*), and a day trip to Edinburgh Zoo. *Both J. Forbes Keith*

Escape route: the Infirmary Bridge, Inverness. *Mike W. Lowson*

recapture. I suspect that the swaying and bouncing motion of the pedestrian suspension bridge must have felt even stranger than normal, having just come out of unconsciousness. Bridges were continuing to feature in many key events in my life.

The memory plays strange tricks, too. My mother, a remedial primary school teacher, told me years later that if she had not been distraught about her son's recovery, my regaining consciousness would have been an interesting experience for her as I spent several hours reciting my spelling homework, including, moments before coming round, the words I'd been learning parrot-fashion from the evening before the bike accident.

My first three years of formal education were at Balloch Primary School. The main building still stands, although the school has expanded its footprint considerably and there have been several applications of whitewash since my day.

Balloch is now a satellite village for Inverness, rapidly becoming a suburb, but in the early 1960s there were just three teachers for seven years of primary schoolchildren. The headmaster, Mr MacLean, taught Primary Six and Seven, his wife taught Primary One and Two, and Primary Three, Four and Five were taught by Mrs MacQueen, a native Gaelic speaker, I recall, although learning Gaelic was not on the curriculum.

Judging by the way the redoubtable Mrs MacQueen reinforced the 'three Rs', with a particularly thorough execution of spelling, punctuation and grammar, she had also learned the English language along the way and was determined that we would do likewise. No wonder I was reciting spelling homework in hospital, even although I was barely conscious.

Balloch Primary's three classes combined totalled just 24 pupils, with only eight in my class. At least my mother could announce without fear of contradiction that 'our Bruce is in the top eight'. To this she would add, much to my merriment, '…and the other seven are brain surgeons.'

Whether any of them became brain surgeons is unknown, but I do know that two of us became chartered surveyors, and on the rural side initially, too. When sitting my Test of Professional Competence for the RICS qualification in 1979 – a gruelling four-day event in a windswept Hampshire – I met again John Robin Bound. We both passed and he went on to a successful career in land agency, becoming senior partner in an important Highland practice. There can be few instances where 25% of a primary school class become chartered surveyors.

My father was by now Divisional Roads Surveyor for Inverness-shire County Council and, in addition to all his involvement with bridges, one of his other responsibilities was the snowcrews. This was especially tough in 1962/63, which was the coldest winter for more than 200 years and is still one of the coldest on record.

One day after school, Mum, Sheelagh and I were visiting our neighbours, the Frasers, well known as having the Duncan Fraser & Sons butcher's shop in Inverness. In fact, our neighbours on both sides were Frasers, which is relatively easy to achieve in a village a few miles from the Highland capital.

While we were visiting, almost 4 feet of snow fell. Dad got a lift home in a snowplough and we were rescued by the snowcrew, which was very exciting for a seven-year-old. On more than one occasion I went out with snowcrews in one of the huge Mack lorries from the depot in Diriebught Road and recall sitting on the driver's knee and steering the snowplough as it made its way down the hill at Daviot on the old A9. I don't think there could have been Risk Assessments and Method Statements in those days.

Incidentally, the bridge across the River Nairn at the foot of the Daviot brae was one of the first improvements on the A9. My father inspected it one day when the ground was snow-covered, and when he returned to his office he couldn't find his pen. Several months later he was back inspecting the bridge and there, lying where he'd dropped it, was his pen, still in working condition.

Dad came home one evening very excited because the contractor excavating the site of a new car park at Culloden Battlefield, just over a mile up the road from our house, had unearthed a musket that had been dated back to the 1746 massacre of the Jacobite army. Enthused by the prospect of further such historic finds, I made the long uphill slog to Culloden Moor on my bike immediately after school the next day, to conduct my own archaeological search. My mother was not too amused when I arrived home with a fusty old plastic comb, claiming it had probably been used by Bonnie Prince Charlie to ensure he was looking his best.

My history knowledge has improved and my evidence-gathering has become more rigorous since then, but my fascination with tangible historic artefacts remains.

Like so many youngsters of my pre-videogame generation, my interest in how things worked was kindled by Meccano and Lego. With my nascent interest in bridges growing as quickly as I was, many hours were spent, often unsuccessfully, trying to create a bridge arch that would stand up on its own in 3D.

My father's idea of an ideal game for a wet Sunday afternoon was a puzzle involving long division or long multiplication. I'm not sure that would go down too well these days, more's the pity, but it certainly gave me an interest in puzzle-solving and fostered an impulsive and enquiring mind, especially when it came to bridges.

Bridges have long fascinated not only young boys but also engineers and lay persons alike. Their structural and architectural challenge create a beauty in design and symmetry that can be viewed and appreciated by all.

National treasures, including our built heritage, have been captured frequently on stamps and coins, and in 2003 the Royal Mint published four new designs by the wood engraver Edwina Ellis for the £1 coin. They celebrate solid British engineering, including the cantilever Forth Rail Bridge and Scottish engineer Thomas Telford's Menai Strait Bridge in Wales.

Even the country's banks acknowledge the importance of bridges. For example, a Bank of Scotland £5 note features the Brig o' Doon, immortalised by Scotland's national bard, Robert Burns, while a Clydesdale Bank £5 note features the Forth Rail Bridge on one side and Sir William Arrol on the other.

Scotland boasts a rich and varied heritage. Its landscape and history combine to provide a legacy of human endeavour, ingenuity and endurance. The diversity of landform and natural features, from rugged mountain terrain to wide productive estuarial carses and firths, has heavily influenced the evolution of Scotland's communication network, be it to military ends or a product of socio-economic development and industrial expansion.

Within that heritage lies a tangible and functional element of Man's Creation – the bridge – linking lands and communities while providing a structural artefact and landscape element that goes beyond its primary purpose. As author John Buchan said:

'The bridge … is a symbol of man's conquest of nature… History – social, economic and military – clusters more thickly about bridges than about towns and citadels.'

Speaking in 1931, Franklin D. Roosevelt, soon to become 32nd President of the United States, said:

'There can be little doubt that in many ways the story of bridge building is the story of civilisation. By it, we can readily measure an important part of a people's progress.'

There are more than 120 place names in Scotland that mark the presence of a bridge, showing that these structures have played a fundamental part in the evolution of the country's history. The numerous references to bridges in naming towns, villages, crossings and meeting places attest to their importance to the very fabric of Scottish life. Many bridges conjure up images of Scotland in their own right, such is their power to provoke a sense of national pride.

Few can fail to be impressed by the iconic Forth Bridges as they span the divide between the Kingdom of Fife and the Lothians, conveying rail and road traffic on majestic structures. Now they are three in number; the 19th-century rail bridge, the 20th-century road bridge and a new road bridge, representing engineering prowess in the 21st century.

As with the Forth, the road bridges that link Easter Ross and Sutherland with Inverness, the Highland capital, are functional conduits for locals and visitors alike, and enhance the scenic vistas as they cross the Beauly, Cromarty and Dornoch firths.

Equally impressive are the many stone-arched curving viaducts spanning wide, deep valleys to carry railways, with their requirement for minimal gradients, to the towns of the north and west. Many date from the Great Age of Railway Engineering in the latter half of the 19th century, and supplanted the canal network, which itself engendered significant engineering works, including the use of aqueducts to traverse differing land contours.

Many of these railway bridges still carry significant passenger and freight traffic, and the canals have been given a rebirth following restoration and their promotion as leisure and recreation routes. This recent reincarnation has itself spawned new engineering development, most notably in the Falkirk Wheel, opened in 2002, linking the Forth & Clyde and Union canals. Part of this impressive structure is an aqueduct, signifying a new era in bridge-building in Scotland with the arrival of the 21st century.

But bridges come in all shapes and sizes and serve many purposes, and they don't need to be on an expansive scale or major engineering designs to be remarkable or impressive in their own right. As Robert Mylne remarked in his 'Observations on bridge-building' in 1760: '… when the magnificent is procured by the simple and the genuine, it pleases universally.'

Writing in 1951, Colonel T. U. Wilson, County Surveyor of Lanarkshire, commented:

'…an attempt should also be made in bridge design to harmonise the bridge with its surroundings – the proportions of the structure and its main architectural features must be such that it is satisfactory in itself and in harmony with neighbouring features.'

11

Fifty fascinating facts...

We all have a curious fascination with 'records', hence the reason why the *Guinness Book of Records* is a perennial best-seller. At university in the 1970s everybody studied statistics – at least, we did at Reading University. My favourite textbook, and one into which I have occasionally delved for a refresher since graduation, is the Pelican classic *Use and Abuse of Statistics* by W. J. Reichmann (1970). But none of that numerical dexterity that passes for insightful analysis here. Just some fascinating empirical evidence that demonstrates the significance of Scotland's bridges and her engineers in a series of straightforward and unambiguous facts.

The oldest...
- surviving single-arch bridge in Scotland – Brig o' Balgownie (c1320)
- surviving multiple-arch stone bridge in Scotland – Auld Brig, Dumfries (1432)
- surviving public railway viaduct in the world – Laigh Milton Viaduct (1811)
- surviving cast-iron bridge in Scotland – Craigellachie (1814)
- surviving suspension bridge in Britain still carrying traffic – Union Bridge, Borders (1820)
- surviving cable bridge in Scotland – Infirmary Bridge, Inverness (1879)

The first...
- bridge to use elliptical arches – Avenue Bridge, Dumfries House (1759)
- bridge across the River Clyde in Glasgow in more than 400 years – Broomielaw Bridge (1772)
- bridge to carry a road on internal spine walls arising from the arch rings – Tongland Bridge (1804)
- bridge designed by Thomas Telford in Scotland – Tongland Bridge (1804)
- wire suspension bridge in the UK – Galashiels (1816)
- combination of suspension and cantilever principles in the UK – King's Meadow, Peebles (1817)
- suspension bridge of sufficient width to carry vehicular traffic – Union Bridge, Borders (1820)
- President of the Institution of Civil Engineers – Thomas Telford (1820)
- President of the American Society of Civil Engineers – James Laurie (1852)
- major bridge structure using steel as the principal component – Forth Rail Bridge (1890)
- female member of the Institution of Civil Engineers – Dorothy Donaldson Buchanan (1927)
- tied bowstring-arch bridge in Scotland – Bonar Bridge (1973)
- lightweight concrete bridge in Europe – Friarton Bridge (1978)
- cable-stayed bridge with a harp configuration in the UK – Kessock Bridge (1982)
- major capital project in Scotland to be funded by the Private Finance Initiative (PFI) – Skye bridge (1995)
- bridge in the world to be constructed entirely of composites – plastics and polythene-clad Kevlar aramid fibre cables – bridge at Aberfeldy golf course (1995)
- rotating boat lift in the world, with associated aqueduct – Falkirk Wheel (2002)

The longest/largest...
- surviving medieval bridge – Auld Brig, Dumfries (1432)
- aqueduct in Europe, when opened – Kelvin Aqueduct, Glasgow (1790)
- single-span granite arch in the world – Union Bridge, Aberdeen (1805)
- span wrought-iron suspension bridge in the western world, when completed – Union Bridge, Borders (1820)
- aqueduct in Scotland (second in the UK) – Avon Aqueduct, near Linlithgow (1821)
- masonry railway arch in the world, when completed – Ballochmyle Viaduct (1848)
- iron bridge in the world when opened – first Tay Rail Bridge (1877) – but it collapsed!
- iron bridge in the world when opened – the existing Tay Rail Bridge (1887), still the longest railway bridge in Britain
- cantilever bridge in the world when opened – Forth Rail Bridge (1890). It remains the second longest, after the Quebec Bridge, which opened in 1917. The cantilever length is measured here, as the Forth Rail Bridge is the longest in overall length.
- civil engineering structure built anywhere in the world in the 19th century – Forth Rail Bridge (1890)

- masonry viaduct in Scotland – Culloden Viaduct (1898)
- concrete viaduct (and the first to use mass concrete) – Glenfinnan Viaduct (1901)
- concrete railway arch in the world – Borrodale Viaduct (1901)
- swing bridge in Europe – Kincardine Bridge (1936)
- suspension bridge outside the USA when opened – Forth Road Bridge (1964), holding the title in Europe until 1966
- cable-stayed bridge in the world when opened – Erskine Bridge (1971)
- cable-stayed bridge in Europe when opened – Kessock Bridge (1982)
- pedestrian swing bridge in the world – Bell's Bridge, Glasgow (1988)
- free-standing balanced cantilever in the world – Queensferry Crossing (October 2016) (This record, upheld by the *Guinness Book of Records*, endured until the connecting viaducts were in place during construction!)
- three-tower cable-stayed bridge in the world – Queensferry Crossing (2017)

The highest...
- bridge in the world when constructed – Old Dunglass Road Bridge (1798)
- aqueduct in Scotland – Avon Aqueduct, near Linlithgow (1821)
- bridge over inland water in Scotland – Cartland Crags Bridge (1822)
- railway bridge in Britain – Ballochmyle Viaduct (1848)
- or rather the tallest bridge in Britain – Queensferry Crossing (2017)

If the above impressive recital was not a sufficient claim to fame, the Kingston Bridge in Glasgow has the **heaviest** steel piles of any bridge in the UK and witnessed the **biggest**-ever bridge-lift operation, involving 128 hydraulic jacks, when it was realigned in 1999.

Beyond Scotland, Thomas Telford built the second-ever iron bridge at Buildwas (1796), the Pontcysyllte aqueduct (1805), which is the longest and highest in Britain, and the world's first large suspension bridge at the Menai Strait (1826). In the Canadian Rockies, James Leveson Ross built the world's highest timber bridge across Stoney Creek in Rogers Pass in 1885.

Scotland has a rich legacy of stone bridges, built initially to achieve military ends but which now serve as an integral part of the highway network or, where bypassed by a new road development, survive as an important heritage or landscape feature. It's usually both. Bridges dating from medieval times built from ecclesiastical funds to bring footweary congregations to church still stand, often in picturesque settings, as a memorial to times past.

Landed estates provided bridges to ease transportation, both vehicular and pedestrian, round their properties. Many also capture symbolism in design and bring a strong element to the environment within which they're set.

That such a relatively small country has such a magnificent portfolio of bridges of all sizes, ancient and modern, is a lasting tribute to the engineers and workers who designed and built them, and those who maintain them. It's also an inspiration to the youngsters of today who, like me all those years ago, will look up at them in wonder and ask, 'How did they do that?'

Bridges continue to play a significant role in my life. In 1981 I was involved in a serious car crash. The injuries sustained, multiple compound fractures to both legs and more bones broken in my hips and left arm, meant that I spent five months in an Edinburgh hospital bed. Further months were spent recuperating and re-learning to walk.

But on the evening of 23 October 1983 I boarded a Greyhound coach in Washington DC to undertake the next leg of a tour of the Eastern USA, an overnight journey to Detroit followed by a local bus to Port Huron in Michigan. From there I walked, unaided and carrying a hefty rucksack, across the St Clair River on the Blue Water Suspension Bridge into Sarnia in Ontario. I had crossed from the USA into Canada by bridge, but for me it was a much greater achievement. It was a key moment. It marked two years and two days since my horrendous accident. I had survived and there would be many more bridges to cross.

Each time I encounter a bridge, whether it's an iconic structure or a humble arch, I never fail to reflect on the countless people who have crossed it, all on a journey and all with a mostly untold tale to tell.

So, in answer to the question 'Why bridges?', with a childhood and background like mine, it couldn't really be anything else.

2. DESIGN AND CONSTRUCTION

From simple planks to spectacular icons

There are many excellent books written on civil and structural engineering theory and design. This isn't one of them. That said, a brief introduction to the basic principles involved allows an understanding of the main designs and how these have evolved together with engineering expertise and experience and the use of different construction materials.

There are only five principal engineering designs used in bridge construction, each of which dictates the shape and character of the physical structure.

Beam

The simplest form of bridge is the beam type, akin to placing a log or plank across a watercourse or ravine to provide a straight line between one side and the other. Many modern road bridges are of this design, carrying carriageways on piers across extensive widths of rivers, such as the Tay Road Bridge and the bridges across the Cromarty and Dornoch firths as well as a multitude of motorway flyovers and service bridges. The beam is supported on piers, which transmit the load forces to the foundations in the ground.

Truss

A development of the beam design is the truss, which has been described as a 'beam with braces'. The design of a truss, usually a variant of a triangle, creates both a very rigid structure and one that transfers the load from a single point to a considerably wider area. A journey through Scotland will encounter several types of truss design, from the lattice truss in railway viaducts such as Dalguise to the Vierendeel-type truss used in the concrete bridge across the River Findhorn at Tomatin. At Dalguise, a substantial number of relatively lightweight elements are used, which eases the task of construction. Across the Findhorn, many of the diagonal elements are eliminated so the openings are rectangular rather than triangular, with fixed joints. A further variation is the bowstring truss, such as that used at Bonar Bridge. The traditional temporary military bridge, the Bailey Bridge, is also a variant of the truss principle.

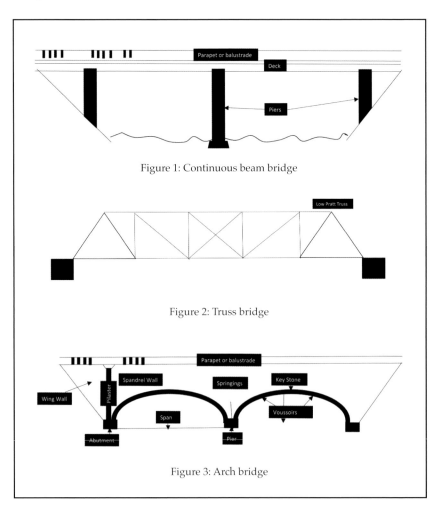

Figure 1: Continuous beam bridge

Figure 2: Truss bridge

Figure 3: Arch bridge

Arch

More geometrically complicated, but used as a design for bridges from Roman times, arch construction involves the individual components, normally stones called voussoirs, being built towards a central keystone at the apex. The load forces are transmitted by direct thrust down the piers. Arches can be built in combination with a series of spans creating a long, low bridge, such as those at Musselburgh and Perth.

With a sizeable single semi-circular arch, the roadway it supports might require to be sloped at either end with ramps, giving rise to the appropriately named 'boo-backit', a bow or hump-backed bridge. Examples of such bridges can be picturesque, particularly against a wilderness backdrop, such as Caulfeild's 1763 bridge at Spittal of Glenshee on the military road between Blairgowrie and Braemar, or set amid the forests, such as at Bridge of Dye, erected in 1680.

But the hump can pose problems, too, and might lead to the bridge becoming obsolete, at least economically. Such was the case with a splendid little bridge in Methven parish in Perthshire. Dating from 1786, rather than the 1619 often ascribed, the Bridge of Ardittie, near Millhaugh, has an unusually high single segmental, almost semi-circular, arch over the River Almond. The resultant humped road became too steep for the horse-drawn carts hauling stone from local quarries, so it was bypassed from the 19th century.

Figure 3a: Semi-circular or full centred arch

Figure 3b: Segmental arch

The use of 'ribbed' arches, as a refinement, allowed for lighter and speedier construction, and reduced the load on the foundations and the quantity of timber centring needed during construction. Examples include Bridge of Dye on the Cairn o' Mount road and the Cramond Brig across the River Almond, which flows into the Forth. Dating from about 1488, the original three stone arches at Cramond witnessed many reconstructions from 1619 onwards but, unlike most arch bridges, the centre arch is narrower than the two flanking arches, rather than the reverse.

Immortalised in the tale of Jock Howieson and the Gudeman of Ballengeich, writer and poet Sir Walter Scott tells of King James V (1512-42) being attacked by a gang of robbers while walking over Cramond Brig. In disguise as the Gudeman of Ballengeich, the King was rescued by a local tenant farmer, young Jock, who farmed at Braehead and was

A series of arched spans can be used to create a long, low bridge, such as Smeaton's Bridge at Perth. *Deborah M. Keith*

Bridge of Dye. *Mike W. Lowson*

15

rewarded by being granted ownership of the farm. But Jock and his descendants were also required to wash the hands of the monarch, and his successors, whenever he or she crossed Cramond Brig. Highly likely to have been a legend embellished by Scott for his *Tales of a Grandfather*, nonetheless he ensured that the practice was fulfilled during King George IV's visit to Scotland in 1822, which Scott himself masterminded. It's been a tradition ever since.

A further development of the arch type came through the building of canals and, more particularly, railways, where the bridge followed the

principal line of the track but with piers constructed parallel to the banks of the river. This is termed 'skewing' and demanded a high standard of stone cutting and a knowledge of solid geometry, as each row of voussoirs lies differently from the others. Good examples of this can be seen at Warriston Viaduct in Edinburgh, dating from 1841, but this type of design was widely used thereafter in masonry bridges.

The use of elliptical stone arches, as in John Rennie's Kelso Bridge, brings an attractive symmetry to the structure. The bridge design creates opportunities for different styling, adding embellishment to the structural purpose. An open spandrel arch with false spandrel walls is used to fine effect on the Invergarry Bridge.

Cramond Brig. *Lewis Matheson*

A skew arch at Warriston Viaduct, Edinburgh. *Lewis Matheson*

Suspension

The fourth type of bridge is of more modern invention, but relies on the reciprocal physics to that of the arch. The suspension bridge is an inverted arch, where the chain or wires hold the carriageway in

suspension – a tensile rather than a compressive force. It's like a washing line, usually with two equally spaced 'props' and the line secured by anchorages at each end.

The suspension bridge had certain advantages over an arch bridge. It was cheaper per length of span, it could be prefabricated and erected relatively quickly, and its span would appear to offer unlimited potential. It was a particularly useful design in a country with a high flood risk, if the piers could be secured properly without undue risk of scour.

Scotland played a significant part in the history of suspension bridge technology. The iron wire cable suspension bridge erected by Richard Lees at Galashiels in 1816 to link parts of his extensive woollen mill was certainly the first of such construction in Britain, and probably only the second in the world.

Several pedestrian suspension bridges were pioneered across the River Tweed in the first quarter of the 19th century, but the most significant, and the first of its kind wide enough to carry carriages, was the impressive Union Bridge constructed in iron in 1820 by Captain, later Sir, Samuel Brown, whose other notable achievement was the chain pier at Brighton.

A product of the newly emerging bridge technology, using wrought-iron bars instead of cables to suspend the deck, the Union Bridge when opened on 26 July 1820 was the largest-span wrought-iron suspension bridge in the Western world. It was a further six years before Thomas Telford completed the Menai Bridge.

Today, the Union Bridge, which spans the border between Scotland and England (Fishwick to Horncliffe), is the oldest surviving suspension bridge in Britain still carrying vehicular traffic, albeit restricted to a single light vehicle at a time. It cost £7,700 in 1820, compared with £20,000 for a masonry bridge of similar span. Major refurbishment plans

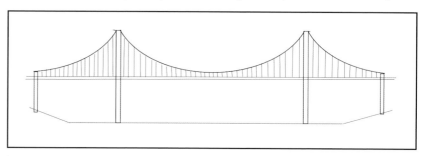

Figure 4: Suspension bridge

17

Union Bridge, Borders. *Lewis Matheson*

are in hand, estimated at £5.6 million, to restore the bridge and provide visitor facilities in time for its 200th anniversary in 2020.

Suspension bridges do have a certain charm. The one across the River Nith at Whitesands in Dumfries, designed by John Willet and erected in 1875 by J. Abernethy & Co of Aberdeen, was described in the local paper as '…an airy graceful thing of beauty that might have been conjured into existence by the wand of an Eastern magician.'

Cable-stayed

Cable-stayed bridges appear similar to suspension bridges, but are more akin to the cantilever design. The deck is supported by a series of individual cables, in tension, anchored on a pylon or tower. The deck is built out from the pylon in a series of cantilevers on either side of the pylon, with the stays arranged in either a fan or harp formation.

In a cable-stayed bridge the deck is in compression, unlike a suspension bridge where it is hung from the suspension cables. The principal advantage of a cable-stayed bridge over a suspension bridge is the ability to increase the overall length of the crossing by multiplying the number of pylons.

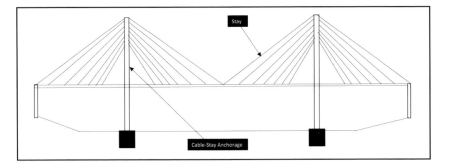

Figure 5: Cable-stayed bridge (fan design)

Cantilever

The fifth method of design is a further development of the truss principle, used in reverse. In a cantilever truss bridge the use of the 'balanced cantilever' method enables the construction to proceed outwards in each direction from a central vertical span. Usually these are built in pairs until the outer sections can be anchored by footings.

The most notable example of the cantilever is the Forth Rail Bridge, with its double balanced cantilevers that support linking short suspended beam spans. This bridge is also an early example of steel

The Forth Rail Bridge design is demonstrated using human 'cantilevers', Baker's assistant Kaichi Watanbe representing the live load.

The timber-built Old Oich Bridge. *Deborah M. Keith*

Broomhill Bridge. *Mike W. Lowson (above) / Lewis Matheson*

used in bridge-building, with its three-yearly cycle of continuous painting of its 145 acres of surface steelwork becoming a hyperbole for structural maintenance programmes.

The magnificent structure, completed in 1890 and probably over-engineered as a consequence of the failure some 11 years earlier of the original Tay Rail Bridge, is the pinnacle of Victorian bridge-building in Scotland, but not the first to use the cantilever principle. Here, the Tweed again played a part. The King's Meadow Bridge, built by Captain Napier in 1817, downstream from Peebles, is the first example using a combination of cantilever and suspension techniques.

Materials

Bridges can be constructed of many materials. Stone was the traditional component, and more durable than timber, which was a common material in early bridge-building. Wood is not as hard-wearing as stone or steel, so examples of wooden bridges are more difficult to find.

One of the oldest timber bridges in the UK, although now in a ruinous condition, is the four-span wooden trestle Old Oich Bridge at Fort Augustus. Originally on the 18th-century military road, Joseph Mitchell constructed the wooden bridge in 1850, following extensive damage to the stone bridge by the floods the previous year. Efforts by the Fort Augustus Preservation Trust to secure funds for the now substantial remediation works required have been unsuccessful thus far.

On an unclassified road at Broomhill, near Nethy Bridge, stands a timber bridge across the River Spey, resting on 15 timber trestles between stone abutments. Built in 1894 and restored in 1987, this bridge is designed to accommodate the substantial floodwaters for which Scotland's fastest-flowing river is renowned, by being significantly longer than the river channel is wide.

In 1895 George Riddoch, of the timber merchants and sawmilling family at Rothiemay in Aberdeenshire, constructed a massive wooden trestle bridge to cross a steeply wooded gorge at Dramlach, near Fochabers, as a means of extracting timber. Considering that he had very limited machinery to hand, this was a noteworthy human endeavour to manhandle and secure the tree trunks, cross-bearers and diagonal braces into position.

That said, the showpiece must be the Aultnaslanach Viaduct on the Highland Railway, just north of Moy. It is a five-span wooden trestle bridge, opened in 1897, and the last of its kind on a main-line railway in Scotland. It has been retained as a wooden structure due to the difficulty in securing foundations for either a steel or masonry bridge.

Cast iron, a product of the Industrial Revolution in the late 18th century, brought greater strength and was improved further with the production of **wrought-iron** girders, used for the first time in a bridge near Glasgow in 1841.

The development of **steel** brought a stronger and more uniformly reliable material. Its use as embedded reinforcement rods to take the tension to match the compressive forces in **concrete** structures greatly lightens the structure, allowing greater height and indeed elegance to be achieved. The Forth Road Bridge, completed in 1964, is an excellent example, incorporating modern techniques of pre-stressing and pre-tensioning the reinforcement rods to deliver a graceful yet functional design.

The principles of design apply to all bridges, mostly singularly, but not uncommonly, in combination. Not all bridges are what they appear, however. Glasgow's George V Bridge gives the appearance of a three-span masonry arch but is actually a continuous beam bridge, the superstructure resting on roller bearings making it independent of the substructure. This was a novel concept when it was built in 1928. The polished granite masonry on this 430-foot-long bridge is merely a façade for the reinforced concrete box-girder construction.

Moveable or opening bridges also use the beam principle, although the demands of road traffic have necessitated the replacement of many of the early swing bridges. At Fort Augustus, for example, a plate girder swing bridge, powered by a petrol engine, was constructed in 1932 to replace the original cast-iron bridge dating from the original Caledonian Canal construction of the early 1800s.

Certain bridges have a dual role. In addition to providing an access route they also act as a barrier to entry. The hinged drawbridge across a castle's fortified moat illustrates this function, and Stirling Castle provides a good example dating from the 15th century. Modern Health and Safety requirements mean that there are no longer any operational

Ben Nevis towers over Banavie Swing Bridge, Fort William. *Canmore*

drawbridges in Scotland, but if safety could be guaranteed I am sure that they would add much to the visitor experience at the likes of Cawdor or Stirling castles.

Construction

Hand-in-hand with the development of bridge engineering, the techniques used in the construction of much of the industrial and commercial infrastructure put in place during the 18th and 19th centuries led to significant advances, which were then applied by the bridge-builder. Most notable were the design and construction of tunnels, sewerage systems and the development of harbours.

Multi-span arches across rivers are going to have wet feet, so to speak, and the task of securing immoveable foundations, where the scouring effect of the current of water channelled between the arches will put the structure in peril, proved daunting. The answer was the **cofferdam**, an idea borrowed from harbour engineering, which provided a watertight temporary structure built to enclose a construction area where the work could be carried out in dry conditions. This allowed the construction of the piers with their lower parts strengthened by aptly named 'cutwaters' or variously shaped 'starlings', which added not only substance to the foundations but longevity to the bridge.

Securing the foundations is paramount in any building, and bridge-builders go to great efforts to ensure that the structures are not at risk from undermining from the strong currents frequently encountered when crossing rivers. If possible, the foundations will be anchored in the bedrock. The use of **caissons** is fundamental to bridge construction across water. These are floated into position and settled onto the river bed, where they remain in situ. By removing their temporary bottoms, the excavations can continue down to a solid foundation beneath the river bed.

So, the difference between a cofferdam and a caisson is that the former is generally temporary, while the latter is permanent.

The beauty of any bridge design is that it is not just about theoretical algebra and geometry, but must also do its job. I learned this self-evident lesson with those fledgling Meccano and Lego bridges I tried to build as a youngster.

The mid-20th century saw my father designing a new generation of bridges that would provide modern road communication links for the forestry, hydro-electric and tourist industries, which were regenerating economic activity in the Highlands and Islands of Scotland.

As a newly qualified civil engineer, he had spent five years designing and building bridges in colonial Nigeria before returning to Scotland and setting up home at Dores. His experiences in West Africa taught him that severe weather can cause significant rivers to change course in a few hours, to leave the bridge he designed and built crossing dry land.

He didn't reckon that he'd experience similar incidents in his native land, but that was the fate of the first bridges he constructed on the ski road that opened up Loch Morlich and the new ski-lift at Cairngorm to the rapidly developing tourist centre at Aviemore. A mighty storm in that vicious winter of 1962/63 brought enormous boulders crashing down the mountainside, becoming lodged under the series of newly completed steel and concrete beam bridges, with the river waters diverted hundreds of yards from their original course. As the accompanying photograph shows, there was a massive rescue operation to recover cars safely, including the rather fine Jaguar Mark IX, which had been caught upstream of the now redundant bridges. Bridge-builders, like enthusiastic youngsters, must always ensure that pragmatism takes precedence over pride.

A Jaguar car being rescued at Cairngorm following the storm of 1962/63. *J. Forbes Keith*

3. MEDIEVAL BRIDGES
From Bannockburn to Burns

As a young secondary school student at Stirling High School, in the very centre of Scotland, I was fascinated by history. It was hard to avoid it, of course, with the majesty of Stirling Castle and the nearby Wallace Monument constantly in view, and the location of the 1314 epoch-making Battle of Bannockburn just a few miles away.

One day we visited Bannockburn and Charles d'Orville Pilkington Jackson's magnificent bronze statue of a mounted King Robert the Bruce. I was excited, as the man who led the Scots cavalry at the battle was a knight called Robert Keith, Marischal of Scotland. I wasn't sure if he was a distant relative of mine, but I was puzzled when I read the National Trust for Scotland (NTS) guide and saw him wrongly called Sir Alexander Keith. Despite my tender years, I wrote to the NTS to point out the error and they wrote back thanking me, saying that no one had ever previously queried that. My enthusiasm as a would-be history detective was ignited and I soon progressed to sleuthing about my passion for the country's bridges and their history.

The move to Stirling followed a five-year stay in Edinburgh, whence we had moved when my father took up a post in the Roads Department of the Department of Transport, based there. It was a move into motorway design and construction when that was in its infancy in Scotland.

In late 1963 we 'flitted' from Inverness to our new home in Barnton on Edinburgh's west side. I had to travel home from school by bus, a very different experience from walking up and down the hill to Balloch Primary School. As a thrifty Scot, however, I often walked the length of Queensferry Road to save the threepenny bus fare.

My new school was very close to Dean Bridge, and exploring its hinterland of Edinburgh's New Town opened my eyes to the power of architecture and how Telford's magnificent bridge added grandeur to the scene. I also came to realise the importance of Telford's structure in providing access to the land beyond the Water of Leith for further speculative building development as Edinburgh expanded in the 19th century. Perhaps it was this experience that sowed the seeds of interest in town and country planning, which was to be an ingredient in my chosen career as a chartered surveyor. Making history come alive through the evidence on the ground was certainly a discovery that has influenced my interests to this day.

In 1964 I pedalled across the new Forth Road Bridge a week or so after its official opening. The bridge brought new horizons for my exploration. The Kingdom of Fife was now on my doorstep and I frequently cycled to Culross, Dunfermline and Aberdour, there and back across the new bridge. Back and Forth, you might say!

My other quest in these 'Special Years' was to find the source of the River Almond. I'd make an early start, immediately after breakfast, at the mouth of the river where it enters the Forth at Cramond. From there I'd cycle on the paths along its banks, crossing over the old Cramond Brig and under the then new bridge carrying the dual carriageway between Edinburgh and the Forth Road Bridge. About a mile upriver I'd cross to the east side again by way of an old narrow stone arched bridge near the Army Scotland HQ and onwards to Edinburgh Airport, or Turnhouse as it was then called.

Past Kirkliston and gazing out over the massive Almond Valley Viaduct, my journey took me to Livingston, only then beginning to be developed around the old village as a major new town serving the needs of West Lothian and a distant Edinburgh.

I'm not sure that I ever did find the source of the river on these expeditions. The Calders certainly featured in my itinerary, but by then the number of tributaries, including Linhouse Water, had become somewhat unwieldy. It was some time in the 1980s, while inspecting a proposal by a hill farmer to plant coniferous trees above Cobbinshaw Loch, in the Pentlands, that I finally had it confirmed that I'd reached the source of the Almond.

My father's subsequent appointment as County Road Surveyor at Stirling County Council in 1968 meant that we moved to Stirling. Having been heavily involved while in Edinburgh in the design of the M8 and the M9 – the Polmont to Falkirk bypass, then the Stirling bypass – he now had the chance to oversee the building of the latter, with its bridges across the meandering River Forth and Bannock Burn and several major interchanges, most notably the link into the M80 to Cumbernauld and Glasgow.

I learned to drive on a motorway – well, at least one that was about to open. We used to go out on a Sunday afternoon when the new motorway was at an advanced stage of construction, for my father to

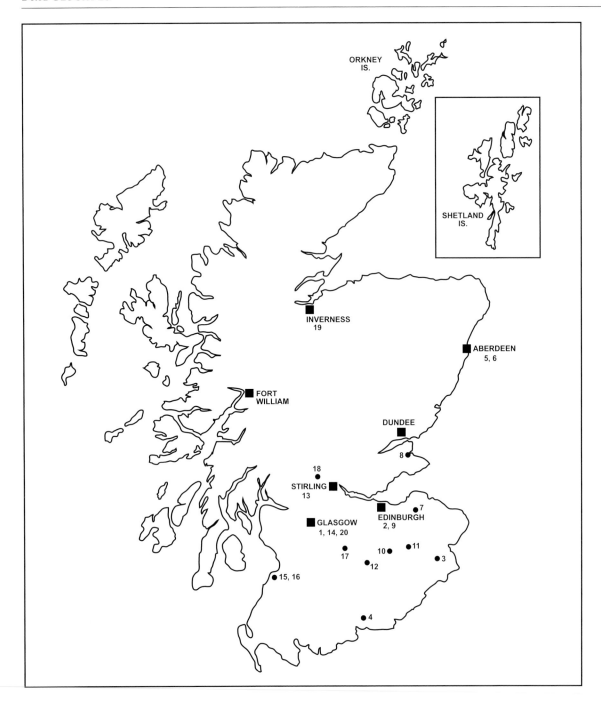

Medieval bridges
Key to bridges mentioned in the text

1	Balmuildy, Bishopbriggs	NS 581 718
2	Musselburgh	NT 340 725
3	Leader Water, Melrose	NT 573 347
4	Auld Brig, Dumfries	NX 968 760
5	Brig o' Balgownie	NJ 941 096
6	Brig o' Dee	NJ 929 035
7	Nungate, Haddington	NT 519 737
8	Guard Bridge	NO 451 188
9	Maiden Bridge, Newbattle	NT 336 665
10	Peebles Bridge	NT 250 403
11	Stow, Gala Water	NT 458 443
12	Cadger's Brig, Biggar	NT 038 376
13	Stirling Bridge	NS 797 946
14	Bothwell Brig	NS 712 576
15	Auld Brig, Ayr	NS 338 221
16	Brig o' Doon	NS 332 178
17	Kirkfieldbank	NS 868 439
18	Doune	NN 721 012
19	Inverness (River Ness)	NH 665 451
20	Great Bridge of Glasgow	NS 591 645

undertake a 'routine inspection'. As a 16-year-old I drove him along the roadway in a Mini 850, learning three-point turns, emergency stops and winding down the window to give exaggerated arm/hand signals to imaginary other motorists.

My dream car at the time was a Mini Pickup. The boy who lived next door, Mitchell Brown, had one. He was training to be a building surveyor.

My favourite subjects at the High School of Stirling, to give it its 'Sunday name', were history and geography. As so often in life, one of the underlying reasons was that my subject teachers were truly inspiring.

Donald MacCallum, aka 'Tinman', taught Higher history and employed the teaching technique of slightly mispronouncing words or names so that his students couldn't fail to remember them. He had a certain way of placing the emphasis on a different syllable than the normal practice. For example, the Tolpuddle Martyrs became the Tolpuddle Mar*tyres*, and we learned that the fertility of farmland was improved during the Agricultural Revolution through the application of farmyard man*ure*. Good old FYM, which featured heavily in my early days as a rural surveyor when calculating the unexhausted manurial value, or UMV, of a field for a farm valuation.

Whether it be the ancient structures of our forefathers that I studied in history classes, or the contemporary constructions of the present day that cropped up in lessons on modern geography, all bridges are built for a purpose. They are a means to an end, to cross a divide, usually a river or ravine, to ease passage between two places.

The Ancient Greeks built arched bridges from the 4th century BC, the earliest example being the Rhodes Footbridge. The Romans were also earnest road- and hence bridge-builders who left a rich legacy of structures throughout most of their former Empire, including the monumentally striking Pont du Gard at Nimes in southern France and the Segovia aqueduct in central Spain.

But the all-conquering Romans had a struggle on their hands when they came to Scotland, known then as the Caledonian kingdom. Hadrian built a high wall at the gateway to Scotland, and Antonine built a second wall, more akin to massive earth embankments and trenches, across the Forth and Clyde divide to keep the Picts beyond the extremity of Empire. Both were significant engineering feats.

The Romans

Sadly, no intact legacy of Roman bridge-building remains in Scotland. Agricola built a bridge over the Forth, presumed to have been to the west of Stirling, to transport his army northwards. The Picts tried to break it down but the Romans managed to return hastily to save it. There were substantial Roman forts at Carmuirs (near Falkirk), Ardoch (Braco), Strageath (Strath Earn), Bertha (Redgorton, near Perth) and Cargill (Perthshire), and a legionary fortress at Inchtuthill (also Perthshire), so presumably there must have been bridges crossing the Rivers Carron, Earn, Almond, Tay and Isla. The Picts reputably built a bridge at Dunkeld.

At **Balmuildy**, near Bishopbriggs, an Antonine Wall fort and camp extending to some 4 acres was extensively excavated by the archaeologist S. N. Miller between 1912 and 1914. It's on the southern bank of the River Kelvin, so one might have expected there to have been a bridge crossing for the Military Way. In 1941 the Board of Agriculture deepened the River Kelvin as part of an arterial drainage scheme and retrieved debris that had formed the stonework of the Roman bridge. The stones included some with obtuse-angled faces, which might have formed part of the cutwater of a free-standing pier, and others are likely to have been part of the abutments and foundations.

The absence of voussoirs led archaeologists to conclude that the bridge platform had been timber. A timber beam recovered from the Kelvin in 1942, which was initially thought to be part of the Antonine Wall bridge, was, however, later carbon-dated and found to be from a tree felled in about 1360! An oak beam does remain, though, and it, together with stones from the bridge and other stones found from a dredging operation in 1982, are in Glasgow's Hunterian Museum.

Two stone abutments found in Polmont Burn in 1992 had channels in the stone, which may have supported horizontal wooden beams, and the old packhorse bridge at Inverkip is alleged to have replaced a Roman crossing. The Old Bridge across the River Esk at **Musselburgh** lays claim to be known as the 'Roman Bridge', but the original foundation was built over with a two-arched medieval structure. Now a cobbled footbridge, it carried the Scots army marching to the Battle of Dunbar in 1296 and the English army in retreat in 1314, following its defeat at Bannockburn.

There must have been several Roman bridges in Scotland. We know there was one taking the great Roman road known as Dere Street over the **Leader Water** near Melrose, as it is referred to by the local minister writing in 1743. It's thought to have been sited between the Leaderfoot Viaduct and the Old Drygrange Bridge, which replaced the even older road bridge in 1780. Several artefacts, including a marble statuette of a Roman god, have been found in the Leader Water, which is not surprising given the significant Trimontium Roman fort and settlement nearby.

The Antonine Wall also passed very close to Clydebank. There was a Roman fort from which several artefacts have been found and most probably a bridge over the Duntocher Burn. The so-called Roman Bridge is, however, an 18th-century creation of Lord Blantyre, including the Latin inscriptions. Substantial repairs to this bridge had to be carried out in 1943 following damage caused by German bombs in the Clydebank Blitz of March 1941.

In south-west Scotland there are several old stone packhorse bridges without parapets over the Water of Minnoch, a tributary of the River Cree, which lies predominantly in the Galloway Forest Park. These structures date from the 17th and 18th centuries but are locally alleged to be Roman bridges. Much more likely is that the name derives from the gypsy, or Romany, people who travelled these lands.

Early Scots' bridges

Devorgilla, the mother of John Balliol, who was to be crowned King of Scotland in 1291, put the first bridge across the River Nith in the 13th century. It was a wooden bridge of 13 arches, but was replaced in 1432 by the nine-stone-arched 'Auld Brig', itself restored in 1620 following a flood. With only six arches remaining, this bridge in Dumfries is now used as a footbridge and is the longest medieval bridge and the oldest surviving multiple-arch stone bridge in Scotland.

The earliest surviving bridges in Scotland date from the late Middle Ages, from the 14th to early 16th centuries. How do we know? Maps have always held a fascination for me. Early recollections of entertaining myself in my father's office in Diriebught Road in Inverness by poring over old Ordnance Survey sheets while he finished his day's work, or creating my own maps of local haunts with coloured crayons, were probably the early glimmerings of my love of geography at school and of my subsequent career as a chartered surveyor.

The symbols used in mapmaking are key to so much information. This is not only critical if you are dependent on the map – your ability to

The 'Auld Brig', Dumfries. *Canmore*

read one correctly could determine whether or not you get safely off that hill walk that seemed a gentle stroll before the mist descended – but they also yield vital clues to the historian researching early settlements, transport routes and customs.

The earliest detailed mapping surveys of Scotland were carried out by Timothy Pont (1565-1614), a Scottish cartographer whose work was published in Joan Blaeu's *Atlas of Scotland* in 1654. Together with Roy's maps of the Military Survey of Scotland, conducted between 1747 and 1755, we gain an insight into the bridges that existed towards the end of the medieval period, albeit that most were small structures and those of wood had a relatively short lifespan.

It is some considerable credit to the engineering acumen of the times that despite horrendous flood events over the centuries, almost 30% of the stone bridges are still standing in substantially the form in which they were built.

Their purpose falls into three distinct categories: ecclesiastical, trade and military.

Ecclesiastical bridges

Ecclesiastical bridges were built to provide access for parishioners to the local church. Examples include one of the oldest and most picturesque bridges, the **Brig o' Balgownie**, at Aberdeen, whose pointed Gothic sandstone and granite arch spans the River Don.

Built in about 1320 by Bishop Henry Cheyne on the orders of King Robert the Bruce, the arch of nearly 70 feet is founded on rock on each side and spans the river where it is constricted into a very narrow, deep channel, just downstream from a 40-foot-deep hole in the river bed known as the Black Neuk Pot.

This bridge, and its setting, has an atmospheric presence, which must have caught the imagination of Thomas the Rhymer, the Borders Seer. His prophecy:

'Brig o' Balgownie, wicht [strong] is thy wa'
Wi' a wife's ae son an' a mare's ae foal
Down shalt thou fa.'

Lord Byron, George Gordon (1788-1824), who was schooled in Aberdeen, must have taken heed of the Seer's advice on his many country walks in this area, for there's no account of him falling foul of the prophecy.

The bridge was extensively reconstructed in 1607 and widened with buttresses added to the approaches in 1912.

Further south in Aberdeen, the **Brig o' Dee** was completed in 1527 by Bishop Gavin Dunbar to a design of Thomas Franche, master mason to King James V. The construction was funded by a bequest of £20,000 by Bishop William Elphinstone, who had died in 1514. In the 1530s there was a chapel to the Virgin Mary built on the bridge, where travellers could 'make their devotions'. In the 1560s the silver statue of the Virgin Mary was smuggled to safety by a local merchant, William Laing, and can be found today in the church of Notre Dame de Finistere in Brussels.

The bridge witnessed the first battle in the Scottish Civil War, known as the First Bishops' War, in 1639, between the Covenanters, led by their then energetic champion James Graham, Marquis of Montrose, and William Keith, the 7th Earl Marischal, against the Royalist supporters of

King Charles I led by James Gordon, Viscount Aboyne. Although successful in his efforts in Aberdeen, Montrose was to change allegiances a few months later with the signing of the Treaty of Berwick, when he came under the spell of Charles I. He was to lead a colourful, if short, life, being hanged and quartered at the old Mercat Cross in Edinburgh in 1650, aged 37.

Although largely rebuilt in the 18th century and widened considerably in 1841, the Bridge of Dee's seven semi-circular ribbed arches of Elgin sandstone, decorated with many coats of arms, make this ancient monument a strikingly good and rare example of this type of construction in Scotland. It continues to carry the busy A90 into the city, although heavy goods vehicles are now diverted via the downstream King George VI bridge, opened in 1941.

The 16th-century **Nungate Bridge** across the River Tyne in Haddington is one of the oldest Scottish bridges on record. Now for pedestrian use only, it takes its name from the old nunnery that stood on the site of St Martin's Church.

Guard Bridge, in the once famous paper-making village of the same name a few miles from St Andrews, was commissioned by Bishop Wardlaw, founder of St Andrew's University, and dates from 1450. It is 443 feet long and comprises six arches of varying spans across the River Eden, at its lowest crossing before becoming an estuary. This Ancient Monument is believed to be as originally built.

At Newbattle, in Midlothian, stands **Maiden Bridge** over the River South Esk. Built for the monks of Newbattle Abbey in the late 15th

Above The Bridge of Dee, Aberdeen. *Canmore*

Left The Brig o' Balgownie. *Lyn Anderson*

27

A detail of arch of Nungate Bridge, Haddington. *Lewis Matheson*

Maiden Bridge, Newbattle. *Canmore*

The Tweed Bridge at Peebles. *Colin L. Shearer*

century, this single-arch bridge is 90 feet long with a ribbed underside, built in sections to save on the centring. The bridge takes its name from Margaret, the eldest daughter of King Henry VII, who crossed it in 1503 en route to marrying King James IV. Accompanied by the Earl of Surrey with 500 men-at-arms, Margaret stopped at Newbattle Abbey for a blessing from the monks before meeting her future husband. The blessing certainly worked, as it was a successful marriage.

King James IV is often cited as the most erudite of the Stewart monarchs of Scotland. He was well-read, multilingual, including Gaelic, and bestowed a legacy of arts and culture on the country. Sadly, his end was not a happy one. He led the Scots in the disastrous Battle of Flodden in 1513 and was killed on the battlefield, becoming the last king in Great Britain to meet this fate. Queen Margaret left a rich legacy, none richer one might claim that being mother of Mary, Queen of Scots, whose French education turned the spelling of Stewart to Stuart. Her great-grandson was King James VI of Scotland, who became King James I of England upon the Union of the Crowns in 1603.

The old five-span stone bridge across the River Tweed at **Peebles** originates from the 15th century; there are records of work being undertaken on it in 1465. It was reconstructed in 1663 using stone from St Andrew's Church, which had been destroyed by the English Army in 1548 during the 'Rough Wooing'. A rather odd name, and one popularised more than three centuries later by Sir Walter Scott to describe the Eight Years' War between the Scots and the English in King Henry VIII's (and subsequently King Edward VI's) attempt to end the Auld Alliance with France and the prospects of Mary Queen of Scots, by putting 'all to fyre and sworde'.

In 1799 someone with an even odder name, John Hisplop, added three arches at the south end of the bridge, but these were demolished to make way for the Peebles railway. It was rather a narrow bridge at only 8 feet wide until John and Thomas Smith of Darnick widened it to 21 feet in 1834. In 1900 a major reconstruction doubled its width to 40 feet. Interestingly there was another, smaller, bridge in Peebles in the 15th century, Cuddy Bridge, across the Eddelston Water, linking the High Street with the Old Town. The present Cuddy Bridge, however, dates from 1857.

Trade bridges

The second rationale for bridges was for encouraging trade, by providing a safe course of passage across a watercourse. Although described as the 'bridge to heaven' on the new information panel, the three-arched stone bridge across the Gala Water in **Stow** was designed in 1655 to provide a link to the trade route between Galashiels and Edinburgh.

The 'Bridge to Heaven' at Stow. *Deborah M. Keith*

The bridge was paid for from subscriptions to the Kirk Session, who managed the project and saw mutual benefit in improving access to the church. Indeed, stone from the old church, now a ruin, was used to complete the construction. It is a pleasing structure, designed with the two smaller arches providing a bridge over the immediate flood plain and with the largest pier shaped to break the force of the main flow of water. The walls are unusually low to allow heavily laden packhorses to cross. Urgent repair work in 2002 incorporated a lime concrete arch to support the central section, without detracting from the skilful masonry that has withstood the test of time.

Another good example of a trade bridge, indeed implied from its name, is **Cadger's Brig** in Biggar. A 'cadger' was a pedlar, or hawker, and this single-arched structure still stands in the centre of this small but bustling medieval burgh in the Southern Uplands. Reputably dating from the 13th century, the name derives from a tale that William Wallace crossed the bridge disguised as a cadger while on a spying mission on the English army, camped nearby.

Military bridges

Stirling Bridge, close to my teenage home and school, held the key to the Highlands and was of great strategic importance as the lowest crossing point over the River Forth. William Wallace (c1270-1305), the Scottish patriot fighting for Scottish independence from England, won a famous victory over King Edward I at the Battle of Stirling Bridge in 1297. Writing about Wallace in 1877, James Paterson relates a narrative on the battle as told by Blind Harry, the Scottish Minstrel, so probably slightly embellished. In turn, Blind Harry (1440-92) wrote his account in 'The Actes and Deidis of the Illustre and Vallyeant Campioun Schir William Wallace', more commonly known as 'The Wallace', in 1477, some 172 years after Wallace's death.

Wallace's stratagem was to position his men on the north side of the river, opposite Stirling Castle and King Edward I's troops. The original bridge was wooden so Wallace engaged a carpenter to saw across the centre of the bridge 'on charnaill bands nald' and to rub it down with clay to disguise the saw marks. The structure was supported on 'thre rowaris of tre' so that when one was withdrawn the other two would collapse. The carpenter was ordered to sit under the bridge in a cradle bound to a beam, with strict instructions to let go 'the pyne' the moment he heard the blast of Wallace's horn.

Some 50,000 English gathered at the south end of the bridge, outnumbering Wallace's army by 50 to 1. Hew of Cressingham led the English vanguard across the bridge, but Wallace waited until the second division, led by John de Warenne, the Earl of Surrey, was 'thik on the bryg', then took his horn and blew the expected blast. Instantly, the

Cadger's Brig, Biggar. *Canmore*

carpenter struck out 'the rowar' and down with a mighty crash went the bridge and all upon it – joined, one presumes, by the faithful carpenter. Hideous cries arose as men and horses tumbled into the river below. The Scots, with newfound confidence, then assailed the troops who had made it to the north bank.

That Stirling Bridge was a resounding victory for Wallace is in no doubt, and Blind Harry's version certainly contains the hallmarks of The Wallace's tactics in countering such overwhelming numerical odds. According to an English chronicler, Hemingford, the bridge remained entire, but was so narrow that only two horsemen could pass at a time. When the English were about halfway over, the Scots took possession at the end of the bridge and prevented them from crossing, but now ideally situated to inflict slaughter on Edward's army.

Whatever the fact, Wallace's victory was certain, but it was savagely revenged by Edward at the Battle of Falkirk the following year.

Stirling was the scene of yet another decisive battle for Scottish independence: Bannockburn in 1314. Here, Wallace's prodigy, Robert the Bruce, King of Scots, won a clear victory over King Edward II's troops in the Carse of Balquhiderock, not a name that springs to mind as rapidly as the waterlogging in the marshy fields that witnessed the major episodes in the battle. The area lies some 1½ miles from Borestone, the traditionally, but incorrectly, held site, and where Pilkington Jackson's statue of 'The Bruce' has stood since 1964.

As a schoolboy at Stirling High School, I was immensely proud to live so close to such an important centre of activity in the history of Scottish independence. Every schoolboy likes a victory. The 'houses' at school were each named after the commanders on the Scottish side at Bannockburn, so there was Bruce, Douglas and Randolph. But there was also Snowden, who I never quite worked out. Why not Keith, after Sir Robert, the Scot's Marischal, who led the 500-strong Scottish cavalry so successfully against the 2,000 English horse? It was 'Scots Wha Hae' that Robert Burns wrote, not 'Scots Wha Don't'.

The bridge of the 13th-century Battle of Stirling Bridge is long gone. They did a reasonable job of destroying it in 1297. The old bridge remaining a short distance downstream from the original, and now without its gateway tower, is still a fine structure, though, dating from

Stirling Old Bridge. *Lewis Matheson*

around 1400. This bridge has four sandstone arches and is 270 feet long with a causewayed carriageway. It was strengthened and reconditioned between 1912 and 1920 and is maintained as an Ancient Monument.

It has also seen its share of Scottish history, most notably in 1571 when gallows were erected on the bridge to hang Archbishop John Hamilton. The loyal Catholic supporter of Mary, Queen of Scots, he had burned the Protestant martyr Walter Myln, aged 82, in St Andrews in 1558. He had published his version of the Catechism in 1551 and followed this with 'The Two Penny Faith' in 1559, much to the ire of the Reformers.

Nearly two centuries later, in 1745, Brigadier William Blakeney, who was commander of the garrison at Stirling Castle, blew up the southernmost arch of the bridge to prevent the Jacobites from crossing en route to Edinburgh. He went on to produce detailed maps of the Battle of Prestonpans fought in September of that year, the first serious battle of the Second Jacobite Rebellion, where the Government troops led by Sir John Cope were heavily defeated.

In these warlike times, bridges were a bastion of defence and, although the use of gunpowder from the mid-15th century rendered many obsolete from a military perspective, they continued to serve a much wider socio-economic purpose down many centuries.

The four remaining arches of **Bothwell Brig** across the River Clyde between Bothwell and Hamilton have also survived since 1400, when the bridge was built by 'Archibald the Grim', the 3rd Earl of Douglas, who had earlier restored Bothwell Castle. Although an Ancient Monument, its appearance has changed somewhat since it was the scene of the Battle of Bothwell Brig in 1679, in which the Royalists under the Duke of Monmouth overcame the Covenanters. This was a very bloody battle, captured by Sir Walter Scott in his novel *Old Mortality*. The Royalists dispensed disgraceful slaughter on the Presbyterian covenanters, with captives pressed into slavery overseas. Much of the bridge was rebuilt in the 19th century, including the addition of the cantilevered iron footpaths.

Cultural connections

The aptly named **Auld Brig** in Ayr dates from the 13th century. Its four slightly pointed sandstone arches with massive triangular cutwaters have carried only pedestrian traffic since 1785, when the New Bridge across the River Ayr was built a short distance downstream. This caused much controversy amongst the population of Ayr, captured by the local lad o' pairts and Scotland's national bard, Robert Burns (1759-96), when

he personified the dialogue between the old and the new bridges in his long poem 'The Brigs of Ayr'.

The New Brig scoffs:

'Will your poor narrow foot-path of a street,
Where twa wheel-barrows tremble when they meet,
Your ruin'd formless bulk o' stone and lime,
Compare wi bonnie brigs o' modern time?'

To which the Auld Brig responds:

'This mony a year I've stood the flood an' tide,
And tho' wi crazy eild I'm sair forfairn,
I'll be a brig, when ye're a shapeless cairn.'

Written in 1786, it contained a strong element of prediction, for the New Brig was destroyed in a storm and had to be replaced in 1877. The bridge was restored in 1910 to commemorate Burns. Far be it for me to point to a slip of the quill by the Bard, but he does attribute the 'New Bridge' to Robert Adam when it was in fact designed by Alexander Stevens.

Another ancient bridge near Ayr is even better known worldwide. The **Brig o' Doon**, the steeply humped single-arch bridge across the River Doon, dates from the 15th century and has a span of 72 feet. It was the scene of Tam O' Shanter's encounter with the devil, warlocks and witches in Robert Burns's epic poem recounting Tam's drunken journey home after market day in Ayr.

After an evening 'bousing at the nappy', Tam passes 'Alloway's auld, haunted kirk', where warlocks and witches are dancing to the devil's piping. Tam, unobserved, watches the spectacle, then applauds. The 'hellish legion' give chase, and he has to race to 'win the keystone o' the brig' where safety lies, since witches dare not cross running water. He succeeds, but not before his foremost pursuer, Nannie the witch, manages to grasp the tail of his mare, and 'Ae spring brought off her master hale, But left behind her ain grey tail.' Sadly, 'The carlin caught her rump and left puir Meg wi' scarce a stump.'

Three bridges now span the Doon in a parkland setting, with the view from the 'new brig', built in 1832, approximately 150 yards downstream, providing the best vantage for Burns's 'banks and braes o' bonny Doon'.

Robert Burns, or 'Rabbie' as we like to call him, captured in verse the virtues of social justice and mankind's liberation, as well as man's –

An engraving of Tam o' Shanter at Brig O' Doon by Thomas Tweedie. *National Trust for Scotland*

including his own – frailties. Voted by the Scottish television-viewing public as the 'Greatest Scot' in 2009, he's celebrated as a national icon, and rightly so. He has left his mark not just on the foundations of socialism and liberal thinking worldwide, but is also honoured in Burns Nights or 'Suppers' on 25 January across the globe and, in a physical sense, sculptured in statues in cities wherever Scots have colonised. I have encountered 'Burns in stone' in Dunedin, in Adelaide, in Vancouver and in Montreal. Indeed, it's claimed that only Christopher Columbus and Queen Victoria as non-religious figures have more statues around the world than Robert Burns.

He was the eldest child of William Burnes and Agnes Broun. His father, born at Clochnahill Farm near Dunnottar Castle, and whose mother was Isabella Keith, retained the Burnes spelling until he died, but Robert favoured the Ayrshire variant.

The 'Supper' is a tradition worthy of maintaining. A meal of haggis, neaps and tatties, with the Address, the Immortal Memory and the Toast to the Lassies, intermixed in a programme of poetry and song, it can be as formal as the 'auld skuil' would dictate, or a mere excuse, if any is needed, for friends to gather socially in the name of culture.

For 20 years as an expat now living in Peterborough, I've enjoyed many convivial January evenings with friends in Oundle celebrating Burns, where the traditions are observed but with licence to digress to other humorous asides. Acknowledgements go always to Blyth Morris, the only other Scot aside from myself normally present, who faithfully delivers a stirring and sincere Address to the Haggis, sgian-dubh in hand.

Anyhow, back to bridges and early attempts to improve communication links.

Several bridges are worthy of note as having provided key infrastructure in their heyday. **Kirkfieldbank** Bridge, otherwise known as Clydesholm Bridge, in the Clyde Valley dates from the late 1690s and replaces a previous ford and ferry crossing, which had itself been sanctioned by Royal Charter granted by King James IV in 1491. The need for the bridge was a result of the considerable expansion of the road network in the 17th century. The application to the Lords of the Privy Council for permission to build the bridge placed emphasis on the perils of the ford crossing, which had claimed the lives of 12 men in the previous four years.

Many bridges replaced ferries, and reputably the bridge crossing of the River Teith at **Doune** was constructed on the orders of the master tailor to King James IV, Robert Spittal, prompted by his wish to hasten his speedy return to his home in Stirling. He could not have made too much use of it himself, however, as it was completed in 1535, the year in which he died.

The bridge, complete with an inscription, has two arches, each spanning 50 feet, with foundations placed on a rock shelf across the river. The tailor, whose house still stands in Stirling, also commissioned bridges at Bannockburn (1516) and two across the River Devon at Tullibody. One of the Tullibody bridges was partly dismantled shortly afterwards, in 1560, during the Reformation, by Sir William Kirkcaldy of Grange (1520-73) to delay the French troops under Henri Cleutin from retreating to Stirling from the Siege of Leith. The French proved resourceful, however – they took the roof off Tullibody Kirk for material to bridge the Devon. Cleutin also led the French at the Battle of Glasgow Bridge the same year, when his troops, in support of Mary of Guise, heavily defeated the Scots Protestants.

A four-arch bridge was erected across the River Ness in **Inverness** in

1680-82 by an architect and builder from Ross-shire. He was James Smith (1645-1731), who married the daughter of Robert Mylne (1633-1710), the last Master Mason to the Crown of Scotland, and the great-grandfather of Sir Robert Mylne (1733-1811), the renowned architect and engineer. When he wasn't building bridges, James Smith was fathering children. He had 32 in total – 18 by his first wife, Janet Mylne, and 14 by his second wife – before he died at the age of 86, presumably of exhaustion.

Glasgow's Medieval origins

At the western end of Antonine's Wall lay a settlement that arose from a fording point on the River Clyde. This small town was to become the industrial capital of Scotland and the 'Second City of the British Empire' – Glasgow. Although it had a population of fewer than 1,000 in the 13th century, Glasgow had a cathedral, standing over the burial place of St Mungo, the city's patron saint. Indeed, the original cathedral had been consecrated in 1136, only to be destroyed by fire in 1175. It isn't known when the first bridge was built, but a charter from 1285 mentions a bridge at the foot of Fishergait, now Stockwell Street.

Henry the Minstrel, also known as Blind Harry – who waxed lyrical about William Wallace's exploits at the Battle of Stirling Bridge – told of a bridge 'Briggit of tre' when he was writing in 1488; this timber bridge was demolished in 1345 and replaced with a stone bridge.

The stone bridge was the **Great Bridge of Glasgow**, otherwise known as Old Stockwell Bridge or Bishop Rae's Bridge, as he funded its construction. And a great construction it was. It comprised eight stone arches and was 12 feet wide. It remained the only structural crossing of the Clyde in Glasgow for more than 400 years. On 8 April 1571 King James VI and the Regent Lennox are quoted as paying this tribute to the bridge:

> 'Considering na thing within our said citie sae precious nor necessary, bayth for the weill of the inhabitants thairof, decoratioun of the same and common weill of the hail cuntre as the Brig of Glasgow over Clyde, quhilk throw the oft inubdations [sic], great fludis and stormis that has occurit and decendit doon the watter in tyme of frost and specialie this last winter, the said brig has bene sa troublit, ding down and dampnageit wit greit trowpis of yis [ice] that gif the saymn be not spedelie redressit and oudourit to the former estait with small tyme, it sall grow to sic point as finallie greitar inconvenience sall follow to the disproffeit of our hail realme.'

This was quite an insightful pronouncement from the King. Young James, who was to go on to become the first monarch of Scotland, England and Ireland following the Union of the Crowns in 1603, was but four years old in April 1571. No doubt the words of wisdom were uttered by his Regent, his grandfather, Matthew Stewart, the 4th Earl of Lennox. The Regent never lived to see whether the necessary repairs were carried out on the Brig of Glasgow, as he was killed in September the same year at a skirmish near Stirling Castle.

By 1585 the bridge had begun to weaken, and a weight limit was imposed. In 1671 the southern arch collapsed, but was repaired. By 1765 the Council sought to close the bridge to carts but, undaunted, the residents of Rutherglen resisted, so the bridge was again repaired and indeed widened. It was judged unsafe in the 1840s, and finally demolished in 1847.

4. COMMERCE REPLACES CONFLICT IN THE 18TH CENTURY

From Wade to trade

As I worked my way through the daily grind of classroom lessons and after-school homework at Stirling High School, when I wasn't thinking about bridges my thoughts began to turn increasingly to the future. I always wanted to have a job where I wouldn't be stuck behind a desk every day – well, at least when it wasn't raining. Rural chartered surveying had appealed to me since I had attended the Forestry Commission's Golden Jubilee in 1969, held at the Bush Estate near Edinburgh.

It seems that my favourite subjects, or the ones where I could scrape reasonable exam results, such as history, geography, English and maths, would not have allowed me to study 'pure' forestry or agriculture at university. A Higher in chemistry was a prerequisite for that and I never did understand chemistry. The RICS advised me that I could be a rural chartered surveyor, with the only stipulation that I had to be able to spell 'chemistry'. That seemed like the career for me.

During school holidays I had the amazing good fortune to gain employment with a young, enthusiastic and hugely knowledgeable chartered surveyor who not only was the factor for several large Perthshire estates, but also had started his own surveying practice and estate agency in Dunblane.

I wrote a carefully crafted letter – in my best handwriting, as there were no spell-checking, variable font, template-providing personal computers in those days – to Marshall MacCallum at Kippendavie Estate Office, imploring him to give me the opportunity to gain some work experience with him that summer. He responded by saying that there were no jobs available, but if I'd like to meet him outside his office in Dunblane at 5pm on Thursday, he'd explain why.

The office was at 1 High Street, just next to the bridge over the Allan Water, and that afternoon and early evening he drove me all round the estates he factored – Kippendavie, Cauldhame, Braco Castle, Doune Castle and Port of Menteith.

He then asked me when I could start.

'But your letter said there was no job,' I queried.

'Well,' he responded in his west coast burr, 'I think we'd get on and just do what you're told.'

On my first day there, a Monday, I asked him if I could have the Tuesday morning off, to sit my driving test. 'You'll be a lot more useful to me with a driving licence,' was his response.

So on 2 August 1972 I passed my driving test at the first attempt. I had not only made myself eminently more useful, but I'd gained a new freedom to explore my native land. I was to spend several very happy summer holidays from school and university at Kippendavie learning so much from Marshall, all of which stood me in very good stead for my career.

It is hard now to recall what I imagined the future held not only for me but for Scotland in 1972. Within a year or so the first discoveries of oil and gas in the North Sea were made, and a generation later the country would not only have its own parliament but also be split by a previously unimaginably close result in a referendum on Scottish independence.

As the riches flowing from the North Sea begin to wane and the UK turns its gaze inwards rather than outwards, Scotland now faces many uncertainties. But if economic conditions look tough for Scotland post-Brexit in the early 21st century, spare a thought for those in the closing years of the 17th century and the dawn of the 18th. Those were wretched times for the Scottish economy. Adding to a run of bad harvests, an investment scheme in the late 1690s by Scottish nobility and landowners, to foster trade by establishing a Scottish colony called Caledonia on the Panama isthmus, left many in financial ruin. It came to be known as the 'Darien Disaster'.

With bankruptcy beckoning, the door to corruption and bribery was open and many saw the signing of the Act of Union by the Scottish Parliament in 1707, creating the union with the English Parliament, as a betrayal of our national cause and of the military successes of both Wallace and Bruce.

Robert Burns certainly held this view and expressed it with vigour in his poem 'Such a Parcel of Rogues in a Nation', written with the benefit of some hindsight in 1791. The penultimate line – 'We're bought and sold for English gold' – still has a pungent ring more than 300 years later.

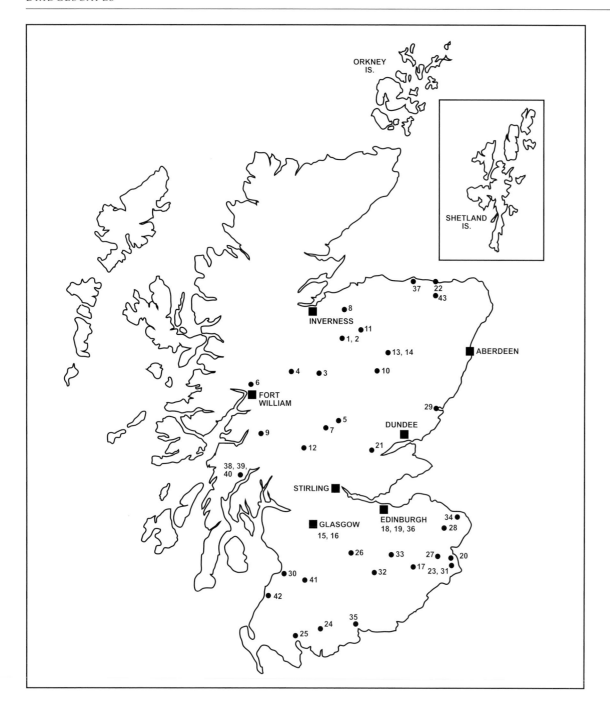

18th-century bridges

Key to bridges mentioned in the text

1	Carr Bridge	NH 905 225
2	Sluggan Bridge	NH 869 220
3	Crubenbeg, R Truim	NN 680 923
4	Garva	NN 521 947
5	Aberfeldy	NN 851 492
6	Kilmonivaig	NN 174 829
7	Kenmore	NN 771 455
8	Dulsie	NH 931 414
9	Bridge of Orchy	NN 273 413
10	Invercauld	NO 186 909
11	Old Spey Bridge	NJ 039 262
12	Killin	NN 571 325
13	Delavine	NJ 280 069
14	Tornahaish and Allt Damh	NJ 271 075
15	Broomielaw, Glasgow	NS 582 647
16	Rutherglen	NS 606 630
17	Yair/Fairnielee	NT 458 325
18	North Bridge, Edinburgh	NT 258 738
19	South Bridge, Edinburgh	NT 259 734
20	Coldstream	NT 848 401
21	Perth	NO 121 238
22	Deveron, Banff	NJ 694 637
23	Kelso	NT 727 336
24	Ken, New Galloway	NX 640 783
25	Cree, Newton Stewart	NX 411 656
26	Hyndford	NS 914 414
27	Drygrange, Melrose	NT 575 346
28	Ancrum	NT 638 584
29	Bridge of Dun, Montrose	NO 663 584
30	Ayr	NS 338 221
31	Teviot, Kelso	NT 719 335
32	Carlow's Bridge, Tweedsmuir	NT 097 243
33	Old Manor Brig	NT 231 393
34	Pease Bridge	NT 791 699
35	Dumfries	NX 968 761
36	Laundry Bridge, Dalkeith House	NT 338 682
37	West Bridge, Cullen	NJ 505 662
38	Aray Bridge, Inveraray	NN 095 094

39	Dubh Loch Bridge	NN 113 105
40	Garron	NN 113 100
41	Avenue Bridge,	
	Dumfries House, Cumnock	NS 537 206
42	Culzean Castle	NS 241 103
43	Bridge of Alvah	NJ 680 610

Civil unrest and outright rebellion

Scotland's geography and topography do not aid easy communication. The rugged and mountainous Highlands in particular, with its tortuously indented western coastline of sea lochs and islands, meant that early trade routes to the central-belt livestock market towns of Falkirk and Stirling comprised drove roads weaving through glens and traversing high moorland. Travelling anywhere was a chore and undertaken as a serious matter only in the interests of securing the sale of livestock at trysts or to engage in neighbouring skirmishes or a grander military campaign. Some of these ventures were by no means a casual exercise.

Clansmen from remote glens rallied to the Jacobite standard raised by John, the 6th Earl of Mar, at Braemar in 1715, at the outbreak of the rebellion against King George I, the 'wee, wee German lairdie'. Travelling on foot across rugged and inhospitable country, some 6,500 men from the Highlands, Perth, Angus and Fife faced 3,100 Government troops under the command of the Duke of Argyll at the Battle of Sheriffmuir, near Dunblane, in November 1715. Although the words of the old song, 'There's some say that we wan, some say that they wan', indicate an indecisive outcome, Sheriffmuir was the beginning of the end for the first Jacobite Rebellion, and those who survived the bloody carnage returned to their homes, the Cause 'not onlie desperate but sunk'.

Following the 'Fifteen, the Government, based at Westminster since the Union of the Parliaments only eight years previously, decided to introduce several measures to establish law and order in the Highlands, thereby hoping to avoid further risings.

Nothing much happened quickly, however, and the failure of a minor Jacobite resurgence in 1719 was down to not uncommon gale-force winds on the west coast, which scattered 6,000 Spaniards and sent them home. Ironically, we must thank those Spaniards for their intervention, for it was this minor incident that finally forced the Government in London to do something about building roads and bridges in the north,

as it was found in 1719 that the Government army, with its cannon and other accoutrements of war, could get no further north than Blair Atholl because of the lack of roads and bridges.

The resultant building of barracks at Kilcumain (later Fort Augustus), Bernera (Glenelg), Ruthven (Badenoch) and Inversnaid (Loch Lomond), together with Fort George (near Ardersier on the Moray Firth) and Fort William, provided a framework for communication that was revolutionary for the Highlands.

Civil unrest gives way to civil engineering

The pioneer of this road- and bridge-building network was an Irishman, **Major General George Wade** (1673-1748), who had seen military service in Flanders and Spain. He came to Scotland in 1724 under orders to prepare a report on the state of the Highlands. The following year he was appointed commander-in-chief and the next 12 years saw the construction, by military labour, of some 250 miles of road and nearly 40 bridges.

Make no mistake about the real intent of his commission from King George I, though. It was to subdue the prospect of further rebellion. Look no further than the UK's National Anthem from the early 18th century. One of the verses, as chronicled in the 1926 *Oxford Book of Eighteenth Century Verse* and now deemed politically incorrect, exhorts:

> 'Lord grant that Marshal Wade
> May by thy mighty aid
> Victory bring.
> May he sedition hush,
> And, like a torrent, rush
> Rebellious Scots to crush,
> God save the King!'

No wonder modern Scots opted for the stirring yet haunting lyrics of Roy Williamson's 'Flower of Scotland' as a national anthem to ring out from the terraces of Murrayfield or Hampden.

Working from May to October each year, roads were constructed from Inverness to Fort William, along the south side of Loch Ness; from Inverness to Dunkeld via the Drumochter Pass; from Fort Augustus to Dalwhinnie via the Corrieyairack Pass; and from Dalnacardoch to Crieff via Tummel Bridge and the bridge at Aberfeldy.

Generally, the roads were approximately 16 feet wide. Only in places did they follow modern routes, but they did provide the first real

'Field-Marshall George Wade', a painting by Johan van Diest. *Courtesy of the National Galleries Scotland*

opportunity to open up the Highlands for discovery and trade, rather than purely military ends.

Most of Wade's bridges comprised a single arch, only 10-12 feet in span, and most were built by contractors for considerably less than £200. Although the contract specification appears to have been very loose about details of design or construction, or even precise location, there was included a somewhat onerous 20 years' maintenance obligation on the contractor. From later records of the condition of some of these bridges, it seems likely that this undertaking was, in many cases, neither honoured nor enforced.

These bridges were largely simple structures, mostly with circular arches, and the style was widely adopted across Scotland, with many bridges being referred to today as 'General Wade's bridges', although they were not, in fact, his commissions.

In Perth & Kinross, the old Rumbling Bridge, some 86 feet above the River Devon, dates from 1713 and was built by local mason William Gray. There was an even earlier bridge – a large stone slab known as a clapper bridge in the gorge, just above the river. Since 1816 this site has boasted a double – or is it treble? – bridge, with a further semi-circular stone arch built 120 feet above the water on the same line. It's atmospheric, as is the name Rumbling Bridge. The story goes that on 13 August 1816 there was an earthquake that shook everything for miles around. Or perhaps the name derives from the sound of the water tumbling from cataract to cataract in the river below?

The old **Carr Bridge** is another example that predates Wade. It originates from 1717 and is a fine structure with a width between parapets of only 7 feet and founded on rock piers that stand proud of the summer water level. Built by the local landowner in response to a petition from parishioners, it is considered to be the oldest stone bridge in the Highlands. This packhorse bridge survived the 'muckle spate', or great flood, of 1829, despite being severely damaged.

A later example is **Sluggan Bridge**, some 3 miles further up the River Dulnain, where the present bridge, built to replace Wade's original, dates from 1769. According to a contemporary source, Sir Aeneas Mackintosh of Mackintosh, this bridge was built first in 1764, being of two arches, but was destroyed in 1768, only to be rebuilt with a single arch the following year. This early bridge was of solid construction for it, too, survived the floods of 1829.

One that is a Wade bridge, however, is the single-arch bridge over the River Truim at **Crubenbeg**, 5 miles north of Dalwhinnie, built of whinstone (schistose) with spandrels filled with gravel or earth. External walls were traditionally built of local rubble masonry, sometimes whin, but often granite. Two such examples remain on Wade's road, now part of the Scottish National Trail from Lagganbridge to Fort Augustus over the Corrieyairack Pass.

Garva bridge, dating from 1732, with its massive stone cutwater buttresses supporting the road for the 180 feet over the River Spey in two widely separate arched spans, is particularly impressive. Originally Wade called this bridge 'St George's Bridge' after the patron saint of England, a name that did not endure for long in the heart of the Jacobite homeland.

Of Wade's legacy of bridges across the Rivers Garry, Tummel, Spean and Tay, only the most architecturally impressive, crossing the Tay at

The Rumbling Bridge. *Iain Matheson*

Aberfeldy, is still in use, but it is a notable monument to Wade's contribution to improving the Achilles' heel of Scottish Highlands, that of communications.

For the Aberfeldy bridge, Wade engaged the architect and builder William Adam (1689-1748), the father not only of his two famous sons, John and Robert, but also of Scottish architecture in the early part of the Scottish Enlightenment. Aberfeldy was his largest bridge, completed in 1733, with its five arches of locally quarried greenish-grey chlorite schist spanning 400 feet, requiring 1,200 piles to be driven into the river bed and banks.

Carr Bridge. *Deborah M. Keith*

Wade's bridge at Aberfeldy.
Deborah M. Keith / Iain Matheson

Garva Bridge. *Andrew Whamond*

Designed from the outset to be somewhat pretentious, the most prominent baroque features, four tall obelisks on the parapets over the middle arch, were added at the late request of General Wade. At £4,095 5s 10d, this memorial to Wade cost more than half of his total spending on Highland bridges.

The bridge still carries the main road north out of the town and is admired by locals and tourists alike as a living monument to Wade's impact on opening up the Highlands. Less sympathetic was Poet Laureate Robert Southey, when he noted in his *Journal of a Tour of Scotland* in 1819: 'At a distance it looks well, but makes a wretched appearance upon close inspection.'

Still visible today at **Kilmonivaig**, near Spean Bridge, are the remains of the High Bridge over the Spean, built in 1736 on Wade's military road. Originally comprising three arches supported on two tall piers, it bridged a deep steep-sided gorge, rising some 100 feet above the river. On 16 August 1745 the first skirmish in the second Jacobite uprising was an ambush on the bridge.

Major Donald Macdonald of Tirnadrish, with 11 men and a piper from Keppoch's Clan, used trees to conceal their lack of numbers to outwit and rout 85 men of the First Royal Regiment of Foot (later the Royal Scots) from crossing the High Bridge. Thwarted in their efforts to travel between Fort Augustus and Fort William on that occasion, the Royalists surrendered, but wrought their revenge on Macdonald, capturing him at the Battle of Falkirk Muir on 17 January 1746 and beheading him in Carlisle. In 2016 a musket ball from the skirmish at High Bridge was found by Paul Macdonald from Edinburgh while exploring the site with his young family.

High Bridge was already in a state of collapse by 1819 when Telford chose another site in Spean for his bridge to carry the Great Glen Road. Although ruinous today, there are plans to restore the old bridge, which is visible from the footpath between the village and the Commando Memorial, erected to commemorate the Second World War commando training unit based at Achnacarry Castle from 1942.

General Wade's experience of bridge-building in the Highlands did not go unmarked on his return south of the border. When the Commission for Westminster Bridge was set up in 1735, Wade was appointed as a commissioner, and he was Field Marshall for the Anglo-Austrian forces against the French in Flanders in the 1740s. Nor did his exploits, including those in Scotland, hurt his wealth. When he died, unmarried, in 1748, aged 75, he left the enormous sum of £100,000 from his investments, including his part-ownership of the lead mines at Strontian.

Following the failure of the 1715 Jacobite rebellions, many of the principal supporters forfeited their estates, among them the 10th Earl Marischal, George Keith, and his brother James, both of whom went on to have distinguished military and diplomatic careers in Europe. James became Field Marshall to Frederick the Great of Prussia and is the only person to have a statue in his honour in both Peterhead and Berlin, the latter inscribed 'Jakob von Keith'.

The Scottish Forfeited Estates Commission was established to administer the forfeited properties, the eventual sale of which helped fund investments in infrastructure for the benefit of the nation. This practice continued after the Battle of Culloden in 1746, and the projects funded from the monies amassed included several significant bridges.

Kenmore Bridge at Loch Tay, built in 1774, is a fine example. Designed by John Baxter, who built several bridges in Perthshire, this three-arched bridge has a circular arched cylinder through each spandrel, which may have been copied from Smeaton's larger bridges at Coldstream and Perth.

Throughout the second half of the 18th century, the extension of the military roads was carried out by a succession of military commanders, following Wade. The most notable was **William Caulfeild**, grandson of the First Viscount Charlemont.

Major Caulfeild – he does appear to have spelled his surname with the 'e' before the 'i', although he would have some difficulty in persuading Mrs MacQueen, my teacher at Balloch Primary School, of the grammatical correctness of this preference – became Inspector of Roads in 1732, based in Inverness. When he was succeeded by **Colonel Skene** in 1767, some 858 miles of military road had been completed,

Kenmore Bridge. *Iain Matheson*

with a further 139 miles under construction. By 1785 there were an estimated 938 bridges on the military road system, a high ratio per mile but a reflection of the topography and river systems of the Highlands.

While these roads were somewhat basic, considering the terrain they crossed they were a huge improvement on the existing drove roads. As one commentator, and it might well have been penned by Caulfeild, put it:

**'Had you seen these roads before they were made,
you would hold up your hands and bless General Wade'.**

The bridges at Dulsie, Feshie Bridge and the old bridge at Invermoriston all date from this period of expansionism in the highway network. Nairnshire's **Dulsie Bridge**, which crosses a deep twisting gorge on the River Findhorn on the old military road between Braemar and Fort George on the Moray Firth, dates from 1755. Standing 60 feet above the summer water level, it is a popular site nowadays for 'tombstoning', an activity in which the hardy or simply mad hurl themselves off the bridge into the deep pool of chilling water below. 'Hardy' is an interesting word often used by Invernessians. It's perhaps too easy to think that it just means bold or courageous, but maybe it's shorthand for 'foolhardy'. Both seem aptly applied to those who go in for tombstoning.

Caulfeild was also responsible for the **Bridge of Orchy** at the gateway to Rannoch Moor, built in 1751. Now a minor public road, it is a remote section of the West Highland Way, the 96 miles of challenging route between Milngavie on the outskirts of Glasgow and Fort William. More than 80,000 walkers and cyclists use the route every year, with nearly 15,000 of them claiming to complete the entire journey. I cannot yet make such a claim, sadly.

The old **Invercauld** bridge, now lying in the Balmoral Estate, was built in 1752 on the Crathie to Braemar road, which for the main part ran along the south side of the River Dee. A masonry structure, 444 feet long on six arches of varying spans, it is an attractive relic in this very scenic area. It only served as a public bridge for just over 100 years, however, with the road along the south side of the river – the Balmoral Estate side – being closed on the passing of the Ballater Turnpike Act of 1855. In 1859 Albert, the Prince Consort, at his own expense, built the new Invercauld Bridge to serve the new road on the north side.

The **Old Spey Bridge** near Grantown is a three-span rubble bridge, dating from 1754. With unusually deep spandrels, the bridge has been strengthened with iron rails, but provides a good vantage point for watching the salmon fishers on this famous stretch of water.

Maintaining the legacy

Building new roads and bridges was one thing, quite another was their subsequent repair, maintenance and upgrading.

In *Life in the Atholl Glens*, John Kerr quotes passages from the Minutes of the Kirk Session in the mid-1700s relating to Struan Bridge (then Strowan). A petition to the Duke of Atholl in 1719 had secured timber for the bridge. It appears that the Session resorted to fining parishioners for misdemeanours to support the maintenance programme.

On 2 December 1758:

'…John Robertson in Tomberaggich gave a joist for the bridge … valued at 14sh Scots, which the Session takes to account in so much of his fine for fornication with Ann Robertson in Auchleeks…'

An etching of Dulsie Bridge by James Fitter (1804) in *Scotia Depicta*. *Courtesy of the National Library of Scotland*

Bridge of Orchy. *Deborah M. Keith*

Invercauld old bridge. *Lewis Matheson*

Above The Falls of Dochart, Killin. *Lewis Matheson*

Left The Old Spey Bridge at Grantown. *Mike W. Lowson*

Such penance was a reasonably reliable source of material and labour, it appears, for on 2 October 1763:

'…Donald Moon at Bridge End of Tilt, for his fornication with Margaret Robertson in Kincraigie, was rebuked and given a communing for repairing the Bridge at Strowan.'

Clearly there was insufficient impropriety to fund all the necessary works. A candid report to the Treasury in the mid-1780s records some 938 bridges, 'many of them insufficient, some ruinous and other of those that were first built, injudiciously constructed and ill-executed.' This lack of proper supervision of construction and maintenance meant that much of the £300,000 of public money expended on roads and bridges in the 18th century was ultimately wasted.

Military labour stopped after 1790 and John Knox, a Scottish bookseller and philanthropist who lived in London – not the Presbyterian who had tormented Mary, Queen of Scots two centuries previously – was highly critical when he wrote in 1786:

'It is hardly agreed upon by travellers which is the line of road, everyone making one for himself. Even sheep follow better routes, understanding levels better and selecting better gradients.'

In his *Tour Through the Highlands of Scotland*, Knox estimates that the rate of travel was 1 mile per hour, so his sojourns must have taken him many months. But they were not in vain, and his far-sighted advocacy for the construction, and maintenance, of new roads for civilian use was to yield results. Knox was retained by the British Fisheries Society and his lobbying resulted in new investments in fishing communities and infrastructure, most notably at Ullapool in Wester Ross.

Other economic drivers were also at work. Large-scale agrarian improvements, displacing cattle rearing with sheep farming, brought two waves of population movements, both coerced. The first was the infamous clearances, initially to the coast. The second was economic migration when industry failed and drove people to the British overseas colonies. The economic and social upheavals brought pressures for improved communication routes. The kelp industry, which came to the fore during the Napoleonic Wars when the cost of the Spanish source of imported alkali used in the manufacture of soap and glass was prohibitive, lasted only a few years, but generated almost 50,000 jobs until its collapse after 1820.

By the second half of the 18th century the Highlands was poised for development of its natural resources. Improved and extended communications were to hold the key to progress in agriculture, fishing, manufacture, social welfare, regional administration and the early signs of tourism. Many bridges from this period are themselves tourist attractions today. An example is **Killin Bridge**, one of the most picturesque bridges in Perthshire, downstream from the Falls of Dochart.

It is a stone and lime structure built originally in 1760, comprising four spans, the widest of which is known as the Big Linn, damaged by flood in 1830 and rebuilt. The piers of the Big Linn rest on natural islands, which are mostly hard rock, but one of them, Inchbuie, bearing more soil than the others, is the ancient burial ground of the Clan McNab. Anyone who can prove direct descent from the clan can claim to be buried on this island!

In the 18th century, communications in the Lowlands and Southern Uplands of Scotland fared a little better than those of the Highlands, but were still rudimentary. Robert Burns aptly sums up the toils of travelling by highway when he announces:

> **'I'm now arrived – thanks to the Gods!**
> **Through pathways rough and muddy:**
> **A certain sign that makin' roads**
> **Is no this people's study.'**

Pre-eminent amongst the emerging professions of road surveyor and bridge engineer was **Charles Abercrombie** (1750-1817), whose legacy of almost 10,000 miles of road in Perthshire, Angus, Aberdeenshire and Ayrshire made a significant improvement to a proper, safe and reliable

communications network, as yet in an embryonic stage. He was also responsible for the Newmills Bridge over the Bluther Burn in Fife, but not until 1814.

Many bridges on the military roads have fallen into disrepair, despite being Scheduled Ancient Monuments. Their restoration and future care provide challenges, both technically and financially. Three bridges on the Braemar to Grantown-on-Spey section of military road, built in 1753 by Major William Caulfeild, have been restored, which, in the case of the small bridge at **Delavine** in 1998, involved jacking up and realigning the seriously distorted masonry arch. This project also saw the restoration of the bridges at **Tornahaish** and **Allt Damh**, on Candacraig Estate.

Bridging the Clyde

Robert Mylne (1733-1811) achieved his greatest successes in England, becoming one of the leading architects of his day and winning the fierce competition to design the original Blackfriars Bridge in London. When he was 40, Robert was engaged as engineer on Glasgow's **Broomielaw Bridge**. A very significant structure, and the first bridge to be built across the Clyde in a rapidly expanding Glasgow for more than 400 years, it merits a mention in the *Encyclopaedia Britannica* in 1797. The description reads: '…32ft wide, with a commodious footpath for passengers, 5ft wide on each side… This bridge is about 500ft in length and consists of seven arches.'

The first weir across the Clyde was also built while this bridge was under construction. This deepened the river immediately below the bridge, necessitating reinforcement of the foundations with rocks at the base of the pillars. In 1781 the father of water engineering on the Clyde, John Golborne (1724-83), and later, in 1799, John Rennie, both recommended removing the weir, but it remained in situ until 1840 and was reconstructed in 1842 under Bishop's Bridge.

In 1775, the new **Rutherglen Bridge** became the first bridge in Glasgow without a toll. It had five spans but was demolished in 1890 when its foundations became unstable following removal of the weir at Glasgow Green ten years earlier.

Another short-lived bridge over the Clyde was the original Hutchesontown Bridge, although it had a longer gestation than a productive life. In 1640 two brothers left a bequest to found Hutcheson Hospital for the relief of the aged and infirm and for educational purposes. This was the origin of Hutchesons' Boys' Grammar School ('Hutchie'), with its motto 'Veritas' – 'truth' – providing a moral compass as relevant to today's students as it has been throughout the school's history. A condition of the legacy was that a bridge be built, a rather grand effort 400 feet long and 26 feet wide with five stone arches.

The foundation stone was eventually laid by Lord Provost Gilbert Hamilton on 1 June 1754, but the foundations proved inadequate due to the soft soil conditions, and a great flood on 18 November 1795 washed the entire bridge away. There were to be successors to this bridge, which also succumbed to a watery grave, of which you will hear more later.

Over in Edinburgh

William Mylne (1734-90), Robert's younger brother who had, with his sibling, benefited greatly from his experience of the European Tour, cut his teeth early on bridge-building. In 1759 he designed the three-arched rubble stone **Yair Bridge**, also known as Fairnielee, across the River Tweed on the Edinburgh to Selkirk road, now the A707. Completed in 1764, the bridge was substantially rebuilt in 1988, using reinforced concrete, so it is not quite as old as it appears.

Yair Bridge, aka Fairnielee. *Colin L. Shearer*

William Mylne's major contribution, however, was in the capital. He was instrumental in plans for the development of Edinburgh's New Town in the mid-18th century, including the original design for the North Bridge. Great plans were afoot in 1760s Edinburgh with the North Loch, now Princes Street Gardens, drained and Lord Provost George Drummond promoting schemes for developing the city beyond the Old Town.

As a schoolboy living in Edinburgh throughout the mid-1960s, I well remember the '200 Summers in a City' exhibition, staged at Waverley Market and an opportunity to promote the many architectural, scientific and cultural aspects manifested in the 'New Town'. Among my childhood souvenirs I still have the oversize exhibition programme, eye-catching in bright red.

The first attempt at the **North Bridge**, which was to comprise three semi-circular arches, each of 72-foot span on tallish piers, proved too heavy, and in August 1769 the great mass of loose fill in the abutment and the approach at the south end of the bridge, derived from previous excavations, forced out the side wall and cracked the short arch and the

abutment wall. The collapsing wall engulfed five pedestrians who were killed by the subsiding earth.

The bridge reopened in 1772, but a further scare about another wall put paid to William Mylne's endeavours with the North Bridge and he disappeared, with his dog, to live on the eastern seaboard of North America, in the backwoods of Carolina, in pursuit of the simple life. By good fortune he missed the end of the American Civil War but did not stay long enough to celebrate the forming of the United States of America in 1776.

Although lacking the ambitionary zeal of his older brother, William did reappear some years later in Dublin, where he ended his engineering career with responsibility for the city's waterworks.

The North Bridge was 1,125 feet long, stretching from the High Street to Princes Street, with three central arches and two side arches. It is not the same bridge that stands aloft Waverley Station today, however. Mylne's bridge was demolished in 1896 to be replaced with three spans of arched girders, each 175 feet long and 75 feet wide, constructed by Sir William Arrol & Co, fresh from the company's massive project on the

A detail of North Bridge, Edinburgh. *Deborah M. Keith*

Forth Rail Bridge. Opened in 1897, it provides a link between the impressive 'Scotsman' building, the former headquarters of the *Scotsman* newspaper at the south end, and the Balmoral Hotel and former General Post Office at the north end, and looks across to the Georgian façade of New Register House. The engineers of the 1897 bridge were Cunningham, Blyth and Westland, who also designed Waverley Station and its bridge.

On the south side of the Royal Mile lies **South Bridge**. This is very much a shopping street along the lines of **Robert Adam**'s Pulteney Bridge in Bath. Indeed, Adam was involved in the design of Edinburgh's South Bridge. I say 'involved' rather than 'engaged' as the latter presumes there to be a contractual relationship. When banker James Hunter Blair became the city's Lord Provost in 1784, the American War of Independence had ended (nearly 20 years earlier, but there was a lot of shouting afterwards), and capital was again available to invest in Edinburgh's development. Plans from 1752 and a scheme from 1775 for bridging the ravine known as the Cowgate were dusted down. Hunter Blair devised a compulsory purchase scheme, empowered by an Act of Parliament in 1785, whereby the development

would be funded by the difference between the existing value of the property and its enhanced value, a sum estimated at £8,600.

The Act also made the construction of the bridge explicitly linked to the reconstruction of the buildings of Edinburgh University, which was urgently required. Hunter Blair discussed the bridge proposals with Robert Adam, who was particularly eager to be awarded the commission. No formal contract was drawn up, though, and it appears that the Lord Provost was keen to pick Adam's brains for ideas about the project, yet avoid engaging an architect whose designs were notoriously expensive. Adam's ideas are certainly transparent in the bridge eventually constructed, a link between the High Street and Chambers Street comprising 19 arches with only one, over Cowgate, visible.

Robert Adam must have felt disappointed and resentful at being used by Hunter Blair, but he was at least successful in being formally appointed to undertake the design of Register House and the new buildings for Edinburgh University.

Back at the South Bridge, local architects Robert Kay and John Baxter completed the bridge with associated properties in 1788. The arches that form the bridge were designed to be business premises for local tradesmen and taverns. They very rapidly fell into neglect, however, and these vaults became Edinburgh's worst slums and were used by Burke and Hare to hide the bodies of people for medical experiments. Today they are a fascinating part of the Edinburgh tourist route, including ghostly tales, and are a major venue during the Edinburgh Festival Fringe in August, which daily hosts more than 60 shows.

Bridging four major rivers: Tweed, Tay, Deveron and Nith

Three very significant bridges from the late 18th century were designed by **John Smeaton** (1724-92), known as 'the father of civil engineering in Britain'. Born in Leeds, his early career was as a maker of mathematical instruments before he turned to engineering. He founded the Smeatonian Society of Civil Engineers, the pedigree of the Institution of Civil Engineers. Responsible for designing the third Eddystone Lighthouse and many canals and harbours in England, his major works are in Scotland, including bridge crossings of the Tweed at Coldstream (1763-66), the Tay at Perth (1772) and the Deveron at Banff (1779).

The **Coldstream** bridge, with five arches each with a 60-foot span, has tunnelled spandrels and pointed cutwaters and starlings. **Perth** has seven principal arches and is 900 feet long. The **Deveron** bridge at Banff, too, has seven arches, is more than 410 feet long, and has a picturesque

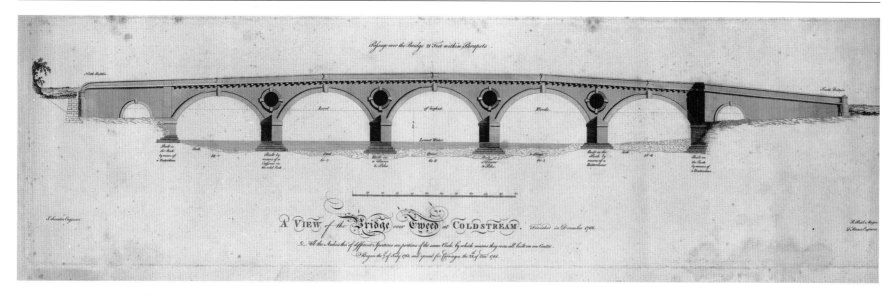

An elevation drawing of Coldstream Bridge. Canmore

setting next to Duff House, home of the Earl of Fife. All three have been widened, Perth by iron cantilevered footways, Banff by additional stone arches, and Coldstream, mostly recently in the 1960s, by cantilevered concrete footways and rebuilt stone parapets.

The Coldstream Bridge once had a 'marriage house' at its northern end, which is in Scotland, allowing marriages for English couples without the reading of the banns, as required south of the border. Gretna Green is world-renowned for this matrimonial activity, but Coldstream got in on the act too. Robert Burns crossed the bridge entering England for the first time on 7 May 1787. Kneeling, he prayed for a blessing on his native land:

'O Scotia! My dear, my native soil!
For whom my warmest wish to heaven sent!
Long may thy hardy sons of rustic toil
Be blest with health, and peace, and sweet content.'

Smeaton's engineering designs for the Forth & Clyde Canal included the Kelvin Aqueduct in Glasgow, which, when opened in 1790, was the largest aqueduct in Britain.

A Scot who was to become predominant as a bridge engineer outside his native land was **John Rennie** (1761-1821), whose 1799 bridge over

the Tweed at **Kelso**, with its five semi-elliptical arched bridge with twin Doric columnar pilasters on each pier, was to be the model for his Waterloo Bridge in London, completed 12 years later. Regarded in style and execution as one of the most handsome and effective structures of its kind, in many ways Kelso Bridge heralded the start of a new era of bridge-building in the UK. In 1921 the south arch was haunched and strengthened and all exposed stonework was cleaned and repointed by engineering firm Blyth & Blyth.

Rennie's other bridges in Scotland included Stenhouse Mills in Edinburgh, of which only the parapets survive; Musselburgh (1808, but widened in 1923); the **Ken** at New Galloway (1811, but rebuilt 1822); the **Cree** at Newton Stewart (1814), and at Cramond (1820, but demolished in 1962).

Alexander Stevens (1730-96), an architect, builder and tenant farmer from Prestonhall in Midlothian, designed several bridges in the late 18th century, based on the Aberfeldy profile. One of his earliest is the handsome **Hyndford Bridge** over the Clyde near Lanark, built in 1773 and comprising five arches. This was followed in 1780 by **Drygrange Bridge** over the Tweed at Melrose, with its three high arches of red and yellow sandstone and central span of 105 feet, which carried road traffic until bypassed in 1975 by the New Drygrange Bridge, by Sir Alexander Gibb & Partners. Stevens's finest piece of architecture was the **Ancrum Bridge** over the Teviot, completed in 1784, with its three segmental arches all in pale pink sandstone.

Rennie's bridge over the Tweed at Kelso. *Deborah M. Keith*

The following year he provided the decorative masonry on the **Bridge of Dun** over the South Esk near Montrose and, in the late 1780s, the new five-arched bridge at **Ayr**, the one that prompted barbed commentary from Robert Burns.

In 1795 he designed the **Teviot Bridge**, upstream from the confluence of the Teviot with the Tweed at Kelso, with its three high arches built by William Elliot. John Rennie was very critical of the Teviot Bridge, saying it was 'the ugliest thing I ever saw' and was 'unlikely to last for any length of time'. He did incorporate the twin columns in his design at his Kelso Bridge, however, and he was certainly wrong on the second count, as it's still there today.

On the Angus coast, the bridging of the River South Esk at Montrose Basin had to await an Act of Parliament in 1790 for what it describes as 'a great publick utility'. The Inch Bridge was a single-span stone structure crossing the southern channel, designed by Alexander Stevens. It was modified in 1830 to incorporate a drawbridge, allowing boats access to the Basin, and continued in use until the 1970s. The northern channel was crossed by a wooden bridge, insecurely founded on piles in unstable gravel, and was repeatedly hit by boats, strong tides and storms. Its life, and that of its successor, were relatively short and problematic, which we'll revisit later.

The River Tweed has only one short section of rocky cascades, near the small settlement of Tweedsmuir. It was first bridged in 1783 by James and Alexander Noble. **Carlow's Bridge** comprises a single stone arch, which has borne the force of the Tweed in spate many times, but despite being much reconstructed it is still in use.

Much as it was originally, when built in 1702, is **Old Manor Brig**, west of Peebles. This is a single narrow segmental rubble arch with a pronounced hump over the Manor Water near its confluence with the mighty Tweed. Designed by the landowner, William, Earl of Queensberry, it was built by his second son, William, the Earl of March.

Ancrum Old Bridge. *Canmore*

The Old Manor Brig, near Peebles. *Colin L. Shearer*

Pease Bridge. *Iain Matheson*

The steep gorges that dissect the eastern side of the Borders presented an obstacle to movement between Berwick and Dunbar. At Cockburnspath in 1786 local architect and mason David Henderson built what was, at the time of construction, the highest bridge in the world. **Pease Bridge** stands 117 feet above water level, the deck supported by four tall semi-circular arches, with the spandrels pierced above each pier with weight-saving hollow cylinders. The spandrels and parapets were extensively rebuilt in 2004, but the bridge still carries the public road.

Across in **Dumfries** a 'new bridge' over the River Nith was built to carry the public road. To a design by architect **Thomas Boyd** in 1791, the bridge, with dressed stone in the segmental arches and rounded cutwaters, was widened by James Barbour and Sir William Arrol in 1892/93. Works to strengthen the bridge in 1935 created an open-spandrel structure, which is masked by the original masonry facing, so the present bridge is not quite what it appears. Further improvements by Baptie Shaw and Morton in 1981 involved broadening the east arch on the south side and renewing the parapets and deck. From a letter in 1794 from the Duke of Buccleuch, it is apparent that landowners were very much alive to the prospect of a ransom strip. The Duke, no doubt encouraged by his astute if not particularly philanthropic factor, declared that access to the new bridge would not be granted until the warrant for £1,000 was paid. The money was found!

The Laird's call

The aristocracy, and even the lesser landed gentry, exercised much control over development in these times. That had upsides, too, for the engineering and architectural professions. Many of the notable bridges from the 18th century are associated with the large country estates that developed extensively during that period. These were welcome commissions and keenly sought, particularly for those wishing to expand their practices by tapping into a wealthy seam of clients.

One such was **William Adam** (1689-1748), an architect, builder and industrialist. Adam was educated at Kirkcaldy High School, but spent his early adult years in the Low Countries. On his return he established an enviable reputation among the landowning fraternity. He designed and built stone arch bridges, including the **Laundry Bridge** at Dalkeith House (1740s) for the Duke of Buccleuch, and the large **West Bridge** at Cullen in Banffshire for the Earl of Seafield in 1743.

His work with the architect Roger Morris on the design of the Duke of Argyll's Inveraray Castle was complemented by a three-arch **Aray Bridge** over the river, with tall castellated turrets in Gothic style. It was destroyed by a flood in 1772, and replaced within three years by the present bridge. Designed by Robert Mylne, it is a magnificent two arched dressed stone bridge with a

'Cullen Castle', a painting by William's son, Robert Adam, showing the West Bridge. *Courtesy of the National Galleries Scotland*

The Aray Bridge. *Deborah M. Keith*

cylindrical opening, known as an oculus, through the spandrel on the middle pier. Mylne also designed the **Dubh Loch Bridge** across the River Shira at the head of the loch.

Roger Morris's **Garron Bridge** at Inveraray dates from 1748 and has a distinctive high segmental stone arch with a 40-foot span, a feature still visible from the present road.

William's elder son, **John Adam** (1721-92), designed the **Avenue Bridge** across the Lugar Water at Dumfries House near Cumnock, for William Dalrymple, Earl of Dumfries, which was the first in Britain to use elliptical arches. Serious mining subsidence in this part of Ayrshire necessitated a faithful restoration, complete with obelisk embellishments, in 1970.

William's second son, **Robert Adam** (1732-94) returned from the Grand Tour of Europe inspired to create bridges as features in the

Garron Bridge. *Deborah M. Keith*

landscape. His paintings depict landscapes, both real and imaginary, in which bridges are a common feature, all with attention to practical detail. He was responsible for bridges on estates where he designed or altered country houses. Each was conceived as a feature of the landscape and structural considerations were secondary, yet rational. His winding 'antique' viaduct approaching **Culzean Castle** for the Earl of Cassills, the Chief of the Clan Kennedy, is not only a landscape ornament, but also forms the principal access to the castle. Sadly, rainwater penetration when the first electricity supply cable was installed in the 1950s led to extensive decay.

James Duff, styled as Earl Fife (the family was not the Earl of Fife until 1885), had the **Bridge of Alvah** constructed over a gorge on the River Deveron in Banffshire. Understood to be the work of Thomas Reid, a local landscape gardener who also built the bridge at Bauchlaw two years previously, the arched structure dates from 1772 and incorporates a room in the west abutment. The bridge lies within the policies of Duff House, which leaves open to doubt the assertion that the room was for the toll collector. More likely is the rumour, reputably never denied, that the room was for Earl Fife to entertain local girls.

By the close of the 18th century, new concepts in bridge-building were being forged, not only in terms of scale and function but also in engineering, science and technology. Ahead lay even more significant developments in infrastructure, which would challenge both the bridge designer and builder alike.

The Bridge of Alvah. *Canmore*

5. The Great Age of Bridge-Building in the 19th century

From road to rail

I left school in 1973 and my career went south. Not professionally, you understand, but a move to England to study at Reading University.

I had originally intended to study at Aberdeen University but the professor who was to launch the new Land Economy course there died prematurely and the course was delayed. I must add that later, during my early professional life in Forfar, I was to benefit greatly from the teachings of Professor Alistair MacLeary, who went on to found the very successful department in Aberdeen, but back then I wanted to get started at university and no one in those days ever contemplated a 'gap year'. Reading University offered what I considered to be the very best of both worlds for a surveyor: a two-year general practice syllabus and a third year on rural specialisms.

The BSc Hons in Estate Management comprised several different subjects: economics, law, building construction, valuation, planning and, of course, statistics. Planning was really the application of all I'd learned about in geography at school, and it captured my imagination. The first-year course was titled 'The Use and Development of Land' with illustrated lectures from Professor Gerald Burke. He explained to us how the countryside and townscapes had developed from early times. I could see so much of what had inspired me during my early exploratory adventures being related as a fascinating history and set in a meaningful context for today.

OK, so his examples didn't get much further north than Oxfordshire, but I could relate to them and translate them into the different but equally captivating stories of Scotland's development as a richly complex web of architecture, engineering, human endeavour and the influence of natural forces.

Professor Burke's secret teaching weapon, akin I suppose to the linguistic dexterity of my school history teacher, 'Tinman', was to illustrate his lectures with a wide variety of photographic slides showing townscapes and village scenes. However, his huge collection seemed to date from the 1950s and early 1960s, as was obvious from the car models that appeared. It was a galaxy of Ford Consuls, Standard Vanguards, Morris Oxfords and Minors, Wolseley 4/44s, Bedford lorries and, in the most recent photographs, the occasional Hillman Minx and Rover 2000. But they were images that captured the moment and left a deep impression of the subject in my mind. They were one reason why I wanted a book on Scottish bridges to be well illustrated.

When I set off for Reading on the bus from Stirling, carrying just a rucksack and a few sandwiches for the journey, it seemed a very long way, but I was always minded to consider how much further it must have seemed to pioneering travellers some 100 years or more earlier.

That said, the 19th century heralded the dawn of a new era in communications, in transport and the means of travel for all in Britain. The greatest benefits, even in the pioneering days, were in the relative ease with which goods and the public could be transported and the time saved in travelling from A to B.

Scotland benefited from these massive innovations and produced several generations of engineers, industrialists and road surveyors who were instrumental in developing these new technologies on a world stage.

The 1800s saw Scotland make the rapid move from a predominantly agrarian economy to a largely urbanised society with the advent of the Industrial Revolution. The novel transport systems that resulted, most notably canals, then railways, gave rise to the Great Age of Bridge Building, with bridges not only serving different purposes, but also made from new, stronger and more versatile materials, which themselves were innovative products of the industrialisation process.

As different transport systems developed, they required differing solutions to bridging the gap, be that across rivers or ravines or as a means of minimising gradient or facilitating easy changes of direction.

Each of the principal means of transporting people, goods and materials developed rapidly in the 19th century, and with them the bridges that provided essential links on each of their networks. Roads, canals and railways were literally to bridge the gulf between the old days and the exciting and fast-moving developments ahead.

As I completed my three-year degree at Reading and looked to the future once more, I could never have imagined how much time in my career I would later spend criss-crossing the country, using almost every mode of transport, and how often I would pause to give thanks to those 19th-century engineers and bridge-builders whose vision and skill made those journeys not simply possible, but scenically impressive and relatively comfortable, too.

6. 19TH-CENTURY ROAD BRIDGES

From stone to steel

The neglect and decay of the roads and bridges built by Wade and his successors in the Highlands, coupled with the loss of many bridges by floods, meant that the highway networks became inadequate to handle the growing economic base. Without huge infrastructure investment the economy would wither and die and with it the population, many of whom had already migrated overseas in significant numbers.

In 1801 the British Government commissioned **Thomas Telford**, a well-respected pioneering engineer for whom greatness was in the making, to survey and report on conditions in the Highlands and to make recommendations for their improvement. He identified that a chief weakness of Highland communications lay in the absence of bridges over the large rivers. Apart from Aberfeldy Bridge and High Bridge at Spean, Wade's other bridges, some 40 of them, had all been relatively small.

Telford's Parliamentary Commissions

As a direct consequence of Telford's findings, two parallel Commissions were established by Act of Parliament in 1803, one charged with 'making roads and building bridges in the Highlands of Scotland', the other with constructing the Caledonian Canal, linking Fort William to Inverness through the Great Glen.

Telford became the permanent consulting engineer and, in the first quarter of the 19th century, more than £1.5 million was expended on these projects. This investment in the vast network of Parliamentary roads and bridges, as they came to be called, is the real foundation and origin of modern communications in the Highlands.

But it was not all public funding. The Treasury made its contribution conditional upon 'match-funding' being derived from the local landed proprietors who would derive benefit from the roads and bridges. They had to put their 50% contribution on deposit in the Bank of Scotland before Telford prepared detailed specifications! In the event, some £233,000 of the total cost of £500,000 for these major civil engineering works was raised from the Highland counties and local landowners.

Thomas Telford was renowned for his attention to detail in his designs. The roads and bridges he built were on a scale far exceeding those by the military. Poet Robert Southey, who travelled throughout the Highlands, recorded in his Journal in 1819 that the

'walled banks, the steep declivities and the beautiful turfing on the slopes form a noble display of skill and power exerted in the best manner for the most beneficial purpose.'

19th-century road bridges
Key to bridges mentioned in the text

1	Craigellachie (Spey)	NJ 288 450
2	Dunkeld (Tay)	NO 026 426
3	Lovat (Beauly)	NH 516 449
4	Conon	NH 541 556
5	Helmsdale	ND 025 153
6	Bonar Bridge	NH 615 915
7	Old Spey Bridge, Fochabers	NJ 340 594
8	Contin	NH 454 566
9	Altnaharra	NC 568 357
10	Calder (Newtonmore)	NN 708 980
11	Spean Bridge	NN 221 816
12	Bannockburn	NS 809 904
13	Cartland Crags	NS 868 444
14	Pathhead (Lothian Bridge)	NT 391 645
15	Dean Bridge	NT 242 739
16	Tongland	NX 691 533
17	Wick Bridge	ND 362 508
18	Thurso Bridge	ND 117 681
19	Cambus o' May	NO 420 976
20	Monymusk	NJ 689 149
21	Cromdale	NJ 665 289
22	Aboyne	NO 352 797
23	Burnhervie (Kemnay)	NJ 735 190

24	Banchory	NO 697 952
25	Larbert	NS 856 820
26	Charlestown of Aberlour	NJ 262 429
27	Crathie	NO 262 949
28	Kirkton of Glenisla	NO 212 603
29	Haughs of Drimmie	NO 170 502
30	Balmoral	NO 261 949
31	Infirmary Street, Inverness	NH 664 445
32	Greig Street, Inverness	NH 663 453
33	Bridge of Oich, Aberchalder	NH 337 036
34	Lochybridge, Fort William	NN 119 755
35	Musselburgh	NT 342 726
36	Leaderfoot	NT 573 347
37	Galashiels	NT 488 358
38	Thirlestane Castle	NT 533 479
39	Dryburgh Abbey	NT 591 317
40	King's Meadow, Peebles	NT 253 401
41	Gattonside, Melrose	NT 545 345
42	Union Chain Bridge	NT 933 510
43	Kalemouth	NT 709 274
44	Duke of Wellington, Aberdeen	NJ 939 059
45	Union Bridge, Aberdeen	NJ 939 061
46	Victoria Bridge, Aberdeen	NJ 964 546
47	Methlick	NJ 857 375
48	Shakkin Briggie	NJ 897 260
49	King's Ford, Cabrach	NJ 381 286
50	Victoria Bridge, Glasgow	NS 591 645
51	St Andrew's Suspension Bridge, Glasgow	NS 600 640
52	Glasgow Bridge (Jamaica Street)	NS 587 647
53	Rutherglen	NS 606 630
54	Dalmarnock	NS 617 626
55	Marykirk	NO 685 650
56	Regent Bridge, Edinburgh	NT 259 740
57	Annan	NY 191 665
58	Stirling New Bridge	NS 797 944
59	Ashietiel	NT 430 351
60	Overtoun	NS 424 761
61	Auchindrean (Braemore)	NH 195 805
62	Corrieshalloch Gorge	NH 203 779

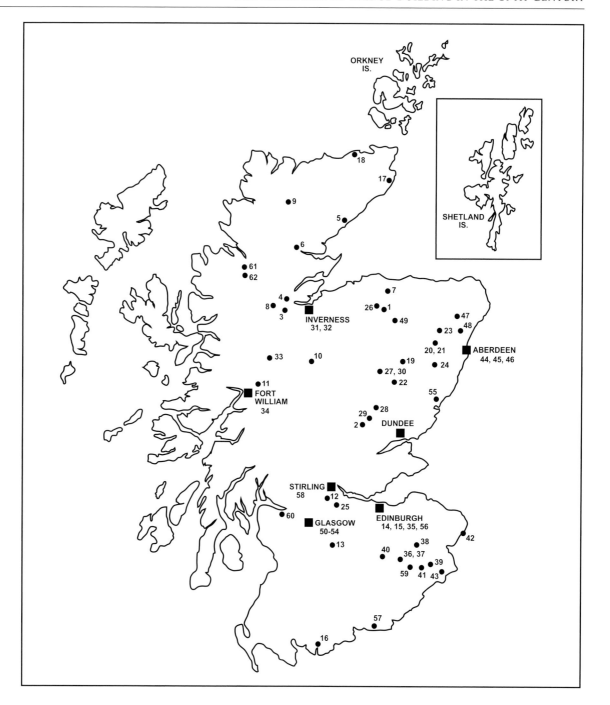

The Telford formula

Thomas Telford described his approach to design in his article 'Practice of Bridge Building', published in 1812. The foundations were of paramount import. Where practicable at a reasonable expense, they were to be sunk and laid upon rock. Where rock could not be found, the foundations were to be sunk to at least 2 feet below the lowest part of the bed of the river. Where the ground was soft a platform of timber was required to be laid under the masonry foundations, to consist of two thicknesses of 3-inch planks laid crossing each other, with driven pile planking where necessary.

On hard ground, Telford required an inverted arch, or pavement, laid and wedged between the abutments, running the full width of the bridge and secured by rows of stones sunk deeply into the bed of the river. His practice was to be liberal with the use of retaining walls and bulwarks.

These bridges were built to last. He believed that a bridge should be placed at a straight stretch on the river and at right angles to the current, but 'where practicable, from the approaches being in a curve, the general outlines of the bridge are seen to most advantage.'

He preferred an odd number of arches, all springing from the same level and increasing in height and span towards midstream, so as to provide a gradient on the road of about 1:24. He did not favour the use of columns as they derived from Greek temples where there were no arches, and described such features as an 'affectation'. That did not deter him from considerable design embellishment on several of his bridges, however, most notably at Tongland Bridge in Kirkcudbrightshire.

Telford's instruction from the Commission resulted in four great bridges: those crossing the Spey at **Craigellachie**; the Tay at **Dunkeld**; the Beauly at **Lovat**, and the Conon at **Dingwall** (only the remains can be seen now, next to the newer railway bridge). Others were also significant. Of the two River Dee crossings, the timber bridge at Ballater lasted until 1885, to be replaced by a granite structure, but Potarch Bridge remains in use, as do his bridges across the Don at Keig and Alford. Telford's bridge in **Helmsdale**, dating from 1811, is also still in use for local traffic.

There had been petitions for a bridge at what became known as **Bonar Bridge** in Ross-shire for many years, but a tragedy on 16 August 1809 prompted action. A ferry, carrying more than 100 people together with goods and livestock for the market town of Tain, sank with the loss of 99 lives, including the Sherriff of Dornoch, Hugh MacCulloch. The disaster relief fund raised more than £2,900, much of it from overseas donors, principally the expat community, which was used to build the first bridge.

The original Bonar Bridge across the River Carron at Ardgay has been replaced, but the structure from 1812 of cast-iron girders with an arch of 150 feet, was described by Southey as 'a spider's web in the air and the finest thing that ever was made by God or man'.

With its foundations laid on caissons, it must have been a solid structure, for it withstood a mass of fir logs consolidated by ice carried by the storms and ensuing floods of the winter of 1813 violently colliding against it. Again, it stood firm five years later when a schooner, caught in a strong tide, drifted under the bridge, losing two masts.

The bridge finally succumbed to the great Highland flood of January 1892, but it was not the iron arch that failed, but rather the masonry arches and the southern abutment that collapsed first. The replacement bridge, a steel structure, was designed by Crouch & Hogg and built by Sir William Arrol & Company in 1893, itself replaced yet again in 1973 by the present bowstring arch bridge.

Telford was fortunate in the superintendent he recruited to assist him in his Scottish commissions. **John Mitchell**, from Forres, was described as 'a man of inflexible integrity, a fearless temper and indefatigable frame'. Nicknamed 'Telford's Tartar', he was physically strong, travelling 10,000 miles each year inspecting his road and bridge works. As that would all have been on horseback, he must have spent an average of 5 hours in the saddle every day to cover this distance.

Mitchell was undoubtedly disliked, to put it mildly, by the contractors of the day, for he enforced the specification to the letter. These contractors and their guarantors lost no less than £68,000, equivalent to many millions today. Telford and his successors, the team of John Mitchell and his son **Joseph** (1803-83), who became the chief inspector of Highland roads, were responsible for some 930 road miles and 1,117 bridges during the 60 years that the Commission functioned. They made an enormous improvement to communications in the Highlands and by the 1820s seven stagecoaches journeyed to and from Inverness every day, and letters were sent three times per week from Dingwall to Skye, where the London Sunday newspaper could be delivered the following Thursday. Given the distances and terrain involved, these represented huge steps forward in social and economic communication.

Telford's bridges remain a monument to this remarkable engineer. Many of them still function today, carrying 21st-century traffic while retaining their individual elegance and enhancing the environment to which they contribute both character and style. The bridge over the Tay

Telford's bridge over the Tay at Dunkeld. *Deborah M. Keith*

at Dunkeld, which Telford described as 'the finest bridge in Scotland', typifies the genre, matching civil engineering ingenuity with creative design. Built on the southern approach to the cathedral city, at the confluence of the Rivers Tay and Braan, it comprises five river and two flood stone arches providing a total length of 685 feet. Two further arches have been built up and used for storage.

The River Braan had deposited so much gravel as it entered the Tay that the old river bed had filled up, allowing the bridge to be constructed over the dry channel into which, upon completion of the work in 1809, the river was again diverted.

The bridge was ornamented at the request of the powerful local landowner, John, 4th Duke of Atholl, who agreed to contribute 50% of the construction cost on the basis that he would receive the tolls, not only as a return on his investment but also to fund repair costs. It appears that the Duke was also the contractor, carrying out the works by direct estate labour.

Telford was not, however, greatly taken with over-ornamentation; his designs were dictated in most cases by the considerations of strict utility. He had, of course, to satisfy the Treasury-funded Commissioners that the scale of expenditure reflected the public purse requirements of functionality at reasonable cost. Only where local landowners were prepared to pay for it did the ornamentation go beyond what Robert Southey described as Telford's 'farthing wisdom'.

In their report on Dunkeld, the Commissioners acknowledged unreservedly that 'the bridge ... is a magnificent edifice ... and altogether worthy of the grandeur of its situation.'

At **Fochabers**, as at Dunkeld, in deference to the wishes and funding of the local landowner, here the Duke of Gordon, some decoration was also introduced into the plans. The Commissioners looked favourably on the result, recognising the contribution that design had on environmental appearance.

Although driven by purpose rather than elaborate design, Telford's bridges make significant statements in the landscape. There are few better examples than in his great bridge over the Spey at **Craigellachie**.

The Spey bridge, Craigellachie. *L. Bruce Keith*

knowledge. These same floods, where 4 inches of rainfall was recorded in one 12-hour period, and described as one of the most grievous natural disasters ever suffered by the Highland counties, claimed the bridges at Fochabers, Forres and Ballater. It took three years to carry out the resultant repair and rebuilding work, but at Fochabers the replacement bridge, which was half masonry and half cast iron, was completed in 1854.

The Craigellachie bridge, which once carried the A941 between Elgin and Dufftown, was restored in 1964 and bypassed by a modern bridge opened in 1972, situated a short distance downstream. The stunning setting of the old bridge is, however, a licensed wedding venue and provides a focus for tourists enjoying the delights of the Whisky Trail round the many Speyside distilleries. The bridge inspired a popular Strathspey tune composed by William Marshall in 1814 and has been captured in several marketing artworks for The Macallan whisky and the Spey Valley Brewery, which brews an 1814 lager. A commemorative stamp was issued in 2015.

The bridge also provided a very fitting location for the colourful and historic ceremony to mark the amalgamation of The Gordon Highlanders and The Queen's Own Highlanders (Seaforth and Camerons) to form The Highlanders (Seaforth, Gordons and Camerons) in 1994, with a plaque now in place.

Many of the Highland bridges incorporated battered wing-walls or buttresses for strengthening, most notably at Calder Bridge, Newtonmore; the three-arch asymmetric rubble-masonry **Contin Bridge** (1812) across the Black Water; and **Altnaharra Bridge** (1815) across the River Mudale on the road between Lairg and Tongue. The **Calder Bridge**, built in 1814, was so solidly constructed that when it had to be demolished following a significant flood in November 1978 it took three explosions to bring it down.

Spean Bridge, which carries the A821 Glasgow to Inverness road across the River Spean, was another of Telford's designs. Completed in

Southey described the bridge as 'of iron, beautifully light, in a situation where the utility of lightness is instantly perceived.' The cast-iron arch structure, perched on stone abutments with castellated granite towers, has a principal span of 152 feet, with a further arch to provide for flood water on the adjoining meadowland. Telford's original plan was for the abutments to rise 7 feet above low water level, but the evidence of local people that the Spey rose in flood by almost 12 feet led to rapid revision and the abutments raised.

Completed in 1814, at a cost of £8,000, with cast iron prefabricated in Wales by William Hazeldine, whom Telford nicknamed 'the arch conjuror', the bridge survived the great floods of 1829 by a narrow margin, for which Telford must have felt indebted to the local

1821 and comprising three arches, this 240-foot-long bridge was widened in 1932 using reinforced concrete with a granite ashlar finish.

In the Lowlands, Telford's circular-arch stone bridge at **Bannockburn**, built in 1819, incorporates a huge circle over the single arch, which has a span of 24 feet – Southey described its appearance as 'singular and

Bannockburn Bridge. *Courtesy of the Institution of Engineers and Shipbuilders in Scotland*

striking'. Telford's aim in the design was to prevent inward earth pressure movement of the tall abutments by means of curved masonry struts – and time is testimony to its effectiveness.

Telford's **Cartland Crags Bridge**, completed in 1822 across the Mouse Water, a tributary of the Clyde, is a splendid three-span dressed stone arch on tall, slender piers, which, at 122 feet above water level, is one of the highest bridges over inland water in Scotland. This huge engineering feat lies on a minor public road leading to the small village of Nemphlar.

Telford's design for the **Pathhead** or Lothian Bridge, south of Edinburgh, commissioned in 1827 by Sir John Dalrymple when he was the Council's convenor for roads, can be considered the prototype for the Dean Bridge's elevation. The use of supplemental, or what Telford termed 'ascititious' or 'external' shallow arches, gave the structure an appearance of slenderness for the five segmental arches across the Tyne Water, best viewed from the valley floor.

The development of the New Town of Edinburgh in the mid-18th century prompted expansion westwards to the farmland across the deep ravine of the Water of Leith. Led by the prospect of speculative residential development value on land owned by Sir John Nisbet, the entrepreneur behind the scheme was John Learmonth, a coachmaker and, later, Edinburgh's Lord Provost. He commissioned Thomas Telford to design and build the **Dean Bridge**, with its four 96-foot sandstone segmental arches towering above the gorge.

The bridge is 450 feet long and has a 23-foot carriageway together with two 8-foot footways. Completed in 1831 at a cost of £18,500, using high-quality stone from the local Craigleith Quarry, each arch has an inset semi-circular arch, adding style to this impressive structure, especially when viewed from below. William McGonagall testified to that point when he described the Dean Bridge as 'a very magnificent sight; because from the basement it is a great height'.

The parapet walls were subsequently raised to 12 feet to deter suicide jumpers. Internally, the Dean Bridge has a hollow chamber that not only allows access for inspection and maintenance, but also significantly reduces the weight of the arches.

This was a technique that Telford first developed at **Tongland Bridge** over a deep gorge on the River Dee on the A711 Kirkcudbright to Castle Douglas road. Built in 1804 in a bold and picturesque castellated style in Annan freestone, Tongland comprises a single segmental arch span of 112 feet, with hollow spandrels between rounded abutments. The steep river banks and the 20-foot rise in tides at this point dictate that the arch is very high, and the bridge incorporates pointed archways in the wing-

Left New Town and Dean Bridge, Edinburgh. *Lewis Matheson*

Telford's Pathhead Bridge. *Lewis Matheson*

Above Dean Bridge is particularly impressive when viewed from below. *Lewis Matheson*

walls and sturdy battlemented parapets as appealing features. Tongland was Telford's first bridge in Scotland and the first in Britain to carry a road on internal spine walls rising from the arch rings. Tongland Bridge also inspired a young Iain Murray, whom we'll meet later as Project Manager at the new Queensferry Crossing. Iain was a frequent visitor when his father worked at the Tongland Hydro-Electric Scheme.

The North

The improved communications leading northwards, first road then rail, provided considerable development scope for the northern towns of Wick and Thurso, with sea links to Orkney and beyond to Shetland. As early as 1805 Sir William Pulteney of the British Fisheries Society commissioned Thomas Telford to design and supervise the construction of a major new herring fishing port and harbour at the estuary of the River Wick. In 1902 the port merged with Wick, a settlement dating from Norse times. The three-arched bridge across the river, leading to **Wick** town centre, was opened in July 1877. It must have been substantially completed by the previous October, however, as a plaque on the bridge records that Their Royal Highnesses The Prince and Princess of Wales, together with Prince John of Glucksburg and the Duke and Duchess of Sutherland, crossed it during their visit to the town. The engineer was John Murdoch from Inverness and the contractor a local builder, Daniel Miller. At the south

Tongland Bridge. *Canmore*

end of the bridge is Ebenezer Place, which holds the world record as the shortest street, at 2.06 metres. It has just one doorway.

The most northerly town on the British mainland, **Thurso**, also has Norse roots as an early trading port for the northern European countries. By the 19th century Scrabster harbour, a mile and a half to the north-west, had become a thriving fishing harbour and Thurso developed along an attractive planned gridiron. The railway arrived in 1874, and on 3 May 1887 the Rt Hon The Earl of Caithness, Lord Lieutenant of the county, opened a magnificent stone bridge across the River Thurso. It was a joint enterprise funded by the Thurso Police Commissioners and the County Road Trustees. The engineers were MacBey and Gordon of Elgin and the contractor John Malcolm.

Wick Bridge. *Deborah M. Keith*

Thurso Bridge. *Deborah M. Keith*

The river is a significant Scottish watercourse, draining both the peatlands of the Flow Country and the agriculturally fertile lands of Caithness, and is a major salmon river. A plaque along the riverside walk records that in 1736 one pool in the lower stretches yielded 2,560 salmon.

Royal Deeside

Two of the best-known footbridges on the Aberdeenshire River Dee are the white-painted suspension bridges at Cambus O'May and Crathie. That at **Cambus O'May**, refurbished in 1988 by the District Council, was a gift in 1905 of Mr Alexander Gordon. The entrances to the bridge add charm, with an unusual swing gate on one side and a turnstile on the other. I wrote this description in the present tense, but on 30 December 2015 the River Dee, swollen from the tempestuous floods from Storm 'Frank', battered Cambus o' May with unprecedented force.

My hope is that it is restored to its former glory as soon as possible, for this bridge is, or was, an excellent example of the legacy of work by **Louis Harper** (1879-1903), a civil engineer who managed the bridge

department at Harpers' Foundry in Aberdeen. His father, John, had established a fencing and gate manufacturing business, but also patented 'a device for straining wire' in 1863, which was to lead the family into the manufacturing of suspension bridges.

The company designed and supplied bridges in many parts of Scotland. Examples include **Monymusk** (1879); **Cromdale** (1881, swept away in 1894); **Aboyne**; **Burnhervie** (Kemnay) (1880, collapsed 1979); **Banchory**; **Larbert**; and, in collaboration with James Abernethy & Co of Aberdeen, the bridges at **Cambus O'May** and, in 1900, across the Spey at **Charlestown of Aberlour**.

The bridges always served a purpose. At Burnhervie it was to give access to the public house there for the thirsty quarry-workers of Kemnay, which was dry at the time. The bridge collapsed in 1979 and has since been replaced twice, most recently in 2005 by a cable-stayed bridge. As for Kemnay, it got its own pub in 1937. As we'll see later, Harper's bridge legacy extended well beyond Scotland.

Royal Deeside is often recognised by its suspension footbridges. **Crathie** is the earliest of these, dating from 1834 but renewed by Queen Victoria (well, Blaikie Brothers, actually, but on Her Majesty's instructions) in 1885, so becoming known as the 'Royal Bridge'. That's not a unique sobriquet, though, as it also describes the 1885 bridge at

The bridge at Cambus o' May.
Lewis Matheson

Ballater. Again painted white, Crathie is an impressive structure, and at 12 feet is slightly wider than normal footbridges, as it was designed specifically to take carriages to Balmoral Castle. The original design was by **John Justice** from Dundee, who did much pioneering work on cable-stay-type suspension techniques, most notably at **Kirkton of Glenisla** in Angus and at **Haughs of Drimmie** near Blairgowrie.

The former dates from 1824 and is a public footpath across the River Isla, being a 62-foot-span wrought-iron suspension bridge with wooden decking and stone abutments. The bridge at Haughs of Drimmie, built in 1830 across the River Ericht, is on a private road, and the 100-foot wooden deck is suspended directly from wrought-iron arches with an under-deck inverted bowed truss built up from circular-section rods. These bridges are the distant ancestor of the major cable-stayed bridges built in Scotland from the latter part of the 20th century.

Isambard Kingdom Brunel (1806-59) is the most celebrated of all British civil engineers, but produced only one bridge on Scottish soil. And it was by Royal Command. The 125-foot-long iron girder bridge across the River Dee at **Balmoral** was built in 1856/57 and incorporated umbrella-shaped flanges into the girders at the top and bottom, so that the rain would run off the iron, preventing corrosion. Although Prince Albert had signed off the plans, Queen Victoria was reportedly not impressed by this Brunel effort. Notwithstanding, the Duke of Edinburgh did unveil a plaque on the bridge in 2006 to mark the bicentenary of Brunel's birth.

If Prince Philip shared his great-great-grandmother's disdain for Brunel's bridge, he bit his lip on that occasion, which is not a characteristic for which he is renowned. I have had the privilege to meet the Duke on three occasions. First was at a garden party at Holyrood, followed by the National Conference of the Duke of Edinburgh's Award Scheme, when I was invited by my good friend Colin Shearer, then the Award's Director (Scotland), to edit a quarterly publication, 'Scottish Award News'. Neither of these meetings provoked other than kind words from the Duke.

Our third meeting, however, was in Buckingham Palace when, as a Trustee of the Chartered Institution of Water and Environmental Management (CIWEM), I was attending the David Bellamy Inaugural Lecture. The more formal proceedings over, we adjourned to a reception room for drinks. The Duke approached a fellow Trustee and me and enquired as to what we did. I said I was there as a Trustee. 'No, no, I mean what do you do for a day job?' he pressed.

When I said I was Head of Property at Scottish & Southern Energy (SSE), the largest renewable energy company in the UK and Ireland,

Above Crathie Bridge. *Canmore*

Below An elevation drawing of the bridge at Haughs of Drimmie. *Canmore*

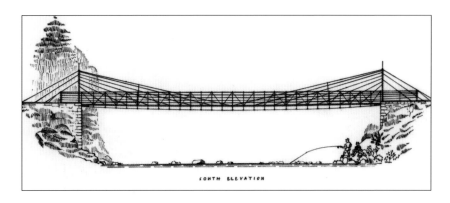

SOUTH ELEVATION

Prince Philip was quick to give me his opinion on those who built wind farms, and it wasn't complimentary!

I don't think I ever related that view back to SSE's Chief Executive, Ian Marchant, although it is unlikely to have lost him any sleep. Ian was an inspiring leader who believed passionately in harnessing the power of natural resources – water, wind and solar – to generate energy. This is a passion I share. Indeed, I believe it is fundamental to the United Nation's Sustainable Development Goals. My Director at SSE, Michelle Hynd, whose unstinting encouragement helped shape my career in its latter years, and paved my way to retirement, certainly found Prince Philip's remark amusing.

Bridging the Ness

Inverness has fine footbridges. **C. R. Manners** was responsible for the design of two of the iron suspension footbridges, Infirmary Bridge and Greig Street Bridge, built in 1879 and 1881 respectively.

The **Infirmary Bridge** is the earliest cable bridge in Scotland still standing. The **Greig Street Bridge** cost £1,400. **James Dredge Snr** (1794-1863) designed General's Well Bridge, to the Ness Islands. Dredge was an English engineer who lived in Bath. A brewer by trade, he had several Scottish bridge commissions, including the **Bridge of Oich** (1854), near Aberchalder, and Victoria Bridge at **Lochybridge**, Fort William.

About midway along the Great Glen, which cleaves its way across the Highlands from Inverness to Fort William, is Dredge's splendid Bridge of Oich. Now maintained by Historic Environment Scotland, it is a very fine example of his use of tapering chains, a principle he patented in 1836. Although at first glance it resembles a suspension bridge, it is in fact a double cantilever bridge, with the continuous deck supported by chains rather than cables. Much less material was required for these bridges, so they were lighter and the rigid chain link also reduced the amount of sway on the timber deck.

Conversely, this design suffers from a low weight restriction, which probably accounts for it not catching on in a major way. The Bridge of Oich, which you come across all of sudden as you drive north on the

The Infirmary Bridge, Inverness. *Mike W. Lowson*

Bridge of Oich. *Deborah M. Keith*

The three bridges at Leaderfoot. *Deborah M. Keith*

A82 near Aberchalder, was left to decay when it was bypassed in 1932 by the concrete bridge still in use. Halcrow Crouch managed the extensive restoration in 1997 and what an excellent result they and the contractor, Morrisons, achieved. It is one of my very favourite bridges.

The bridges over the Ness have had a chequered history. In 1410 Donald, Lord of the Isles, burned down Inverness and with it an oak bridge described as 'one of the finest in the Kingdom' on his way to the Battle of Harlaw. This was one of the bloodiest battles between the barons of north-east Scotland led by the Duke of Albany, the Regent of Scotland, and the Earl of Mar against the Western clans, fought near Inverurie in 1411.

Inverness's fortunes with bridges did not improve. A wooden bridge collapsed in 1663 with more than 200 people on it; the great flood of 1849 swept away a stone bridge; and the railway bridge was irreparably damaged by flood in 1989. Local folklore has it that disaster will strike when there are too many bridges. The Brahan Seer, that great Highland prophet, predicted in the 17th century that there would be a worldwide tragedy if ever it was possible to cross the Ness dry-shod at five places.

A fifth bridge was erected temporarily in August 1939 – the month before Hitler invaded Poland…!

The South

John Rennie has an impressive legacy of bridges in Scotland following his success at Kelso. They include the five segmental arches spanning the River Esk at **Musselburgh** (1809, but widened in 1924) and the bridge over the River Ken in Dumfries & Galloway. This was Rennie's second attempt at this bridge; the first, built in 1811, was destroyed by flood. Of granite masonry, its five arches were completed in 1822 and carry the A712 Dumfries to Newton Stewart road via the village of New Galloway.

Some bridges, although magnificent in their own right, are enhanced by their setting beside other bridges spanning the same river. Such is the case at **Leaderfoot** across the River Tweed, downstream from Melrose. Here, three bridges from different eras span the Tweed, collectively producing a stunning visual effect. The backdrop of the Eildon Hills, after which the Romans called their local settlement 'Trimontium' – a rather obvious translation being 'place of the three hills' – adds to the landscape quality.

The largest bridge is the former viaduct, dating from 1863, with slender sandstone columns, while just downstream, is the old road bridge, the Old Drygrange Bridge, built in 1780, overlain with the modern road bridge, from 1973, on the A68. The former viaduct stands 116 feet above the river on 19 arches, each of 43-foot spans. Collectively the bridges are sometimes referred to as 'Tripontium', which must rank as a pun to equal the very best the Marx Brothers could muster.

Valerie Gillies, the Edinburgh Makar, or poet laureate, from 2005 until 2008, captures the beauty of the place in her 'Ballad of Leaderfoot':

> The river runs from west to east
>   roads south to north
> from bank to bank three bridges span
>   three centuries worth
>
> before these the Fly-boat Brae
>   led down to its ferry
> near the ghost-line of the Roman way
>   on the outward journey
>
> salmon sandstone pillars rise
>   above Leaderfoot
> the meeting of two singing streams
>   by leafy Ravenswood
>
> builders pay attention to the piers
>   so the arch can spring
> taking you far from what you see
>   to what you're not yet seeing
>
> for when the Tweed is running high
>   from wintry moor and moss
> old Drygrange Bridge is standing here
>   to carry you across

The structure of the poem brings to mind the shapes of the piers and arches. The poem is carved freehand in stone seats that chime with the shape of the bridge, created by the sculptor, Garry Fay.

The first wire suspension bridge created in Britain was across the Gala Water in **Galashiels** where, in 1816, woollen cloth manufacturer **Richard Lees** conceived this single 111-foot-span iron wire cable footbridge to ease communication between parts of his works. It cost £40 and spawned many suspension footbridges in the area.

The Hon Captain Napier designed a 125-foot-span bridge with stiffened stays to replace a ropework footbridge at **Thirlestane Castle**, near Lauder, in 1820, while **John and William Smith** built a 260-foot single span with a 4-foot-wide walkway across the Tweed at **Dryburgh Abbey** for David Stewart Erskine, the eccentric 11th Earl of Buchan, in August 1817. This cable-stayed design proved somewhat ambitious and was destroyed by a gale the following January. It was later restored on the catenarian principle using eye-bars for the first time, but this, too, was destroyed in 1838.

There is quite a tradition of significant landowners building bridges on their estates. Sir John Hay, Bart, commissioned **Redpath and Brown** in 1817 to build the **King's Meadow Bridge**, a 110-foot-span footbridge across the Tweed on his estate below Peebles. This has since been demolished and should not be confused with the replacement, Priorsford Bridge, dating from 1905. The present suspension bridge was designed by local engineer R. J. M. Inglis and built by Somervail of

Priorsford Bridge, Peebles. *Colin L. Shearer*

Dalmuir. It is a picturesque bridge because of the engineering detail, with inclined wires forming different angles against vertical supporting bars.

Also visually appealing is **Gattonside Bridge** over the Tweed near Melrose. Built in 1826, it has a 296-foot span, being a chain link suspension bridge. It has been described as 'the most elegantly futile structure conceivable', although it does serves to link the village with the parish church in Melrose. The designer was **J. S. Brown** of Redpath and Brown and the masonry was by **John Smith** of Darnick, who built Abbotsford for Sir Walter Scott. Some claim that major refurbishment in 1992 changed the bridge's appeal irreversibly.

The River Tweed also bore witness to further developments in bridge design technology. Britain's first suspension bridge for road traffic was designed and built by **Captain Sir Samuel Brown** across the Tweed in 1820. The **Union Chain Bridge** – for it does indeed link Scotland to England – lies near Norham Ford and incorporates Brown's

Gattonside Bridge. *Deborah M. Keith*

revolutionary technique of using iron rods linked together to form rigid chains, which allowed the development of bigger and heavier suspension bridges. The bridge opening was a spectacle, with Captain Brown in a curricle towing 12 carts followed by 700 enthusiastic spectators. With a cable span of 449 feet and roadway of 378 feet, it is still in use today, only slightly modified, and is the oldest surviving suspension bridge in Britain still carrying vehicular traffic – one car at time, but the proposed refurbishment should see it back to full strength.

There is a story that the bridge blew down six months after it opened, but there is no evidence, rather the testimony of Captain Brown himself writing to Sir David Brewster some 18 months later, that 'the fact is paramount to all other, that ever since it has been opened, it has given entire satisfaction and has been in constant use without any restriction.'

Brown's 180-foot-long suspension bridge across the River Teviot at **Kalemouth**, near Eckford, was completed in 1835 and is also still in use today on a minor road.

Brown's bridge over the Teviot at Kalemouth. *Callum Black*

The Union Chain Bridge across the Tweed.
Lewis Matheson

East to Angus

Captain Samuel Brown's bridge-building endeavour in Montrose was not his finest hour. As seen earlier, the wooden bridge across the northern channel through the neck of the Montrose Basin lasted only about 40 years. Captain Brown was engaged in 1828 to design its replacement, a suspension bridge of considerable visual appeal and called the Chain Bridge, costing £25,000. Not that it was universally welcomed. That year the *Montrose Review* published 'The Lament of the Wooden Brig':

'An I, a brig with age sair worn,
And now forsaken and forlorn,
For they who once did muckle prize me
In haughty mood so now despise me;
They say I'm but rotten clotch
Unfit to carry cart or coach;
They scoff, they sneer, they jibe and spurn me,
And vow ere lang that they will burn me;
Oh sirs what modern alteration
Takes place in every form and fashion.'

Just as the Auld Brig of Ayr had predicted adversity ahead for its replacement, so the wooden bridge rants:

'Had my successor only been
A brig composed of lime and steen
I should have gladly left my station
And wished him joy of his succession;
But thou a silly simple coof,
Suspended hanging from the roof,
Mair supple than a frosty tangle
That we see from house top dangle
Ye frantic bodies of Montrose,
Ye're fain about him, I suppose;
But by my soul, yet need na brag –
He'll prove, I'm feared, a Willie Wag.'

This prediction proved uncannily correct for Captain Brown's Chain Bridge. In 1830 a large crowd gathered on it to watch a boat race, and up to 700 people were estimated to occupy the central portion of the structure when one of the principal suspension cables snapped,

trapping and crushing the spectators. Three perished in the ensuing panic, the local newspaper describing it as 'such a scene of wailing, lamentation and grief perhaps never before witnessed in Montrose and, we fervently trust, will never be witnessed again.'

Repaired and with strengthened chains, a second disaster was avoided by good fortune in 1838 when a gale badly damaged the roadway, which was blown into the sea only minutes after the mail coach had crossed. Again, the bridge was strengthened and lasted until the late 1920s.

The Granite City

In the Granite City, Aberdeen, Captain Brown was also responsible for the suspension bridge named in honour of the Duke of Wellington, following his success at the Battle of Waterloo some 15 years earlier. Commissioned by the Heritors of the Church of Nigg, near Aberdeen, to replace the Craiglug ferry and provide access to a new church, Brown's **Wellington Bridge** across the River Dee is a single span of 217 feet supported by two cables consisting of wrought-iron eye-bar links with shackles and pins, with massive granite masonry towers.

An elliptical arch was added to the north side in 1886 to allow passage of Riverside Drive below the bridge approach. The bridge was reconstructed in 1930 when the old T-section road beams were replaced with rolled steel joists, but the original towers and chain survive, little altered. It has been a pedestrian bridge since 2002.

Aberdeen had been substantially improved in the early 1800s under the auspices of a plan for Georgian civic design by **Charles Abercrombie**. This included the construction of **Union Bridge**, at 130 feet the world's longest single-span granite arch. The architect was **James Burn** of Haddington and it was built by **Thomas Fletcher**, under some influence from Thomas Telford. Spanning the Denburn and completed in 1805, it was widened in 1908 by **William Dyack**, the burgh surveyor, with Sir Benjamin Baker as a consultant.

The view from atop the bridge on Union Street gives not only a vista of the railway and Union Street Gardens below, but also of the impressive structures on Rosemount Viaduct, a little to the north-west. Three beautiful granite buildings there house the Central Library, St Mark's Church and His Majesty's Theatre. The trio is known, with typical Aberdeen wit, as 'Education, Salvation and Damnation'.

The Bridge of Don is an impressive five-span dressed granite bridge with rounded cutwaters built by **John Gibb** and **John Smith** in 1830, the helping hand of Thomas Telford again evident. The existing bridge

Wellington Bridge, Aberdeen. *Bill Harrison*

Union Bridge, Aberdeen. *Mike W. Lowson*

is considerably wider, however, than the original, with an adjacent concrete bridge added in 1959, taking it from 24 to 66 feet wide.

A ferry disaster in 1876, which resulted in the loss of life for 32 passengers returning from a visit to the Bay of Nigg, was the catalyst for the **Victoria Bridge** across the River Dee, completed in 1881. Designed by Edward L. J. Blyth of Edinburgh, this fine five-arched granite bridge was instrumental in developing the city to the south of the river.

J. & W. Smith built several bridges in Aberdeenshire in the 1840s. The firm's bridge over the River Ythan at **Methlick**, dating from 1844, was restored in 2004 by Aberdeenshire Council, which found it impossible to source granite to match the original stonework.

The remains of the Shakkin Briggie. *Canmore*

Remarkably, the council had to import granite from China to effect the required appearance – talk about 'coals to Newcastle'! There is a certain irony in this tale, for Aberdeen's Rubislaw Quarry, which at a depth of 465 feet had been the deepest quarry in Britain and had supplied granite for the Forth Rail Bridge, the terrace of the Houses of Parliament and London's Waterloo Bridge, had closed in 1971. The quarry was known, again with north-east humour, as 'the hole that Aberdeen came out of'.

John Smith also built the **Shakkin Briggie** over the River Dee at Cults, which provides a good example of local patronage. In 1836 the local church Minister, the **Reverend Dr George Morison**, financed personally the cost of a fine 250-foot-long chain suspension bridge with a wooden deck, whereby his 'flock' could attend church without resort to a boat. Its formal name was St Devenick Bridge, but the resting of the stone piers on shifting beds of shale, strong river currents and autumn floods in 1914 and 1920 severely damaged the structure, which was substantially rebuilt in 1922 after the *Aberdeen Daily Journal* opened a public fund for its repair.

In the 1950s and '60s major repairs were again required, but political wrangling over responsibilities for upkeep (the Morison Trust fund for maintenance yields about £12 a year) has precluded the crippled wreck from restoration. The bridge is a Class A Listed Structure, seen as a rare piece of engineering archaeology, and plans are afoot to make it once again safe for pedestrian passage, although erosion in the 1980s caused the approaches to be washed away. Given its perilous condition, it is hoped that local pleas for its salvation will be heeded. Aberdeen poet Ken Morrice (1924-2002) even composed an ode to the Shakkin Briggie:

'Aince a lovers' tryst ablow the hill,
Aftimes a family jaunt across the stanes
and water (afore a walk gaed oot o fashion)
noo look at ye! Fa noo wad chance his banes?
A clatter o win l'se warren ye're cowpt intil
the Dee. Brods hing lowse. Fat's left
atween the spales and roost has shaky trimmles.
Ill-trickit loons hiv lowped and rived
their way through snorls o barbs and brammels
tae vandalise and rape your denty weft.

Elegant aince and lichtsome, trig
As ony quine, soople as the river,
(squatted here nae humphy-backit brig!)
Noo the deid-chack's in your timmer.

Steek and streekit, fa gaes a fig?
Weel, I for ane! Short o ae span,
Gappit-toothed, negleckit, still ye stan –
Nae brig your marra – ye thrawn, aul limmer!'

The Cabrach

Through the area known as 'The Cabrach' runs the A941 road between Rhynie and Dufftown, notorious together with its A939 sister road from Cockbridge to Tomintoul over The Lecht as one of the first roads in Scotland each year to be blocked by winter snows. Early surviving bridges at Bridgend, across the Charroch Burn, and at Blackwater, date from 1827.

The one across the River Deveron at **King's Ford** dates from 1851, although the King referred to is in fact Edward I of England (1239-1307), who found travelling in these parts in 1296 somewhat troublesome, in large measure due to the lack of bridges. Quite why the locals thought it fitting to commemorate the English monarch's visit is questionable. Edward I was on the rampage following the signing of the treaty between Scotland and France in 1295, which has become known as the Auld Alliance. A recent research thesis by Dr Siobhan Talbott demonstrates that the treaty remains extant – an interesting point in the Brexit negotiations!

The king was living up to his sobriquet as 'Hammer of the Scots' ('Scottorum malleus'), wreaking havoc throughout the country, including purloining the Stone of Destiny on which hitherto Scottish Kings and Queens had been crowned. It remained in England for seven centuries. An attempt by Ian Hamilton and three accomplices to bring the Stone back to Scotland from Westminster Abbey on Christmas Eve 1950 ultimately failed. On 11 April 1951 it was discovered in the grounds of historic Arbroath Abbey, adjacent to where Scotland's epoch-making Declaration of Arbroath had been signed by King Robert Bruce in 1320, and returned to Westminster. But on St Andrew's Day, 30 November 1996, the Stone was returned to Scotland, this time to Edinburgh Castle, with reasonably good grace and great ceremony. It now lies behind armoured glass, surrounded by a sophisticated security system, despite persistent rumours that it is not the Stone that was stolen in 1950, the whereabouts of which remain unknown. It is a classic conspiracy theory, the truth of which will perhaps never be known.

By the 1880s construction rather than destruction was the intent, and a group inspired by **Mr Robertson**, the schoolmaster in Lower Cabrach, raised funds for the building of six bridges. Mostly of single-arch stone construction, these were a huge benefit to farmers, traders and travellers in the district. The bridges crossed the Fiddoch at Bridgehaugh, the

The Cabrach Monument. *L. Bruce Keith*

Balloch Burn at Ballochford, the Lewie Burn near Bridgend, and across the Alltdauch, Bank and Auchmair Burns. Mr Robertson was evidently an excellent fundraiser. With surplus funds from a bazaar, a somewhat grand drinking trough was erected at Alltdauch burn, near the boundary between Upper and Lower Cabrach.

Glasgow's Victorian heritage

Glasgow, already well established as the industrial capital of Scotland by the 19th century, also had its share of significant bridges, which is hardly surprising for a bustling and energetic city dissected by the River Clyde, the mother of shipbuilding and with a vibrant international trade. It truly was the second city of the British Empire. By the 1850s Glasgow's population had risen dramatically to more than 400,000 and would exceed 800,000 by the 1880s.

The **Victoria Bridge** is the most handsome and the oldest surviving of a series of bridges built in the city centre. Its five flat segmental sandstone arches carry a roadway 80 feet wide, which is still one of the widest in Britain.

Victoria Bridge, Glasgow. *Iain Matheson*

Designed by **James Walker** of London and named in honour of Queen Victoria's memorable visit to Glasgow, tens of thousands watched the opening on New Year's Day 1854. Given the history of bridges across the Clyde, it was fitting that the toast at the banquet held that evening was 'The Stability and Prosperity of Victoria Bridge'.

St Andrew's Bridge, built in 1856, provided a safe crossing for workers to cross the Clyde to factories in Hutchesontown. This suspension footbridge, designed by **Neil Robson**, has cast-iron classical pylons with paired fluted Corinthian columns, each 27 inches in diameter and 20 feet high, with light lattice girder spans of 220 feet. The bridge, which is still in use at Glasgow Green, has been substantially refurbished in recent years, the parapets and decking being replaced in

1997, while a repaint in 2005 has enhanced its appearance.

One of Glasgow's most prestigious bridges, the work of the renowned Scottish engineer **Robert Stevenson**, had a short life, however. Built in 1829 to replace the original Hutchesontown Bridge, which had been a casualty of the 1795 floods, and a timber footbridge built in 1803 to a design by **Peter Nicholson** (the author of *Principles of Architecture*), Stevenson's Hutcheson Bridge was the third on this site, and was a handsome five-span sandstone masonry bridge with segmental arches. At 407 feet in length, it was described by mathematician Stephen Fenwick of the Royal Military Academy as 'one of the best specimens' of its type.

Concerns over the effect a weir upstream would have on the bridge's foundations, which were later proved unfounded, led to the decision in 1868 to demolish Hutcheson Bridge. It was replaced in 1872 by the fourth bridge on this site, the wrought-iron Albert Bridge, which stands to this day.

Three years previously, some 30,000 people had gathered on a temporary bridge, erected to maintain traffic flows, to witness the last public hanging in Glasgow, outside the Greek Revival-style High Court building. The case was notorious. Dr Pritchard had been found guilty of poisoning his wife and his mother-in-law and had been dubbed the 'Human Crocodile' as he had opened his wife's coffin so that he could kiss his victim on the lips. There's no record of whether or not he wished to carry out the same gruesome ritual with his erstwhile mother-in-law.

By the 1820s, Mylne's Broomielaw Bridge had become unstable due to the increasing flow of traffic, and the trustees appointed **Thomas Telford** to design a replacement. At 560 feet long and 60 feet wide – twice the width of Mylne's bridge, and with foundations 10 feet deeper – Telford's seven-arch bridge opened on New Year's Day 1836, one year ahead of schedule. Even the deeper foundations proved inadequate, however, and had to be reinforced, causing a navigation hazard on the Clyde. This bridge became known as **Jamaica Street Bridge**, and is now Glasgow Bridge.

Glasgow has its own 'Bridge of Sighs'. Designed by **David Hamilton** and completed in 1836, it spans the ravine that once carried the Molendinar Burn. The bridge received its name from the many funeral processions crossing it carrying coffins from Glasgow Cathedral to the Necropolis, Glasgow's most spectacular graveyard, boasting 3,500 monuments and the final resting place for 50,000 deceased individuals.

Crossing the Clyde would always bring conflicts of interest. The city witnessed a burgeoning population and thriving trade and industry based on the river – the first the product of the success of the latter. Architect **T. L. Watson** described the problem:

'…it is not too much to say that Glasgow is rent in twain by its harbour for more than half the length of the city and that for more than half of its area there are not adequate means of communication between large and populous districts on opposite sides of the river.'

Many solutions were proposed. An idea for a swing bridge came to nothing, as neither bridge nor river passage could guarantee a continuous service. A survey in December 1881 showed that during the 18 hours between 6am and midnight a bridge would have to be open for a total of 9 hours. Bell, Miller & Bell devised a Duplex bridge, shaped like a 'Y' in plan so that, when a ship sailed through, the traffic could be diverted on to the branch of the top portion of the 'Y' that was closed. Alexander George Thomas suggested a high-level bridge with elevators at each end to provide access, but it would have cost £140,000. So there remained 4½ miles of the Clyde flowing through Glasgow that was without a bridge, which remained a problem until the Clyde Tunnel was opened in 1963 and the Kingston Bridge in 1970.

Of course, bridges still needed replacing. The **Rutherglen Bridge** dating from 1775, closed in 1890, and a replacement, designed by **Crouch & Hogg** with steelwork by Sir William Arrol & Company, opened in 1896. With a total length of 301 feet over three arches, and using masonry facings of granite sourced from Aberdeen, Dalbeattie and Cornwall, the bridge cost £64,690.

Crouch & Hogg was also responsible for the design of the **Dalmarnock Bridge** in 1891. With five spans of 54ft 8in each, this bridge has a 32-foot-wide roadway and two footpaths, each 9 feet wide. It was the first major bridge in Glasgow to have a completely flat surface. And Telford's Broomielaw Bridge, which had been rebranded the Jamaica Street Bridge, was replaced by Glasgow Bridge, which opened on Queen Victoria's 80th birthday, 24 May 1899, and stands to this day. Using the old bridge as a constructing platform, the current bridge is supported by four steel cylinders, each 19 feet in diameter, filled with concrete and sunk under each pier. Glasgow City Council brought in Sir Benjamin Baker and Sir John Wolfe Barry to double-check the engineer's structural calculations. Fortunately, they agreed!

Stevenson's legacy

Although **Robert Stevenson** (1772-1850) is most famously remembered for the Bell Rock Lighthouse and the legacy of lighthouses he designed around Scotland, he was also responsible for some fine Scottish bridges. In addition to Hutcheson Bridge, he worked as a consulting engineer with John Rennie Snr, Thomas Telford and Alexander Nimmo. That said, Marykirk Bridge, Regent Bridge, Annan Bridge and Stirling New Bridge are all testimony to his independent efforts.

Although his bridge legacy is of masonry arches, Stevenson was clearly interested in the innovative idea for suspension bridges being built in the Scottish Borders in the first quarter of the 19th century. His paper 'Description of Bridges of Suspension' was published in the *Edinburgh Philosophical Journal* in 1821.

Robert's father died of an epidemic fever when he was an infant, and he was educated at a charity school. When he was 15 his mother married Thomas Smith, an ingenious mechanic who, in 1786, had been

Far left Robert Stevenson. *Courtesy of the Institution of Civil Engineers*

Left Regent Bridge, Edinburgh. *Lewis Matheson*

to the Greek Revival design by the architect Archibald Eliot. A magnificent 50-foot semi-circular arch, the platform for this bridge forms part of Waterloo Place and is ornamented with two open arches supported on elegant Corinthian columns. The bridge was opened during the visit to Edinburgh by Prince Leopold of Saxe-Coburg.

Annan Bridge in Dumfries-shire is of dressed sandstone with three segmental arches and rubble spandrels. Robert's son Alan, who went on to create the Hebridean Skerryvore lighthouse off the coast of Tiree, worked with his father on the bridge. Its completion in August 1826 was celebrated by the workers drinking a gallon of whisky. How many workers there were is not known, but I am sure they all had at least one dram.

Stevenson's **Stirling New Bridge**, with its five stone arches, provided a more substantial crossing of the River Forth at this Gateway to the Highlands when it opened in 1831.

appointed engineer to the newly created Northern Lighthouse Board. Robert not only succeeded his stepfather in this role, which he fulfilled industriously for 50 years, but he also married his stepsister, Jean, and started the Stevenson dynasty of lighthouse engineers. His grandson, Robert Louis Stevenson, author of the adventure novels *Kidnapped* and *Treasure Island*, never met his grandfather, however, as Robert Snr died in July 1850, just four months before RLS was born.

Stevenson's Bell Rock Lighthouse, in the North Sea some 11 miles south-east of Arbroath, is justly included as one of the Seven Wonders of the Industrial Age, but his bridges are also a worthy testimony to his skills. As early as 1814 he built **Marykirk Bridge** across the River North Esk between Angus and Kincardineshire, using the same team that had completed the Bell Rock Lighthouse some years earlier. It is a handsome, dressed sandstone, four-arched structure featuring recessed circular embellishments in the spandrels.

In 1819 Stevenson built the **Regent Bridge** in Edinburgh's New Town

Bridges renowned for different reasons

This journey through history is largely one of imagination, innovation and impressive success, but not all bridge construction went to plan. **Ashiestiel Bridge** across the River Tweed on the unclassified Innerleithen to Caddenfoot road was built in 1847 for Sir James Russell of Peel. At 133 feet, it claimed to be the largest arch ever constructed of rubble whinstone. Upon completion, however, the contractors, **J. & T. Smith** of Darnick, removed the centring, the keystone shot up in the air and the bridge collapsed. The contractor rebuilt it at his own expense and, unsurprisingly, subsequently went bankrupt. The second attempt still stands, however, being a single elliptical arch of common whinstone rubble and, except in the cornice and coping, contains not one hewn stone.

Right Ashietiel Bridge. *Colin L. Shearer*

Below right Auchindrean Bridge. *Lewis Matheson*

Some bridges are renowned for quite sinister reasons. **Overtoun Bridge** near Milton in Dunbartonshire is a granite arch bridge built in 1865 by the Calvinist Lord Overtoun to serve his property. Since the 1950s the bridge has been the scene of suicide jumps by numerous dogs from the 50-foot-high deck. There have been several investigations, including by experts on wildlife habitats and the paranormal, and the only common theme seems to be that the dogs are all long-snout breeds such as Labradors, collies and retrievers.

The Braemore Estate at Loch Broom in Wester Ross was bought in 1860 by **Sir John Fowler**, later of Forth Rail Bridge fame, where he entertained the Archbishop of Canterbury and other dignitaries. He experimented with several engineering works, including creating a lenticular iron-truss bridge, to a design by his colleague, **Benjamin Baker**. With a span of 102 feet across the River Broom, **Auchindrean Bridge** is a unique design in Scotland, although it is similar to Brunel's Royal Albert Bridge at Saltash in Cornwall.

He also had a wire rope cable suspension bridge constructed in 1875, with an 82.5-foot span across the steep **Corrieshalloch Gorge**, providing dramatic views of the Falls of Measach on the River Droma beneath. The bridge, now on property owned by the National Trust for Scotland, has since been replaced and a new access and car park opened, but it still offers impressive views of the gully beneath.

Repairing, renewing and replacing bridges of old is an ongoing process, but needs to be carried out with deference to our architectural, social and cultural heritage. Upgrading works on bridges can yield some interesting artefacts. In 2015, for example, works to replace the old bridge across the River Spey at Ruthven on the single-track road that links the B970 to Kingussie and the trunk road, unearthed a 121-year-old time capsule containing items from the 1800s. This included a bottle of whisky, a folded newspaper dated Saturday 29 September 1894, and a paper scroll. All are now held safely at the Highland Folk Museum.

7. 19TH-CENTURY CANAL AQUEDUCTS

From towpaths to tourism

In our increasingly hectic world of instant meals, instant emails, instant chat, instant TV and any number of instant gratifications, there is something to be said for slowing the world down to a maximum of 4 miles per hour, with no movement between dusk and dawn.

One of my close friends, retiring after many years of high-speed, high-pressure work, invested in a share of a traditional English narrowboat so that he and his wife could spend much of their new-found leisure time meandering gently along the canal network at a rate hitherto absent from his professional career.

Another friend chose to spend his honeymoon on the canals in preference to some exotic blue-sky, sun-kissed, golden-beached resort abroad. After almost 40 years of marriage, he and his wife have holidayed on and beside canals many times since then, most recently for a family break cruising the Caledonian Canal on a hire-boat arguably better equipped than their own home, but they have yet to be tempted to join the hordes seeking cheap flights to sun, sand and sangria. Each to their own, of course, but perhaps the largely gentle pace on today's canal networks has much to commend it.

It wasn't always thus, however. Indeed, canals were the ultra-modern high-speed super-highways of their day.

The Great Age of Bridge Building has its roots in the Industrial Revolution, when the need for cheap and effective means of transporting bulky cargo and iron around Britain was paramount to entrepreneurial success.

The development of the canal system in the latter part of the 18th century, firstly by James Brindley (1716-92) on the Bridgewater Canal followed by the Trent & Mersey Canal, then by John Smeaton, spawned a remarkable line of civil engineers whose expertise was applied to pioneer innovative designs and, literally, ground-breaking techniques in construction. Scottish engineers who had cut their teeth on projects in their homeland were engaged to design and build major civil engineering works in England as industrialists and investors began to appreciate their potential.

Thomas Telford and John Rennie both won commissions south of the border; Telford's first canal at Ellesmere was 112 miles long, while his masterpieces on the Shropshire Union Canal and Menai Straits were yet to come.

Scotland's first canals, such as the **Monklands Canal**, begun in 1720, were primarily for the transport of coal. The **Forth & Clyde Canal**, surveyed in 1763 by John Smeaton, had the more general purpose of providing a trade and supply link across the central belt of Scotland where industry was developing rapidly. It was extended in 1818 to Edinburgh, via the **Union Canal**.

Perhaps the most ambitious canal-building operation in Scotland, although not the most commercially successful, was the **Caledonian Canal**, through the Great Glen between Corpach at Fort William and Clachnaharry at Inverness, which enabled shipping to avoid the dangerous northern seas. **Thomas Telford**, commissioned in 1804, in parallel with his work on Highland roads and bridges, designed a canal with numerous locks and other engineering works, as well as a few swing bridges.

The **Crinan Canal** was designed by **John Rennie** between Crinan and Ardrishaig and opened in 1801, providing a navigable route between the Clyde and the Inner Hebrides to avoid travelling round the exposed Mull of Kintyre. Subsequently improved by Thomas Telford, the canal has six swing bridges as well as a retractable bridge at **Dunardry**. The latter replaced a swing bridge in 1900 and operates by a rotating handle and a cogged wheel, which causes the bridge deck to roll forwards and backwards on rails and come to rest on the lock chamber.

A bridge over a canal has two possible functions. One is to carry a road or track across the canal, and the other is as a roving bridge, where towing by horses was the principal means of propulsion of the barges and the horse had to cross the canal to the towpath on the opposite bank.

Canal-building did produce another much more spectacular type of bridge structure – the aqueduct – whose purpose was to carry the canal itself and its exceptional weight of water across landform features. These often presented a unique challenge to the engineer and the physical requirements often produced massive structures.

The **Kelvin Aqueduct**, designed and constructed under the supervision of Smeaton's chief engineer, Robert Whitworth (1734-99),

19th-century canal aqueducts
Key to bridges mentioned in the text

1	Dunardry	NR 819 912
2	Kelvin Aqueduct	NS 516 689
3	Luggie Water	NS 657 739
4	Avon Aqueduct	NS 965 758
5	Almond	NT 104 706
6	Slateford	NT 220 707
7	Muirshearlich	NN 143 806
8	Fort Augustus	NH 379 093
9	Clachnaharry	NH 648 466
10	Banavie swing bridge	NN 119 755
11	Scott Russell Aqueduct	NT 184 706
12	Falkirk Wheel	NS 853 802

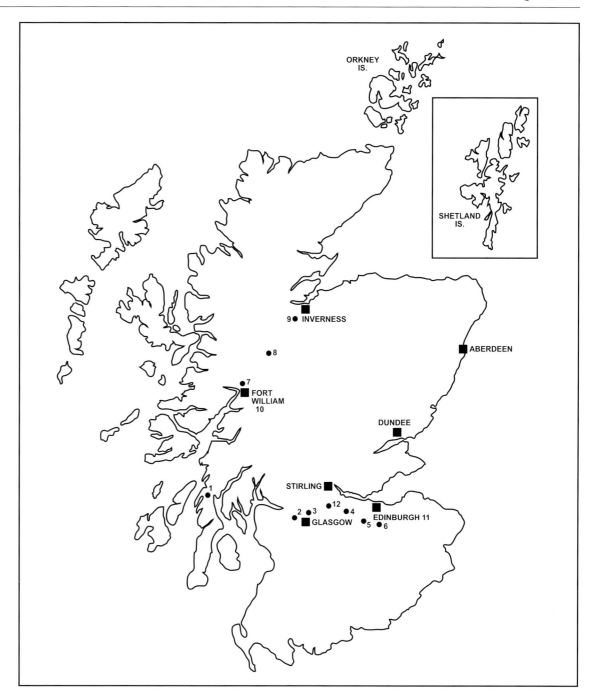

was 400 feet long and 68 feet high and had four arches each spanning 50 feet, supported on huge triangular piers. When completed in 1790 this aqueduct, carrying the Forth & Clyde Canal, was the largest yet built in Europe. John Smeaton also designed the **Luggie Water Aqueduct** at Kirkintilloch, being an impressive 124-foot-long single arch that opened in 1775.

Hugh Baird (1770-1827) was responsible for much of the engineering work on the Union Canal. Born in Bothkennar in Stirlingshire, Baird designed the aqueducts, receiving advice from Thomas Telford. His examples use an iron trough to achieve watertightness, as well as to contain the outward pressure of the water, allowing the viaducts to be more slender than a purely masonry aqueduct such as Smeaton's at Kelvin. The results were impressive.

To the west of Linlithgow, the **Avon Aqueduct**, which carries the canal across the valley through what is now Muiravonside Country Park, is both the longest and the highest aqueduct in Scotland. It is also the

Left The Avon Aqueduct. *Canmore*

Above The Almond Aqueduct. *Canmore*

second-longest in Britain after Telford's epic at Pontcysyllte in Wales. The Avon, completed in 1820, is 810 feet long and stands 86 feet above the river, carried on 12 segmental arches each of 50 feet. The cast-iron trough is supported on three internal longitudinal masonry walls.

The **Almond Aqueduct** carries the Union Canal across the River Almond at Kirkliston on five segmental arches with tall tapering piers of rock-faced stone. Completed in 1821, and frequently referred to as Lin's Mill Aqueduct, it is 420 feet long and 76 feet above the river.

Slateford Aqueduct, completed in 1822 and spanning the Water of Leith in Edinburgh at a height of 76 feet, is carried on eight arches for its 500-foot length. At the side of the aqueduct is a reinforced concrete aqueduct from 1936, which crosses the A70 Lanark Road.

The Baird family is yet another of these Scottish families steeped in our engineering heritage. Baird's elder brother Charles we will encounter later as he established a thriving business, and was building bridges, in Russia. Baird's son, **Nicol Hugh Baird** (1796-1849), who joined his father on the Union Canal project, emigrated to Canada, earning a significant reputation as a canal engineer around the Great Lakes.

We should not forget the human toil that went into these engineering feats. It wasn't all honest labour, however. Two of the construction workers in Baird's labour force on the Union Canal's aqueducts were Burke and Hare, Irish immigrants who undertook some serious moonlighting. Together, they murdered 16 people in Edinburgh and sold to Dr Robert Knox for dissection for his well-attended anatomy lectures, the pair gaining immortal infamy in the process and spawning many gruesome and ghostly tales thereafter.

On the Caledonian Canal, which passes just a few miles from my

The Scott Russell Aqueduct, Edinburgh. *Canmore*

At the southern end of the canal, the swing bridge at **Banavie**, carrying the railway to Mallaig, is set against a backdrop of Ben Nevis to the east, Britain's highest mountain. Immediately to the north of the bowed-truss swing bridge lies 'Neptune's Staircase', a spectacular and scenic series of eight locks on the canal, and themselves a significant testimony to Telford's design prowess.

A more modern aqueduct owes its name to a Scottish naval engineer, **John Scott Russell** (1808-82) who, in 1834, observed a bow wave continue to travel forward at about 8 miles per hour when a boat stopped moving on the Union Canal. He called it the 'wave of translation', but it is now referred to as a soliton or solitary wave. The **Scott Russell Aqueduct**, opened in 1987, carries the Union Canal over the Edinburgh city bypass and affords new recreational users of the restored canal route unparalleled views across the western side of Edinburgh. As a teenager, I frequently cycled through this area when it was undeveloped countryside. It is unrecognisable from those days in the 1960s and is now a mixture of housing developments and retail centres known as Baberton and Wester Hailes

Aqueducts are more than just bridges, of course. They include the whole infrastructure system conveying water supplies, so include miles of tunnels, piping and bridges, spanning the physical barriers presented by the terrain. When Scottish Water undertook its ambitious project to upgrade the Katrine Aqueduct, completed in 2013, it involved the maintenance and repair of two aqueducts, each 26 miles long, which supply water from Loch Katrine to 1.3 million people living in Glasgow and the Central Belt. This included engineering works on 21 bridges, most notably where the aqueduct crosses the deep valleys of the Duchray, Endrick and Blane watercourses.

This is yet another example of a significant engineering project that enabled a piece of Victorian design and construction, originally completed on 28 December 1859 and opened by Queen Victoria, to continue to serve its purpose well into the 21st century.

The original project, which had been enlarged at least twice by increasing the capacity of Loch Katrine and the compensation reservoirs at Loch Vennachar and Loch Drunkie, had been the responsibility of the chief engineer to Glasgow Corporation Waterworks, James M. Gale (1830-1903). I am sure he was not exaggerating when he said:

> 'It is a work which will bear comparison with the most extensive aqueducts in the world, not excluding those of Ancient Rome; and it is one of which the city may well be proud.'

childhood homes at Dores and Balloch, Telford built several aqueducts, of which the one carrying the canal over the River Loy is a good example. Completed in 1806, near **Muirshearlich**, it has three low arches, the central one accommodating the river while the other two have cobbled floors and can be used by pedestrians and animals.

While the Caledonian Canal remains today a living monument to the genius of its great engineer, the infrastructure does require to be renewed and replaced occasionally to enable it to function. The original cast-iron swing bridge carrying the A82 across the canal at **Fort Augustus** was replaced in 1932 by a steel plate girder single-span swing bridge powered by a petrol engine, designed and erected by **Sir William Arrol & Co Ltd**. The road surface is laid on timber and galvanised steel decking.

The **Clachnaharry** swing bridge, which carries the railway across the Caledonian Canal close to its northern end at Inverness, dates from 1909, but was built to the same design as that by **Joseph Mitchell** in 1862. It is a massive bowed-steel box-girder structure on a 65-degree skew, and has always been painted white to reduce expansion of the metal in hot weather.

The Falkirk Wheel. *Iain Matheson*

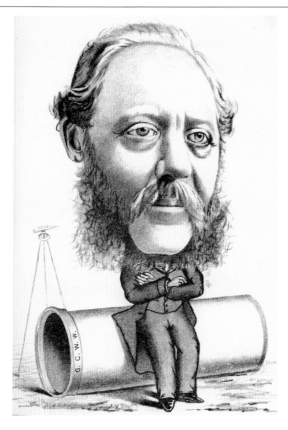

A caricature of James M. Gale. © *CSG CIC Glasgow Museums and Libraries Collection: The Mitchell Library, Special Collections*

There were 25 substantial iron and masonry aqueduct bridges on the original schemes built between 1855 and 1901, of which six are Listed Category A, five are Category B and two are Category C.

Where the aqueduct crosses the Endrick Water, special protection measures were needed to safeguard silting of the river as it is designated a Special Area of Conservation (SAC) under the EC Habitats Directive on account of the Atlantic salmon and lamprey populations.

A book celebrating Scottish engineering achievements in bridges cannot omit an opportunity to venerate the biggest canal restoration

project ever – the 69-mile sea-to-sea ship canal linking for the first time in 60 years the cities of Glasgow and Edinburgh.

For nearly two centuries from 1822, the Forth & Clyde and Union canals created a key commercial transport corridor across central Scotland. Transport demands changed, however, and road-building during the 1960s resulted in at least 32 obstructions, effectively severing the link.

The ambitious Millennium Project to restore the link to its former status included as its centrepiece the magnificent **Falkirk Wheel**. Part functional boat lift, part visitor attraction, this impressive structure, completed in 2002, replaces the flight of 11 locks from the 19th century that formed the historic link. The only rotating boat lift in the world, the Falkirk Wheel has two water-filled caissons that can transport at least eight boats at one time – the approximate weight of 10 African elephants – up or down the 79 feet between levels, using only as much electricity to do so as would be needed to boil water in eight domestic kettles.

The Falkirk Wheel is a living testimony that the imagination, vision and skill of the master engineers of past centuries has not been lost in our mad, modern desire for instant solutions to everything. It has a feeling of solid permanence that would have brought a satisfied smile to the face of any Victorian bridge-builder.

The link from the canal to the Falkirk Wheel is, of course, an aqueduct, and it passes through a tunnel under the Antonine Wall dating from AD142. I wonder what the Romans would have made of that?

But it's not just the Falkirk Wheel that moves in a circle. The canals have come full circle, too. Built originally as major transport corridors at the birth of the Industrial Revolution, they are today once again being increasingly recognised and valued as arterial channels, but now largely for the thousands of recreational users, be they visitors or locals, who enjoy them for boat cruising, canoeing and angling, or walking and cycling along the former towpaths, or perhaps just pausing to rest awhile beside their fascinating charm.

With a proud and beneficial heritage, Scottish Canals is today the body responsible to the Scottish Government for the management and development of these Scottish waterways, which include 251 bridges, in addition to the iconic Falkirk Wheel.

8. 19TH-CENTURY RAILWAY BRIDGES AND VIADUCTS

From Milton to magic

The canal era was relatively short-lived, despite its enormous achievements and impact. Technological advancements in steam power meant that their economic viability was rapidly eclipsed by the Railway Age. The opening of the Stockton & Darlington Railway in 1825 laid the foundation for significant investment in private railways, funded by industrialists and in which the major Scottish engineers had a major part to play.

It is estimated that between 1830 and 1860 the railways added more than 25,000 bridges to the British scene. Many of the most spectacular of these bridges and viaducts were in Scotland, whose many rivers and mountainous terrain added a scenic beauty to these impressive engineering achievements. Some 65 of the viaducts in Scotland are listed as being of architectural or historic importance, testimony to the engineering skills employed in their design and construction, in addition to the significant positive impact they create as landscape features.

The oldest surviving public railway viaduct in the world – not just Scotland – dates from 1811. Known as the **Laigh Milton Viaduct**, it crosses the River Irvine near Gatelea in Ayrshire and was originally on Scotland's first public railway, the Kilmarnock & Troon Railway. In 1816 it became one of the first structures to carry a travelling steam engine. The bridge was bypassed as early as 1847 when the route was converted from a horse-hauled plateway to locomotive working. A four-span masonry bridge with segmental arches, the engineer was **William Jessop** and the railway was commissioned by the Duke of Portland to carry passengers and coal in horse-drawn wagons. The bridge was extensively and very finely restored in the 1990s, retaining the character of the original, and it is now open to the public again as a footbridge. The contractors responsible for the restoration were Barr Construction, and the job included significant but effective masonry replacement and repair.

The economic imperative to construct railways in what was a fiercely competitive market in the mid-19th century is evident from the history of railway development by private companies. While the industrial Central Belt, with connections to England, was well provided with a railway network from the 1840s onwards, the railway did not reach the northern towns of Wick and Thurso until 1874. On the west coast, the line to Oban was completed in 1880, but the Mallaig line was not open until 1901, and only then after a massive Government subsidy during the construction phase.

The organisation of the railways has been through several incarnations since these early days. The private companies were grouped together into different parcels, with the North British and the Great North of Scotland becoming part of the London & North Eastern Railway (LNER), while the Caledonian, Glasgow & South Western and

19th-century railway bridges and viaducts
Key to bridges mentioned in the text

1	Laigh Milton	NS 383 369
2	Dunglass	NT 770 721
3	Hurlford	NS 447 371
4	Kilmarnock	NS 429 381
5	Ballochmyle	NS 508 253
6	Almond, Kirkliston	NT 112 721
7	Avon Viaduct	NS 981 769
8	Lothianbridge (Newton-grange or Newbattle)	NT 325 649
9	Larbert	NS 858 819
10	Linhouse Water	NT 076 647
11	Braidhurst	NS 219 707
12	Slateford	NT 219 707
13	Nairn (town)	NH 886 562
14	Findhorn	NJ 020 586
15	Conon Bridge	NH 539 557
16	Spey, Newtonmore	NH 711 979
17	Ardgay	NH 599 904
18	Invershin/Oykel	NH 578 952
19	Dalguise	NN 994 479
20	Tilt	NN 873 651
21	Tay Viaduct (Logierait)	NN 968 518

Chapter 9

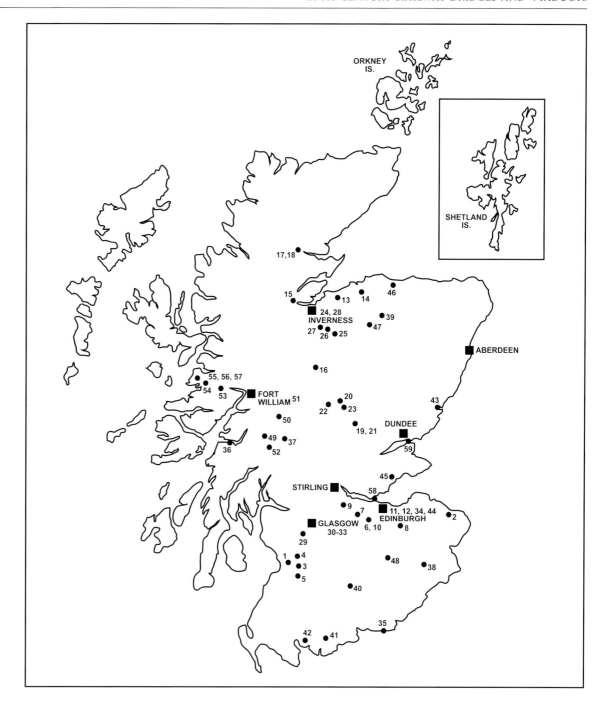

The restored Laigh Milton Viaduct. www.geograph.org.uk

Highland were incorporated into the London Midland & Scottish (LMS). But between the 1930s and the Beeching cuts, or rather amputations, of the 1960s, rationalisation exercises involved major closures of lines and, of course, the infrastructure such as the viaducts that were an integral part of the track system. The Scottish railway system of the early 21st century is a skeleton of its former self, but the operational routes that remain, together with the surviving relics of the closed lines, comprise some of the finest railway inheritances in Britain.

Two Scottish engineers were responsible for much of the early railway network in Scotland: **Thomas Grainger** (1794-1852) and **John**

Miller (1805-83). The partnership was formed in 1825 and endured for 22 years, operating out of the ground floor of Grainger's house at 56 George Street, Edinburgh. Many of the finest viaducts surviving from the 1840s, some still in use, form part of their rich legacy. Their work on viaducts includes Dunglass Viaduct at Cockburnspath (1846), the Hurlford Viaduct across the Irvine Water in Ayrshire (1848), the Kilmarnock Viaduct (1848), and the acme of early Scottish railway engineering, the Ballochmyle Viaduct south of Mauchline (1846/48).

The oldest viaduct in the Borders, and still in use, is **Dunglass Viaduct**, a magnificent structure, well-proportioned with a central span of 135 feet and two smaller arches on one side and three on the other. Its juxtaposition with the A1 road makes for a pleasing photograph of different communication routes bridging this steep gully at Cockburnspath, the third being the Dunglass New Bridge designed and built by James Burn of Haddington and opened in 1800.

Hurlford Viaduct, otherwise known as Crookedholm, is a modest seven-span structure with semi-circular arches and superb ashlar masonry, and is a good example of the Grainger and Miller style.

Kilmarnock Viaduct is on a much larger scale, with 23 masonry arches carrying the railway across the town centre and the Kilmarnock Water. Completed in 1850, it remains a dominant feature of the rebuilt townscape and is listed.

Spanning the wooded gorge of the Water of Ayr, John Miller's **Ballochmyle Viaduct** near Mauchline is a very distinguished red sandstone structure, with its semi-circular central arch of 181 feet, rising

The undersides of the three bridges at Dunglass. *Lewis Matheson*

Top left Ballochmyle Viaduct. *Canmore*

Top right and above Almond Viaduct. *Lewis Matheson*

some 169 feet above the river. That span was the world's largest masonry railway arch at the time of the bridge's completion in 1848, and it remains the highest railway bridge in Britain. The masonry detailing on the bridge reflects the technology, with moulded voussoirs and tapering piers on either side of the main arch. The viaduct appeared in the Tom Cruise movie *Mission Impossible* in 1996.

Grainger and Miller were also responsible for two other very handsome viaducts, both constructed in 1842 and now Listed Grade A. The **Almond Viaduct** near Kirkliston has 36 spans, with 32 masonry

arches on a wide curve spanning the shallow valley of the River Almond and a further seven arches lying to the west of an embankment. At 2,100 feet, it is the longest arched viaduct in Scotland. The **Avon Viaduct**, lying to the west of Linlithgow, has 23 spans of ashlar. Both viaducts have been strengthened for modern use.

John Miller was employed by the North British Railway as engineer on the 23-span viaduct over the River South Esk at **Newtongrange**. Also known as Newbattle or Lothianbridge, it was built in 1847 and was a critical part of the infrastructure for the local coal-mining and other industries in the second half of the 19th century and much of the 20th. The semi-circular arch rings of all but one of the spans are, unusually for Scotland, of brick, and form an imposing wall to the A7 main road. The viaduct also has a new life. Since 2015 it has been an integral part of the new Borders Railway, linking Edinburgh to Galashiels.

Thomas Grainger bestowed another legacy on engineering in an international context. As we'll see later, his apprentice, James Pugh Kirkwood, emigrated to the USA together with his friend, James Laurie. The first James went on to design several bridges on the American railroad and become a pioneer in water treatment. The second James also designed bridges, and became the first President of the American Society of Civil Engineers.

Although **Joseph Locke** (1805-60) stands alongside the Stephensons and Brunel as one of Britain's leading railway engineers, he did not undertake major works such as tunnels and viaducts unless absolutely necessary, preferring more circuitous or steeper routes. The steep incline at Beattock, for example, proved a severe test for locomotives in the pre-electrification era. An uncle of a friend of mine was a Glasgow engine driver for whom a regular turn was to man the 'Beattock Banker', a locomotive based at the foot of the bank that was attached to heavy trains to push them up and over the summit. Not every train required this assistance, so in moments of inaction he loved to collect the copious berries growing wild on the railway embankments there. His wife's resultant raspberry jam and bramble jelly were the envy of many.

Scotland presented a number of challenges on this front, and Locke's 23-span viaduct at **Larbert** (1848), and the viaducts over the **Linhouse Water** at Midcalder (1842), which forms a notable feature in open country, are good examples of his albeit limited ventures into viaduct construction.

In 1845 he was jointly responsible for the **Braidhurst Viaduct** of unusually slender appearance, bridging the North Calder Water where it runs through Strathclyde Park, a recreational area created in the 1970s from derelict land.

In Edinburgh, Locke designed the viaduct at **Slateford** for the Caledonian Railway in 1848. Situated immediately against the Union Canal's Slateford Aqueduct, it has 14 masonry arches spanning the Water of Leith.

The Highland Railway Company produced some splendid engineering works and was unique in not relying on wealthy English sponsors. Led by **Joseph Mitchell**, whose father John had succeeded Thomas Telford in his role as chief inspector of the Highland roads, he engendered huge support amongst Highland chieftains and other landowners anxious to see their remote country opened up. He was responsible for several important viaducts in the Highlands, including those at **Nairn** (1858, in the town of the same name); **Findhorn**, west of Forres (1858); **Conon Bridge** (1862); the **Spey Viaduct**, south-west of Newtonmore (1863); **Ardgay** (1864); and the **Invershin Viaduct**, otherwise known as the Oykel Viaduct (1867).

During the 1860s Joseph Mitchell built the

Locke's Larbert Viaduct. *Robert Murray*

Dalguise Viaduct. *Deborah M. Keith*

Highland Railway through the Monadhliath Mountains and the Drumochter Pass (1,482 feet above sea level – and the highest point on the British main-line railway network). The original section of the Inverness-Aviemore route went via Forres and Grantown, but it was shortened in the 1890s when a more direct line was constructed.

Among Mitchell's viaducts are two excellent examples of the lattice-girder bridges that he pioneered in Scotland. Dating from 1865, **Dalguise Viaduct** is a monumental structure in the valley of the Tay, between Dunkeld and Pitlochry, comprising two spans of 210 feet and 141 feet with piers carried up to form castellated stone towers. **Tilt Viaduct**, which dates from 1863, has a single 150-foot span with castellated arches at each end in deference to its proximity to Blair Castle, the ancestral seat of the powerful Dukes of Atholl.

On the Aberfeldy branch of the Inverness & Perth Junction Railway, Mitchell built the **Tay Viaduct**, a lattice girder bridge on 8-foot-diameter cast-iron piers, reminiscent of locomotive funnels. It is 420 feet long and was one of 23 bridges on the 9-mile long branch line, constructed in 1863. When the lined closed in 1964 the viaduct passed to the Kinnaird Estate, which gifted it to the Logierait Bridge Company. With substantial effort, and grant aid, this community-owned bridge was comprehensively restored in 2001 at a cost of £400,000. By way of comparison, the original 1860s bridge cost £13,772. It is in regular public use for vehicles and forms part of the Sustrans National Cycle Network.

At **Calvine**, north of Blair Atholl, Mitchell constructed his semi-

Tay Viaduct, Logierait.
Iain Matheson

Two of the 'Struan bridges' at Calvine. *Deborah M. Keith*

circular masonry-arched viaduct across an existing road bridge, which makes an impressive feature, with a steel girder bridge added on the eastern side in 1898.

These are known collectively as the 'Struan bridges', and the location was a popular picnic spot for my family travelling south on the A9 from Inverness-shire to visit the grandparents in Dundee and Forfar. At that time, the late 1950s and early '60s, it represented a challenging journey of 4 hours or more, not to mention the seasonal problems caused by unpredictable weather.

The viaduct through the Pass of **Killiecrankie** has 10 semi-circular masonry arches, each with a 35-foot span and set on a slight curve, blending with the striking and historic scenery of the heavily wooded ravine, the scene of the Battle of Killiecrankie in 1689. In the area around the Pass, the Government troops supporting William of Orange but led by a Highlander, General Hugh Mackay of Scourie, were routed by the Jacobite army, which occupied the high ground, led by John Graham of Claverhouse. Affectionately known as 'Bonnie Dundee', Graham's success at Killiecrankie claimed his own life when he was killed in the charge on the Government troops.

This battle pre-dated what is referred to as the First Jacobite Uprising by some 26 years, and the success was short-lived, for the Jacobites were defeated less than a month later at the Battle of Dunkeld.

The **Findhorn Viaduct**, near Mitchell's birthplace at Forres, is a three-span box-girder bridge inspired by Robert Stephenson's tubular bridges and stands on stone abutments and piers of solid ashlar.

Mitchell's viaduct across the River Ness in **Inverness** was a well-proportioned bridge with five segmental arches of sandstone ashlar of the highest quality. Severe flooding in February 1989 swept away a major part of the bridge, but it was such a key link in the network that it was replaced by another viaduct by May 1990.

North of Inverness, the railway is carried over the River Conon by the large and handsome bridge that originally ran parallel to Telford's

Conon Bridge of 1809, of which only the distinctive octagonal tollhouse survives. The viaduct, built in 1862, is skewed, with each 73-foot span comprising four staggered ribs.

Heading north through Ross & Cromarty, the railway line detours inland from the coast towards the rugged upper reaches of the Kyle. Reminiscent of Thomas Telford's designs, Mitchell's bridge over the River Carron at Ardgay, built in 1864, is an elegant two-span masonry bridge with segmental arches. The central pier has a rounded cutwater.

Onwards to the border with Sutherland, the Oykel Viaduct provides a link between the two stations of Culrain and Invershin, some quarter of a mile apart as the crow flies across the Kyle of Sutherland. The alternative route involved a trip of 10 miles, and when the basic 3rd Class fare was a penny a mile, travelling over the viaduct was much the preferred choice for the locals. Built in 1867, it spans the 230 feet in a

The Oykel, or Invershin, Viaduct *Deborah M. Keith*

wrought-iron lattice truss design, with semi-circular arched approaches on each side and the deck secured on top of the trusswork. There is now a metal footbridge bolted to the west side of the viaduct, erected in 1999 to provide a pedestrian route. There are magnificent views to Carbisdale Castle, a Scots Baronial-style mansion with 365 windows, which was built for the Duchess of Sutherland in 1907 following a family feud.

The Salveson family, the shipping magnates, owned the castle from the 1930s and afforded safe refuge to King Haakon VII of Norway and his son, Crown Prince Olaf, during the Second World War, subsequently donating it to the Scottish Youth Hostel Association. Sadly, due to the excessive cost of repairs, Carbisdale Castle ceased in that role in 2011 and was sold in 2016 to an investment company whose aim is to refurbish it as a 'world-class residence'. I have many happy memories of ceilidhs held in the castle, a hallmark of the camaraderie of the hostelling movement.

Joseph Mitchell had been schooled in Inverness and later studied at Aberdeen University. He was the author of several books, including *Reminiscences of my Life in the Highlands*. Although he died in his London property in 1883, he and his family lived for many years in the Highland capital, where his home was Viewhill House at the top of Castle Street. Coincidentally, this property also became a youth hostel. I stayed there while rediscovering Inverness in the 1970s and '80s and while I had the privilege of serving on the National Council of the Scottish Youth Hostel Association. The hostel later moved to new premises and Mitchell's house was seriously damaged by a fire in 2007.

In the late 1890s the new route from Aviemore to Inverness brought new and dramatic viaducts to the Highland line, engineered by **Murdoch Paterson**, who had been Joseph Mitchell's professional partner. The viaducts included that near **Allt Slochd Mhuic**, the second highest summit after Drumochter. It is an attractive eight-span masonry viaduct with semi-circular granite arches and tapering piers, spanning a wooded gorge some 109 foot above the water.

In and around the village of Tomatin there are three viaducts dating from 1897. The **Tomatin Viaduct** has nine semi-circular spans of rock-faced ashlar with voussoirs of brick and external facing stonework. The viaduct over the River Findhorn is striking in character and most

Culloden Viaduct. *Lewis Matheson/Iain Matheson*

unusual for that part of the world in having nine light-steel trusses supported on slender, tapering masonry piers, in turn supported by abutments pierced by small semi-circular arches. It is, however, very well proportioned and sits proudly in the broad river valley.

Aultnaslanach Viaduct across the Dalriach burn near Moy is the only wooden trestle bridge on a main-line railway in Scotland, constructed where ground conditions did not permit more solid foundations. In 2001 a steel beam structure supported on concrete columns was built within the existing bridge.

By far the largest engineering work on the Inverness to Perth line is **Culloden Viaduct**. Also known as the Nairn or Clava Viaduct, it is the longest masonry viaduct in Scotland, at 1,785 feet, with 28 spans of red sandstone, some 132 feet above the river. Built in 1898, the viaduct strides the wide valley of the River Nairn in a graceful curve. It lies a short distance from both my childhood home at Balloch and the site of the Battle of Culloden in 1746, the last battle fought on British soil, which effectively brought to an end the Jacobite cause.

Glasgow, or rather the Admiralty and the Bridge Trustees, had a somewhat hostile relationship with the early railway companies. The problem was how to bridge the Clyde without impeding navigation. The oldest viaduct dates from 1847, when Neil Robson designed the **Pollockshaws Viaduct**, with its five segmental arches, two of them skewed over the White Cart River, for the Glasgow, Barrhead & Neilston Direct Railway. Pollockshaws West station, lying adjacent to the viaduct, is the oldest in Glasgow.

From 1847 it was then a further 23 years until the City of Glasgow Union Railway opened its first railway bridge, in 1870. It had taken 11 years and cost £2 million to build the 6¼ miles of track, the bridge and the related infrastructure.

In 1878 the **Caledonian Railway Viaduct** was constructed with its piers exactly in line with the Jamaica Street (now Glasgow) Bridge, in accord with the Clyde Trustees' requirements. It is built on a skew, with five spans, some 32 feet above high water mark. The **Dalmarnock Railway Bridge** dates from 1897, and remains in use today.

A year later the second **City Union Railway Bridge** was constructed. The engineer was **William Melville** and the contractor was **Sir William Arrol & Company**. The endeavours to ensure the foundations were sound and the superstructure girders robust were intense. In order to minimise disruption to river traffic, the new columns were founded a few feet from the piers of the original bridge. Each abutment is founded on three large caissons sunk under air pressure to a depth of 54 feet below Ordnance Datum (OD) and four smaller caissons sunk to a depth

Connell Ferry Bridge. *Deborah M. Keith*

of 30 feet below OD. All seven caissons were then filled with concrete to a height of 6 feet above OD. The cost was £67,970.

Such was the attention to detail in the design and testing of these railway bridges that when the **second Caledonian Railway Bridge** was completed in 1905, it was tested by running 19 of the company's heaviest locomotives, weighing about 1,167 tons, on to the middle of the bridge. The structure was judged a success as the maximum deflection was recorded as 7/8ths of an inch! This bridge was designed to carry eight tracks for a length of 702ft 6in. Designed by D. A. Matheson, the Chief Engineer of the Caledonian Railway, with advice from Sir J. W. Barry, it was built by Sir William Arrol of steel lattice girders on granite piers, and was believed to be the widest railway bridge in the world when it opened.

On **Argyle Street**, the glass-walled bridge carrying the platforms of Central Station has long earned the nickname of 'The Hielanman's Umbrella' for its reputation as a meeting place for Glasgow's large Highland community taking shelter, and the opportunity for a blether, during one of the not infrequent downpours. That is certainly a more welcoming name than its Network Rail reference – Bridge WCM2/085 – and the whole precinct is now much improved through works carried out under the Public Realm Project in 1999, including re-glazing of the Venetian windows.

Leith has been an industrous port for Edinburgh for centuries, but its major development occurred with the building of dockyards in the 19th century. In 1874 the longest swing bridge in Britain, the **Victoria Swing Bridge**, engineered by Rendel and Robertson, was constructed to carry two dock rail tracks together with a road. With hydraulics powered by a nearby power station, the wrought-iron bridge was 212 feet long and swung to allow shipping passage up the Water of Leith. It held the length record until 1937, when the Kincardine Bridge was opened. Now a public footpath, it was restored in 2000.

Another bridge that broke records when it was completed in 1869 was the **Solway Viaduct**, linking Scotland and England between Kirtlebridge in Dumfries-shire and Brayton in Cumbria. At 5,790 feet in length, it was the longest viaduct in Britain until the opening of the first Tay Rail Bridge. It took three years to construct at a cost of £100,000. Both bridges suffered from extreme weather conditions, although the Solway not so tragically as the Tay. Built initially to carry iron ore from Furness to the steel mills of Lanarkshire, it was severely affected by ice floes in 1875 and again in 1881, when 45 of the 181 cast-iron piers were destroyed. Following extensive repairs, the bridge continued in use until 1921, by which time its industrial purpose had waned. Thoughts were given to

converting it to a road bridge, but these did not materialise and the bridge was demolished in 1934/35. The principal objection to demolition evidently came from the residents of Kirtlebridge, who had enjoyed a leisurely walk across the Solway Firth on a Sunday to enjoy the then more relaxed alcohol laws south of the border.

I first became aware of this viaduct when I was working with several nature conservation bodies on the Solway Mosses National Nature Reserve. Walking through the peatlands of Bowness Common, the evidence of a previous railway line was obvious, heading out towards the Solway Firth. I asked the ornithologists and botanists about the history of the site and they related the fascinating tale of the Solway Viaduct and how Nature had wrought havoc on its structure.

On the Callander & Oban Railway, the branch from Connel to Ballachulish was completed in 1903, but fell victim to the Beeching cuts in 1966. The **Connel Ferry Bridge**, a splendid steel cantilever bridge over the Falls of Lora at the narrowest part of Loch Etive, was designed by **Sir John Wolfe Barry** (1836-1918), the engineer who 15 years earlier had designed London's Tower Bridge. His assistant was Henry Marc Brunel, IBK's younger son.

The contractor at Connel was Arrol's Bridge & Roof Company and, with a span of 500 feet, it is the second largest of its type in Britain. It comprises 2,600 tons of steel and cost approximately £43,000. A roadway was incorporated in 1914 and following the closure of the railway the bridge was converted for use by road traffic and pedestrians only.

Connel Ferry Bridge holds a commanding position, and in 1944 three Fairey Barracuda aircraft of the Fleet Air Arm, destined for service in the Far East, made a farewell gesture to Scotland by flying under it in line astern. With a wingspan of 60 feet, this was not an exercise for the faint-hearted. The bridge featured in the 1981 film *Eye of the Needle*, starring Donald Sutherland and based on Ken Follett's Second World War spy thriller.

Also on the disused Callander & Oban Railway is the viaduct at **Glen Ogle**, where the railway climbed the 1:60 gradient for 6 miles north of Lochearnhead to the summit at 944 feet above sea level. Designed by B. & E. Blyth as a 20-arch structure across a depression in the hillside, the viaduct, as built between 1866 and 1870, comprises 12 segmental arches carrying the track some 450 feet. Now forming part of the Rob Roy Way, good views of this viaduct, and the military road constructed by Caulfeild in 1749, are gained from the A85 road.

Two other viaducts are worthy of mention as striking examples of major engineering that impact beneficially on the landscape quality. **Drygrange Viaduct**, otherwise known as Leaderfoot, across the River

Glen Ogle Viaduct. *Deborah M. Keith*

Tweed at St Boswells, comprises 19 tall semi-circular arches on tapering masonry and brick piers. Built in 1863 by **Jopp, Wylie & Peddie**, it was described as 'immense' by Queen Victoria in her Journal and functioned as a railway viaduct on the North British Railway's line to Reston until the late 1940s. The spans are each 43 feet and the bridge towers 123 feet above the river. The viaduct forms a fine group alongside the 18th-century Drygrange road bridge and its modern concrete successor.

The tall piers of Drygrange, or Leaderfoot, Viaduct. *Lewis Matheson*

Carron Viaduct, Speyside. *Mike W. Lowson*

Designed by Alexander Easton Gibb and built in 1863 to carry both rail and road, **Carron Bridge** in Speyside was Scotland's last cast-iron railway bridge. Its three ribbed arches, flanked by segmental flood relief and access arches, span the River Spey between massive stone abutments with triangular cutwaters. Still an impressive sight when viewed from the river walk, the bridge now serves vehicular traffic for Dailuaine Distillery and walkers on the Speyside Way.

Serving the highest village in Scotland, the eponymous **Wanlockhead** or Rispin Cleugh Viaduct was a well-proportioned eight-span arched bridge with terracotta brick spandrels and piers and concrete arch rings. It was built in 1891 by **Sir Robert McAlpine & Sons** to a design by Charles Foreman and stands as a monument to the lead-mining industry that once prevailed in this part of the Southern Uplands. It was not only lead, however, for zinc, copper and silver were all mined in this area too, as well as some of the purest gold in the world; at 22.8 carats, it was used to make the Scottish Crown. Unfortunately, there was just not enough of this valuable resource to ensure viability of the mining activity. The Wanlockhead & Leadhills Light Railway branch line, also the highest in Scotland, closed in 1938 and mining was over by the 1950s. The viaduct was demolished in 1991.

Further west, the viaduct that carried the Portpatrick Railway from Glasgow to Stranraer across **Loch Ken**, near Parton, is one of earliest surviving examples of three wrought-iron bowstring lattice girder spans. The bridge is built on a curve with a radius of 880 yards, with the masonry of the piers resting on cast-iron tubes, up to 42 feet deep, which were sunk to their final depth by a novel use of screw-piles. Designed by **B. & E. Blyth**, consulting engineers, the bridge cost £13,000 when it was constructed in 1859. The line closed under the Beeching cuts in 1965.

The largest viaduct on the 'Port Road', as the Portpatrick & Wigtownshire Joint Railway was known, is the **Big Water of Fleet Viaduct**. At 900 feet in length and towering as high as 70 feet, the 20 segmental arches stride across the remote countryside of the Cairnsmore of Fleet National Nature Reserve, north of Gatehouse. The structure was designed by B. & E. Blyth and opened in 1861, but required strengthening with brick piers in the 1940s. This was probably essential work, given that the viaduct carried millions of tons of ordnance and supplies and many thousands of US troops during the Second World War, when Cairnryan was purpose-built as a major military port, with a rail link to Stranraer.

To see the viaduct without the brick reinforcements, however, watch the 1935 film version of John Buchan's *The 39 Steps*. The railway line was closed in 1965, but the viaduct remains in use as a cycle and walking route. Its 'wee sister', the Little Water of Fleet Viaduct, which had only nine arches, was, however, blown up as part of an Army training exercise.

On the east coast, at **Montrose**, the original wrought-iron viaduct across the mouth of the Montrose Basin was designed by Thomas Bouch for the North British Railway in 1870. It was demolished in 1880, to be replaced by the 14-span structure by Sir William Arrol, which is still in operation.

Disused and dismantled railway lines might no longer reverberate to the sound of hard-working steam locomotives, but nowadays they make excellent recreation areas for walkers and cyclists, such as the 40-mile Formartine and Buchan Way, in Aberdeenshire. It runs along the route of the former line from Dyce to Maud, where the track split into branches to Fraserburgh and to Peterhead.

The former railway line south of Edinburgh and beyond Dalkeith, built in the 1830s principally to haul coal from the Midlothian coalfields, also now provides a walk/cycle route incorporating the **James Jardine Viaduct** at Glenesk. With its elegant late-Georgian style incorporating fine ashlar masonry, extensive curved wing-walls and tapering pilasters and archivolts, it has strong resemblance to some of Telford's bridges in the Highlands. Professor Roland Paxton states that it is the finest pre-Victorian railway bridge in Scotland, and it is certainly several cuts above the purely functional design.

James Jardine (1776-1858) was an associate of Thomas Telford, but much else besides. A brilliant mathematician, he carried out a series of studies on the Firth of Tay, from which he was the first person to calculate Mean Sea Level. Jardine built bridges, tunnels, harbours and the reservoirs that provide Edinburgh with its water supply. He lived at 18 Queen Street, a most prestigious address in Edinburgh. As with Telford, he never married and had no children. That's a shame, as we can only wonder what their offspring would have achieved with such distinguished genes.

The railway viaduct at **Leslie**, in Fife, stands on tall slender piers and, unusually in Scotland, has elliptical arches. Built in 1861 by **Thomas Bouch** – a successful venture before his ill-fated bridge over the Tay – it now serves as a footbridge. Likewise, the grand viaduct at **Speymouth** (Garmouth) is now used as a footbridge over the meandering course of the River Spey, disused for a long period after serving the fishing ports on the Banffshire coast. Built in 1886, its 350-foot bowed central truss is flanked by six 100-foot plain truss approach spans, carried on cylindrical masonry piers. On the former Strathspey Railway, the

Neidpath Viaduct. *Colin L. Shearer*

Ballindalloch Viaduct, dating from 1863, has seen countless whisky barrels transported over it, but now provides a route for walkers and cyclists since it closed in 1968.

The magnificent **Neidpath Viaduct**, carrying the former Symington, Biggar & Broughton branch line of the Caledonian Railway across the Tweed to the west of Peebles, is now part of a heritage trail. Opened in 1864, the line operated for 90 years before the cutbacks spelled closure.

The local architect engaged in the design, Robert Murray, is said to have carved a rough builder's model of the eight ashlar skew arches from a turnip. The Scottish turnip, which is what the English mistakenly refer to as a swede, is a versatile vegetable. That said, anyone who has tried to fashion a lantern out of a neep for Hallowe'en will appreciate Mr Murray's manual dexterity.

The West Highland Railway, from Craigendoran to Fort William, and its extension to Mallaig on the west coast, runs through some of the most spectacular mountain, moor, loch and coastal scenery in Scotland

Glenfinnan Viaduct viewed from a steam train. *Iain Matheson*

Inset Moor of Rannoch (Cruach) Viaduct. *Alan Reid*

and contains many railway viaducts of impressive construction and outstanding landscape qualities. Completed in 1894, the most elite structures on this section of the line are the two steel **Horseshoe** and **Gleann** viaducts on the Horseshoe Curve between Bridge of Orchy and Tyndrum, where the line crosses two valleys as it follows the contours of the hillsides.

The largest single viaduct, however, is across the **Moor of Rannoch** (Cruach), carrying the line over a depression in a tight curve. The viaduct, now commonly referred to as Rannoch, has nine latticework steel spans, each of them 70ft 6in, on masonry piers.

At Fort William, the **Lochy Viaduct** has four 80-foot steel trusses. The ground conditions over much of the track length did not make for ease of preparatory construction, and at **Fillan Viaduct**, north of Crianlarich, piles were driven in to a depth of 30 feet and the central pier required a cofferdam to be formed mid-channel in the River Fillan.

The newer extension to Mallaig, opened in 1901 after much lobbying by the Crofters Commission, affords colourful views along Loch Eil and Loch Shiel, then spectacular vistas westwards from Lochailort to the islands of Eigg, Rhum and Muck and north to Skye. The White Sands of Morar and those at Arisaig have been used in beach scenes in many movies, most notably *Local Hero*, Bill Forsyth's brilliant 1983 comedy-drama about the oil exploration business, starring Burt Lancaster and Scotland's own stable of exceptionally talented actors including Dennis Lawson, Fulton Mackay, Rikki Fulton, Alex Norton and Peter Capaldi.

Mallaig was founded in the 1840s when the landowner of North Morar Estate, Lord Lovat, divided his farm of Mallaigvaig into 17 parcels of land and encouraged his tenants to diversify into fishing. By the 1960s Mallaig was the busiest herring port in Europe.

The route of the railway, some 41 miles, is enhanced by large and prominent railway viaducts, most notably at **Glenfinnan**, **Lochailort** and **Morar**. The engineers were **Simpson and Wilson** and contractor **Sir Robert McAlpine**, who brought early prominence to the use of mass concrete in such large structures. In fact, this pioneering work with concrete on the railway was a consequence of the rock encountered locally being micra-schist, quartz and gneiss, admirably suited for concrete, but quite impossible to cut for use in masonry on a large scale, certainly in terms of economic cost. Although this had been determined by the engineers at the pre-contract stage, the contractor used his work to publicise this form of construction, earning him the sobriquet of 'Concrete Bob'.

Glenfinnan must rank as one of the most magnificent viaducts in Britain, perched on a remote hillside at the head of Loch Shiel. It is the longest concrete railway bridge in Scotland with its 21 arches in a spectacular curve stretching over 1,248 feet. The tallest arch stands 100 feet above ground level. The mass concrete still shows the imprint of the grain of the wooden shuttering into which the concrete was poured. The viaduct is popular with photographers and captured in many calendars, providing a fitting backdrop to the monument to the raising of Bonnie Prince Charlie's standard at the start of the fated 1745 Jacobite Rising. It also appears to great effect in the 'Harry Potter' movie *Harry Potter and the Chamber of Secrets* by Scottish writer J. K. Rowling, where the 'Hogwarts Express' is seen steaming across the viaduct chased by a Ford Anglia.

The viaduct at **Loch nan Uamh**, also known as Gleann Mama, at Lochailort, comprises eight spans in two groups of four, each of 50 feet, which is the standard on this line. Again built of mass concrete, it has a magnificent setting amidst rugged, rocky hinterland and the sandy estuary.

Loch nan Uamh Viaduct. *Canmore*

This viaduct has a strange tale to tell, which has only recently been proven accurate. According to legend, during construction (1899-1901) one of the horse-drawn carts engaged to carry rubble used for backfilling the deep and cavernous piers on these mighty viaducts reversed into the offloading position, overbalanced, and cart and horse disappeared down into the structure. As time went on, the story was subject to the twists associated with such tales and the scene of the incident became unclear.

In 2000 Professor Roland Paxton from Heriot-Watt University in Edinburgh located the metal remains of the cart and the shod horse using an infra-red camera technique being developed by engineers for establishing whether rock formations at depths were suitable as foundations. This attracted much publicity and Professor Paxton, who also chaired the Panel on Historical Engineering Works at the Institution of Civil Engineers, described the find as exciting, not only because it demonstrated the application of this new scientific technique as being an effective tool for the civil engineer, but also that it finally put to rest the speculation over the tale and proved beyond doubt that it did occur, and where.

The Morar Viaduct is a 90-foot mass concrete bridge spanning the River Morar just below the spectacular Falls of Morar. It has a single large span and two smaller arches on the north side. At about 1,000 yards long, the River Morar is the shortest river in the British Isles, linking the Atlantic Ocean to Loch Morar, the deepest freshwater body in the British Isles. Its 1,017-foot depth is also home to 'Morag', who gives 'Nessie' a run for her money in the monster stakes.

In its short length the River Morar has three bridges and a hydro-electric power station. The latter dates from 1948, the heyday of the vision of the country's wartime Secretary of State for Scotland, Sir Tom Johnston, for renewable energy from Scotland's abundant water resource – a rich legacy indeed.

The viaduct at **Borrodale** has one large span some 86 feet above the river level and is flanked by single 20-foot arches. At the time of building, this bridge was the longest concrete railway arch in the world. The whole structure is encased in rubble masonry and has a castellated parapet, which was a condition stipulated by the landowner.

The pioneering work by 'Concrete Bob' on massed concrete on the West Highland Railway viaducts does have a sobering legacy. As with any innovative material, time alone is the greatest test of its durability and longevity. At some point the concrete will show some evidence of cracking and that will be a telling sign of its life expectancy. The implications, of course, will be enormous, as this will put a 'sell-by date' on the many thousands of similarly constructed structures worldwide. Engineers engaged in monitoring the viaducts have an imperative on attention to detail!

The route of the railway from Fort William to Mallaig is as majestic as it is beautiful. It deserves to be viewed, which is exactly what two of my closest friends, Colin Shearer and Mike Lowson, both then in their 20s, not only envisaged but brought to fruition in 1984.

As Area Operations Manager of the then under-threat lines to Oban, Fort William and Mallaig, Mike was convinced that their scenic and tourism potential could be greatly enhanced, and worked up plans for a wide range of line-saving enhancements, the key to which was the reintroduction of steam-hauled services on the Fort William-Mallaig extension.

When Colin arrived as Area Manager, then one of the youngest on British Rail, these plans, and more, secured the considerable support and impetus they needed to become reality. Together, they created the 'West Highlander', BR's only scheduled main-line steam-hauled service, opening up stunning vistas of Lochaber to the delight of tourists from around the world. This quickly caught the public's imagination; the 'West Highlander' later became 'The Lochaber', which in turn became 'The Jacobite', and a whole new exciting and hugely successful chapter in Scottish tourism was written. From those uncertain days in the early 1980s, it is now marketed, without too much exaggeration, as one of the greatest railway journeys in the world. Its added identity as the route of the 'Hogwarts Express' from the 'Harry Potter' films has brought a new generation of young enthusiasts for the service, too.

The magic that the pioneer bridge-builders brought to creating Scotland's railway system has today been extended and, indeed, re-energised as they continue to serve the public not only on rail lines but also in many other ways, including their role in the life of a modern-day but fictional young wizard.

Scotland's engineering and industrial achievements, which left our forebears gasping in amazement, continue to astonish and inspire new generations, and their heritage will do so for many generations to come.

9. BRIDGING THE FORTH AND TAY

From tragedy to triumph

In my graduation year of 1976, together with my fellow students I was keen to put into practice all the knowledge and experience we'd gained. We'd surely be snapped up as enthusiastic young graduates and offered employment where we could undertake training for our professional qualification as chartered surveyors.

I went to a Civil Service interview at Basingstoke for the Ministry of Agriculture, Fisheries & Food (MAFF) and was offered a post as a graduate surveyor at what seemed at the time a significant salary of £3,200 per annum. It was a lot after a student grant where I had to eke out a living in a world where beer was 14p a pint and my hall of residence charged £9 per week for full board!

Fortuitously, I was simultaneously contacted by David Wardhaugh, a past-Chairman of the RICS Scottish Branch, who had spotted my name as a young hopeful on the RICS's Jobs Enquiry Register. Mr Wardhaugh and his son Robin ran a land agency partnership in Forfar and they were looking for a new 'assistant'. This job offered a rather lower salary of £2,400 per annum. It was 25% lower – you can tell I'd studied statistics – but had two or three key advantages.

First, it was a chance to return to Scotland; second it was a job in private practice, as I really didn't want to be a white-knuckled civil servant back then; and third, although it may have paid less, the job offer included a car – a Simca 1100 GTX. I'd be living in Forfar, a town I'd known from visits to my Keith grandparents, and I'd have a car with which to explore. It was no ordinary Simca 1100 either. With metallic paint, the GTX suffix meant that it had a clock!

It was no contest; I took the job.

I concentrated on the factoring of rural estates, several in Aberdeenshire, such as Knockespoch and Grandholm, the Forneth Estate in Perthshire and the Mylnefield Estate near Invergowrie. This meant that the Simca was put through its paces. Early-morning starts to cross the Cairn o' Mount via Bridge of Dye, Potarch Bridge and Bridge of Alford to Knockespoch one week, then Marykirk Bridge, Bridge of Dee and Bridge of Don to Grandholm the next week, all indelibly etched on my mind as I made my way to meet charming if occasionally other-worldly landowners and handle sensitive rent reviews or requests for landlord's improvements with tenants I had difficulty understanding

until my ear became attuned to their native Doric. A firm handshake proved a useful ally here, though. It was interpreted as meaning that you were sincere, if nothing else.

One of Forfar's great joys was the genuinely friendly atmosphere in the office. The Wardhaughs were kind and considerate employers and embraced me as one of their own, which was more than I could expect for I was certainly a bit 'green around the gills' and given plenty of opportunities to 'learn from my mistakes'.

But I did work hard. My position as 'assistant' was actually quite fluid. I occupied a rather splendid office next door to Mr Wardhaugh Senior and on many occasions I heard him discussing instructions with clients. As the talks concluded, I overheard either, 'I'll get my senior assistant to deal with this for you,' or 'I'll get my junior assistant to…,' depending on what level of professional fee had been negotiated.

One thing was certain – the work would be coming my way and I wasn't being paid two salaries. But I revelled in it all and one real advantage of working in a small country practice was that it was a diverse workload and I had considerable responsibility early on in my career.

I qualified as a chartered surveyor in 1979 and got a new car as a reward, this time a bright red Chrysler Sunbeam hatchback.

Among the rich variety of different professional tasks, I was also involved in Forfar's community spirit. People were genuinely surprised when I told them that my grandfather was Jim Keith, who had been Treasurer of Forfar Athletic Football Club in the early 1960s, although few people made any connection between me and anyone associated with sport, even in an official capacity.

While Robin Wardhaugh and I were keen Round Tablers and participated fully in 'dominoes and stovie supper nights' with the older generation of Forfarians, David Wardhaugh was a well-respected Rotarian. He returned from a lunch meeting one Tuesday to announce that the local retired GP, Dr Gibson, was embarking on a study of all the doo'cots (dovecots) in Angus and he'd 'volunteered' me to visit, measure and produce drawings – elevations and plan – of each of them. And this was all to be done in my own time!

There were 66 dovecots in the county of Angus. I know, as I measured them all. Some were magnificent structures, others were in ruinous condition, but they all made it on to the draughtsman's board in my flat and were reproduced as ink drawings at a scale of 1/8th inch to the foot. There were no laser measuring devices in those days so my then girlfriend, Linda, obliged by holding the end of the measuring tape. Oh boy, did I know how to treat a girl!

I'm pleased to say that Dr Gibson was thrilled with the result. A few years ago I visited the Finavon Doo'cot, which has been faithfully restored and is open to the public. Part of the display included my drawings! Perhaps the doo'cot experience fuelled my idea for a book on another part of our Scottish heritage, the bridges, although I've drawn the line, so to speak, at attempting to replicate each of them as an elevation or a plan.

The Forestry Commission has done excellent work in providing facilities for public access and recreation on land in its ownership, and as a young surveyor in Forfar I was fortunate to be involved in the creation of several of the Commission's visitor facilities, including providing reduced levels from my dumpy level (a simple theodolite – no lasers in those days) for proposed car parks at Glen Doe in Angus and Oldman Wood at Maryculter in Aberdeenshire. They are still there and well used to this day.

One particular Forestry Commission property I would recommend visiting is in Glen Affric. Set dramatically above the 100-foot Plodda Falls, which plummet to the River Abhain Deabhag below, the previous owner of Guisachan Estate, **Lord Tweedsmouth**, built a wrought-iron bridge in 1889. This afforded striking views over the falls, but time took its toll and the Forestry Commission's replacement viewing platform now seeks to give the walker the same experience but in a safe environment.

Glen Affric is a truly magnificent area, with walks through stands of Douglas fir and larch near Tomich. It was from this forest that the timber was harvested that formed the masts of Robert Falcon Scott's research ship *Discovery*. In 1986 she returned to Dundee, the city where she was built and launched in 1901, and is now on permanent display at an excellent visitor centre at Discovery Point, which lies between the road and rail bridges over the River Tay.

Of course, almost every journey south from Forfar in my well-travelled Simca or Chrysler Sunbeam would take me to and through Dundee, and I would never fail to marvel at the sight of the Tay Rail Bridge, a tale of triumph and tragedy that would change bridge-building in Scotland for ever.

Eventually the Forth Rail Bridge would come to be recognised worldwide as the classic icon of Scottish engineering, but its history is so much wrapped up with that of the Tay Rail Bridge that I have brought them together in this chapter.

Crossing the Silvery Tay

The first rail bridge to link Fife with Dundee across the River Tay was designed by **Sir Thomas Bouch** (1822-80) for the North British Railway Company. Initially a well-respected and experienced engineer, he was renowned for his arrogance and economic frugality. These traits were to prove fatal for the 75 people on board the 5.20pm train from Burntisland as it crossed the high girders, some 79 feet above the water level, on Sunday 28 December 1879, when 13 of the 84 spans collapsed in a vicious storm, sending the train into the river beneath. In the strong currents of the River Tay, the bodies were swept away and 29 were never recovered. (Research by the Tay Rail Bridge Disaster Memorial Trust claims that the death toll was 59 rather than 75, but in any event it was very substantial.)

The Tay Bridge had been a significant landmark when it opened in 1877. Of lattice girder construction, on iron columns, it was the longest iron bridge in the world. It had been crossed by Queen Victoria and the US President. Its collapse was one of the worst disasters in British railway history.

Much has been speculated about the cause of the collapse, but it was probably a combination of poor design by insufficient allowance for wind pressure in a channel renowned for its funnel-like effect on winds; low-grade cast iron from the suppliers; poor supervision during construction; and a poor maintenance record. The subsequent inquiry concluded that these, combined with extraordinary weather conditions, created the tragic event.

William McGonagall (1825-1902), the Dundee writer oft cited, with some justification, as the worst poet in the history of the English language, put pen to paper to record the tragedy in his own inimitable if numerically inaccurate fashion. The first stanza, which by McGonagall's own admission 'will probably be as much as you can stand', set the scene:

'The Tay Bridge is a beautiful span,
And the River Tay runs through it;
A wonderful work by the hands of man,
Many strangers come far to view it.'

Above Fallen girders after the collapse of the Tay Rail Bridge. *Courtesy of the National Library of Scotland*

Above right The last resting place of Thomas Bouch. *Kim Traynor*

And so to the disaster:

> 'Beautiful Railway Bridge of the Silv'ry Tay
> Alas I am very sorry to say
> That ninety lives have been taken away
> On the last Sabbath day of 1879
> Which will be remembered for a very long time.'

While more attention to detail at all stages might have averted the disaster, blame was laid predominantly at Bouch's feet.

He had long held an ambition to bridge both the firths of Tay and Forth, even when he was manager and engineer of the Edinburgh & Northern Railway, a post he had attained in 1849, at the age of 27. He realised that the Tay would be the more straightforward proposition

and said of the project, 'It is a very ordinary undertaking,' and, as if to emphasise the claim, he produced a very ordinary design for the bridge.

A Board of Trade Inquiry in 1880, itself not very thorough, found that 'the bridge had been badly designed, badly constructed and badly maintained'. The bridgemaster appointed to oversee maintenance was unqualified and he repaired defects using material bought over the counter from a Dundee ironmonger. While the cast-iron columns were supplied as 'best iron', the foundry omitted to mention that this was, in fact, grade-three material.

Referring to Bouch's arrogance in a postscript to his book *The High Girders*, John Prebble asserts, perhaps slightly unkindly, that

> 'Thomas Bouch was a little man on stilts … the great storm of 28th December blew the stilts from beneath Bouch as cynically as it plucked the stilts from beneath his bridge.'

Bouch's reputation shattered, only six months after receiving his knighthood from Queen Victoria, his contract to design a rail bridge

Today's Tay Rail Bridge. *L. Bruce Keith*

across the River Forth was cancelled and work was put in hand in 1880 to design a new bridge over the Tay. Bouch died the same year, broken-hearted and dismayed, at the age of 58, and is buried in Edinburgh.

With a considerable amount of debris from the bridge and the engine and six wrecked carriages landing in the icy waters of the turbulent river, well-known for its strong currents and tidal flows, it is not surprising that it took several weeks for the bodies that were eventually recovered to be found. The wood debris was washed up on local beaches for months afterwards, collected as driftwood and some of it used to make furniture.

My mother's family hailed from Dundee and my great-great-grandfather, David Whamond, a skilled carpenter, made a grandfather clock from the wood salvaged from one of the carriages that crashed that night in 1879. Somehow it went out of the family – perhaps one of my forebears found it rather callous – and my aunt, on a visit from Canada, found it in an antique shop in Montrose in the 1970s. Obviously it was not that much of a sentimental heirloom, however, because she declined to buy it. The clock was last heard of in San Francisco.

The Tay needed a replacement crossing. The engineers second time round were **William and Crawford Barlow**, whose bridge was opened in 1887. Built on entirely new piers, it reused many of the old girders, but the high girders were replaced by two massive trusses.

The bridge comprises 85 spans, 74 over water, and with a length of 2 miles 56 yards it was, like its predecessor, the world's longest railway bridge at that time. It remains the longest railway bridge in Britain. Following completion, the piers of the old bridge were cut down to just above high water level, where they can still be seen downstream of the new structure.

In 2003 a project to strengthen and refurbish the rail bridge won the British Construction Industry Civil Engineering Award. Costing £20.85 million, hundreds of thousands of rivets were removed and replaced and more than 1,100 tons of bird droppings were scraped off the ironwork lattices using hand tools, all in very exposed conditions over a firth with very fast-running tides.

Lessons learned at the Forth

Given Thomas Bouch's failure across the Tay, it is perhaps not surprising that the engineers chosen to take over his contract on the design of the Forth Rail Bridge, **Sir John Fowler** and **Benjamin Baker**, should produce a bridge of striking appearance and immense grandeur but, by all accounts, grossly over-engineered.

Crossing the expanse of the River Forth, to link the Lothians with the Kingdom of Fife – by which stage it has already transformed from a meandering river on the Carse of Stirling into a major watercourse at the modern port of Grangemouth and the naval dockyard at Rosyth, and at the neck of a significant estuary – is no mean feat.

From the days of Saint Margaret, Queen of Scotland (1045-93), after whom the small towns at either end of the Forth bridges are named, there had been a ferry linking the communities and providing an invaluable trade route. The original ferry was provided by Queen Margaret, wife of King Malcolm III, for pilgrims journeying to the religious centres at St Andrews and Dunfermline Abbey, founded by her son David I, and it had operated through the generations until the opening of the Forth Road Bridge in 1964.

It's worth recording that, ironically, it was Thomas Bouch who had designed the world's first train ferry, which plied between Burntisland in Fife to Granton in Edinburgh between 1850 and 1890 as part of the Edinburgh & Northern Railway's cross-estuary service.

As early as 1818 the land surveyor and civil engineer **James Anderson** (1793-1861) had published proposals for a wrought-iron chain suspension bridge with 1,600-foot spans over the Forth, although his plans were well beyond the capability of structures at that time and, at an estimated cost of £175,000, was considered profligate for a country still recovering from the recent Napoleonic Wars.

Indeed, reflecting on that suspension bridge proposal at the opening of the eventual structure, Wilhelm Westhofen, one of the bridge's engineers and chroniclers, opined that it was 'so light … that on a dull day it would hardly have been visible and, after a heavy gale, no longer to be seen on a clear day either.'

But it was the growth of the railways that provided the catalyst for the iconic structure, known in railway parlance as 'The Bridge' – all other railway bridges have a number!

Four railway companies – the Midland, North British, Great Northern and North Eastern – backed the bridge project financially; each could see the commercial rationale for this vital artery across the firth. The Forth Bridge Railway Company was a joint venture, with proportionate contributions of 32.5%, 30%, 18.75% and 18.75% respectively.

The bridge, designed by **Sir John Fowler** (1817-98) and **Sir Benjamin Baker** (1840-1907), and engineered by **Sir William Arrol** (1839-1913), ranks as one of the wonders of the Industrial Age.

As early as 1873, Fowler had published *Building Long Railway Bridges*. The engineers calculated that the bridge design would work both

Sir John Fowler. *Courtesy of the Institution of Civil Engineers*

Sir Benjamin Baker. *Courtesy of the Institution of Civil Engineers*

theoretically and scientifically, before it was constructed on the shoreline and then erected in situ.

It was a revolutionary solution: three huge double cantilevers with the upper section being in tension and the lower section in compression, with the piers providing a balance at each end. A bridge had never been built on this scale before. It took three years to construct the foundations beneath the water and the granite piers above. Six caissons, each of 400 tons, were floated out into position and concrete poured in to make

The Forth Rail Bridge *Deborah M. Keith*

Above The Forth Rail Bridge. *Lewis Matheson*

Left The Forth Bridge, Inchgarvie South Cantilever, photographed by Evelyn George Carey on 1 September 1889. *Courtesy of the Institution of Civil Engineers*

them sink. They were then levelled and the 7-foot-deep chambers filled with compressed air to enable the workers to build the foundation.

With a total length of more than 1½ miles, two clear spans each of 1,710 feet, two of 675 feet, 15 of 168 feet and six of 50 feet, it was three times longer than anything of its design that had ever been built before, and the first major bridge structure using steel as the principal component. It was the largest bridge of its kind in the world until the Quebec Bridge in Canada opened in 1917. It is still the longest cantilever bridge in Britain, and the second longest in the world.

The towers, each built on four piers, are 361 feet high and the railway deck is 158 feet above the high water level. The six (three double) cantilevers are each built out 680 feet from the towers and carry the central supported spans. The main columns are 12 feet in diameter.

Some 4,600 men took seven years to build the bridge, at a cost of £3.2 million, equivalent to some £250 million today. There are 54,160 tons of steel, including 4,200 tons of rivets, which equates to 6½ million in number. There are approximately 100 rivets per foot and, to hasten erection, Arrol invented a hydraulic riveting machine. The last rivet was solid gold and was driven home by the Prince of Wales.

The stonework is some 640,000 cubic feet of Aberdeen granite. The bridge was built to exude confidence and solidity. It is enormous and hugely over-engineered, being built to withstand a wind pressure of 56lb per square foot, whereas 30lb per square foot is today regarded as sufficient. Sadly, the first Tay Rail Bridge had been designed to withstand only 20lb per square foot. With the memory of the tragic loss of life when the Tay Bridge collapsed still fresh when HRH The Prince of Wales, later King Edward VII, opened the Forth Bridge on 4 March 1890, the design underpinned that restored confidence. And that was just as well, for there was a gale blowing that day too.

One problem encountered with the use of steel, in the corrosive environment of a major estuary, was that the 145 acres of steel surface required continual painting. This repetitive process, with red oxide paint, which admittedly kept squads of painters employed for generations, gave birth to the familiar *bon mot* of anything that seemed endless and ongoing as 'like painting the Forth Rail Bridge'.

A new product described as a 'glass-flake epoxy paint', which is similar to that used in the offshore oil industry, has now been applied together with a primer and a red top coat to create a virtually impenetrable layer to protect the bridge's steelwork from the weather. This

The Forth Bridge from the Hawes Pier, photographed by Evelyn George Carey on 15 April 1889. *Courtesy of the National Galleries Scotland*

project itself took more than nine years to complete, cost £134 million and employed a 200-strong team of painters and 4,000 tonnes of scaffolding. This painting product is expected to last up to 25 years before a revisit is necessary, so time will tell if the old saying has outlived its origins. The new chemical treatment, however, does preserve the bridge's famous trademark red colour.

That the Forth Rail Bridge was the largest civil engineering structure built anywhere in the world in the 19th century – you can lay eight Eiffel Towers along its length – is in no doubt. Impressive and iconic though it certainly is, it was not universally acclaimed as a thing of beauty. The arts and crafts designer William Morris (1834-96) called it 'the supremist specimen of all ugliness'.

Scotland's leading Modernist architect, Professor Andy MacMillan (1928-2014), did, however, see architectural beauty in the bridge, highlighting 'the close link between the bridge's technical and functional design, visible in its appearance so that the stresses that balance the bridge form part of its aesthetic appeal.'

Whatever your view, the world's first all-steel bridge makes a strong statement about the development of civil engineering. This is a view upheld by the UNESCO panel in July 2015 to designate the bridge as a World Heritage Site, awarding it the same status as the Taj Mahal and the Great Wall of China. The Forth Rail Bridge is the sixth World Heritage Site in Scotland; the others are Edinburgh's Old and New Towns; the Heart of Neolithic Orkney; New Lanark; the Antonine Wall; and St Kilda.

This award recognises the contribution the rail bridge makes to engineering history. What had gone unmarked for 129 years, however, was the human endeavour and cost that had been invested in the project, not only in its initial construction but the continuous programme of maintenance, including the celebrated painting regime, which ensured that the structural steelwork remained fit for the purpose of conveying rail passengers and freight north and south across the Firth of Forth.

In 2012, the completion of the 10-year major refurbishment project, including the coat of paint that is expected to last 25 years, was the opportune moment to salute the 'Briggers'. Two monuments by local artist Gordon Muir, one at each end of the bridge, were unveiled by then First Minister Alex Salmond. The memorials are each 7-foot bronze plaques on a stone base, bearing the name, age and occupation of the 73 men (rather than the 57 officially recorded at the time) who died building the bridge, with the engraving: 'To the Briggers, past and

present, who built, restored and continue to maintain this iconic structure.'

Being a cantilever design, the bridge was constructed in sections pivoting on the principal towers. This is a captured well in historic photographs, which gave rise to a piece of German propaganda during the Second World War. Sir Tam Dalyell, the former politician and highly respected writer and commentator, who died in 2017, told a story arising from the state visit to Scotland of the Sheikh of Bahrain in the 1930s. Tam's father was a diplomat representing the British Government in Bahrain and a dinner was held to which the higher echelons of society were invited, including Joachim von Ribbentrop (1893-1946), who was at the time German ambassador to Britain.

They were entertained by Lord Lothian and the subject turned to Scotland's engineering prowess, in particular the magnificent Forth Rail Bridge. The German ambassador was intensely interested in the bridge, so Tam's mother, who sat next to him during the dinner, presented von Ribbentrop with a framed print of a photograph of it under construction – the view that shows the towers before the addition of the platform connecting the cantilevers.

Von Ribbentrop was to make clever use of this gift. On 16 October 1939 Luftwaffe Ju88 bombers carried out the Second World War's first bombing mission in the UK in the Firth of Forth, a prime target being the naval dockyard at Rosyth, lying a very short distance upstream from the bridge.

What a propaganda opportunity! That same photograph was published in German newspapers, this time claiming that it proved the Germans had successfully bombed the bridge, destroying Scotland's most iconic structure. Fortunately, it wasn't true, but a clever ruse.

In September 2016, however, Network Rail discovered detailed drawings in an old box file under a desk in Glasgow. These were dated 1945 and show plans for a second Forth Rail Bridge, to be located a short distance downstream from the existing bridge. Just why the plans had been drawn up is unclear. Strategic thinking that the Forth Rail Bridge may become a target for the German V-Bombers then blitzing London could have produced plans for a replacement in the event of substantial damage. Alternatively, perhaps the transport planners of the day were thinking about yet further increases in traffic in the years following the war.

The jury is out, but the discovery of the plans opens yet another chapter in the history of 'The Bridge'.

10. 20TH-CENTURY BRIDGES

From cars to Claret Jug

It is highly probable that the 20th century will be regarded as the Age of the Automobile. From early beginnings grew a vast industry producing vehicles to meet the demands of an expanding and increasingly mobile population, whose horizons were widened by the use of cars, vans and lorries to conduct their personal and business transportation needs.

On my own personal journey, 1981 was time for my career to take a new road and bid farewell to Forfar. A move to the Department of Agriculture in Edinburgh as a Lands Officer brought many new challenges. Now I was a civil servant at The Scottish Office, which required me to learn certain protocols.

Based initially at the area office covering Fife, the Lothians and the Borders, I had the opportunity to get to know in detail both the topography and the underlying soil of the countryside. Maps produced by Aberdeen's Macaulay Land Use Research Institute (MLURI) drew on climate, soil and topographical information to produce a Land Capability for Agriculture (LCA) classification for the whole of Scotland. Excellent stuff, and just the sort of practical application of science and statistical data that appealed to me.

The draft maps required to be 'ground-truthed' so, with colleagues from the MLURI and the Scottish Agricultural Colleges, I spent several months digging trial holes across south-east Scotland. Some might question whether my skillset was employed to best effect in moving a hole from one side of the field to the other, but let me assure you that in all the 30 years since I've never encountered an approach to land classification that could surpass that developed by my friends in the MLURI.

The other piece of experience that came from doing the sort of work that takes you to remote hill farms and the far-flung extremities of agricultural businesses, with sites that are the subject of a planning application, is that I built up an almost encyclopaedic knowledge of certain parts of the countryside. This included the back roads, the rivers and the burns that traverse the landscape and, of course, the bridges that cross them.

Just five weeks into my new job, however, my life came to a dramatic and shuddering halt. I had a serious car accident in the Borders, suffering multiple compound fractures to both legs, and more bones broken in my hips and left arm. The injuries meant that I spent five months in an Edinburgh hospital bed. Further months were spent recuperating and undertaking the painful and often frustrating process of relearning to walk.

The crash resulted in me being off work for eight and a half months, not a glorious start to my new job in the Department. It did, however, present an unexpected opportunity to renew my experience of going with my Dad to visit some of his road and bridge projects.

After I was discharged from hospital, I went to live at my parents' home in Stirling to recuperate. It must have been quite an adjustment for them. I'd left home for university some eight years earlier and here I was, back in the 'nest'. My father, ever the straight but fair talker, remarked one day that 'the joy of having you home has begun to wear a little thin.'

That said, we did spend a lot of quality time together, especially on days out inspecting major road improvement schemes near Tyndrum, which involved a new bridge across the River Fillan, and on the road to the north end of Loch Lomond through Glen Falloch, as far as the boundary between Central Region and Strathclyde Region.

Local government reform in Scotland in the late 1970s had meant that Stirlingshire was now part of Central Region and my father, who had to apply for basically the same job in the new authority, was now styled the Director of Roads. It was on such trips that we stopped at the Green Welly restaurant at Tyndrum for a bite to eat. Invariably it was lasagne, a dish we both enjoyed but never got at home as my mother was not partial to pasta. It has now become a tradition for my wife Deborah and me to stop there en route to regular holidays in Argyll, and I never fail to tell her the story about those 1982 sojourns with my Dad, which I deliberately time to coincide with crossing the bridge over the Fillan.

My initial work on estate management on the Secretary of State's smallholding schemes, land use planning case work, farm capital grants schemes and such like, was all very interesting, but I was becoming increasingly interested in the environmental agenda and an opportunity to work not just at a practice level, but to be involved in policy work, too.

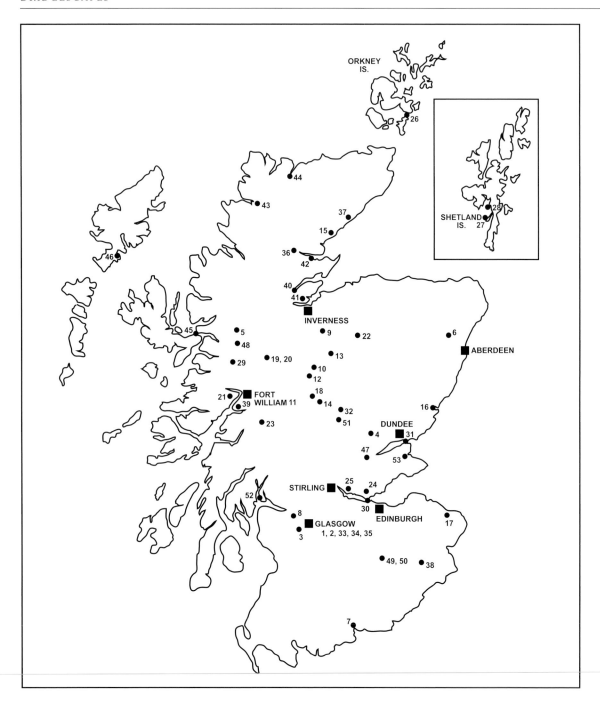

20th-century bridges

Key to bridges mentioned in the text

1	King's Bridge, Glasgow	NS 600 637
2	George V Bridge, Glasgow	NS 586 648
3	Inchinnan Bascule Bridge	NS 493 678
4	Kinclaven	NO 159 380
5	Cromdale	NH 065 289
6	Inverurie	NJ 782 205
7	St Michael's Bridge, Dumfries	NX 973 756
8	Duntocher Burn	NS 490 730
9	Findhorn	NH 804 277
10	Newtonmore	NN 708 980
11	Lochy, Fort William	NN 124 755
12	Crubenmore	NN 676 914
13	Loch Alvie	NH 870 092
14	Dalnamein	NN 755 695
15	Brora	NC 906 039
16	Montrose Basin	NO 709 572
17	New Dunglass	NT 771 721
18	River Kiachnish	NN 671 690
19	Oich	NH 337 036
20	Invergarry	NH 307 107
21	Righ	NN 012 637
22	New Spey, Grantown	NJ 039 266
23	Etive	NN 252 548
24	Glen Bridge, Dunfermline	NT 088 875
25	Kincardine	NS 924 871
26	Churchill Barriers	HY 484 010
27	Trondra/Scalloway	HU 475 414
28	Brig o' Walls	HU 265 515
29	Glen Quoich	NH 015 040
30	Forth Road Bridge	NT 125 795
31	Tay Road Bridge	NO 408 301
32	Garry Bridge	NN 914 609
33	Kingston Bridge	NS 579 647
34	Erskine	NS 462 724
35	Bells Bridge	NS 568 652
36	Bonar Bridge	NH 615 915
37	Helmsdale	ND 026 151
38	Galafoot Bridge, Melrose	NT 509 347
39	Ballachulish Bridge	NN 051 597

40	Cromarty	NH 589 611
41	Kessock	NH 665 475
42	Dornoch	NH 747 852
43	Kylesku	NC 233 330
44	Kyle of Tongue	NC 590 568
45	Skye	NG 765 275
46	Scalpay/North Harris	NG 214 965
47	Friarton	NO 130 216
48	Athnamulloch	NH 132 206
49	Fotheringham Bridge	NT 242 403
50	Priorsford Bridge	NT 253 401
51	Aberfeldy golf course	NN 853 491
52	Linn Gardens, Dunbartonshire	NS 223 826
53	Swilken, St Andrews	NO 499 171

There was one man dealing with agricultural pollution in the Department at that time – the indomitable Tom Brownlie. Because his interests covered silage effluent, slurries and sewage sludge, he became known to his colleagues, I think affectionately, as 'Mr Stinky'.

I volunteered to join Tom in this task, and became 'Mr Stinky's Assistant'. I quickly became immersed in the subject, sometimes literally, while also doing an Open University course in Environmental Control and Public Health, and working with River Purification Boards – the predecessor to SEPA – on the Scottish Farm Waste Liaison Group. Rivers and watercourses then became important to me for what was in them, rather than how one crossed them, but it did give me a valued insight into the Scottish river systems and their part in the nation's history.

That history revolved round the uses of the riparian land and the water that flowed along its course, with the linkages between communities inextricably bound by the built infrastructure, including bridges, viaducts and aqueducts.

One of the most complex designations with which I dealt was the Nitrate Vulnerable Zone (NVZ) over the catchment of the Ythan River in Aberdeenshire. It is a rich agricultural area, particularly for livestock. At the time the catchment of some 66,000 acres was home to 25% of Scotland's pig population and several intensive dairy farms, producing some of the best ice cream I've tasted. But the nitrate levels, perceived to originate from the farming practices, were held to cause, or at least to exacerbate, the occurrence of algal blooms in the Ythan estuary. This

was a feature known as eutrophication, or nutrient enrichment, and it was one of several criteria set by the EU Nitrates Directive for establishing an NVZ.

I spoke at meetings in village halls in Methlick, Auchterless and Fyvie to farmers and land managers rightly anxious to learn what restrictions might be imposed by Government on their businesses to reverse, reduce or merely mitigate the effects of the nitrate on the watercourse and its ecosystem.

A scheme was devised that at least moved both parties in a direction of travel that produced some results, but as all this was going on I took respite on several occasions on the Newburgh bridge crossing the estuary. There I could stand on a late summer's evening, looking inland to the catchment beyond Ellon, then seawards across to the Sands of Forvie, a National Nature Reserve and a Special Protection Area, famed for its birdlife. 'Where,' I pondered, 'do these birds go to the toilet?' Standing on a bridge, especially after a long evening in a village hall, can bring some reflective thoughts to bear.

There was another exciting development wearing my land-use hat. In 1988 The Scottish Office announced the creation of three Environmentally Sensitive Areas (ESAs), where farmers and land managers entered into management plans with the Department of Agriculture (probably in its Scottish Office Agriculture & Fisheries Department – SOAFD – nomenclature at that time).

The exciting thing for me was that I was involved in shortleating (a good Scottish word) the original ESA candidates and working up policy and statutory designations, the management prescriptions for the individual areas, training the staff, writing the 'handbook', then developing the individual farm plans with local agricultural staff colleagues. Oh yes, and the budgets too!

The first three ESAs were in Breadalbane, Loch Lomond and the Trossachs (it wasn't a National Park at that juncture), and the Eildon Hills at Melrose. There was a considerable amount of collaborative work with the archaeologists in the RCAHMS and Historic Scotland – then two separate bodies – and, boy, was it interesting! I had no idea hitherto that there had existed human settlements and farming activity at significant altitude in Scotland at and beyond the 1,000 feet contour at very early periods in our history. What a hard life it must have been!

During visits to these ESAs, and there were many, I travelled through countryside that boasted many splendid bridges, perhaps none more so than the 'Tripontium' across the Tweed, Wade's bridge at Aberfeldy and the stone arches at Kenmore. Each is an intrinsic part of the ESA's rich heritage.

Later, in the early 1990s, there was the second tranche of ESA designations and again I was fortunate to be heavily engaged in this work with the well-deserved designations of The Stewartry ESA in Dumfries & Galloway, and the Machair lands of the Uists and Barra.

Some property matters, too

I've never had any problem with having more than one master. If I had, I would have had a tough time. In addition to my pollution/environmental role, I also had the good fortune to have a role in managing the Secretary of State's extensive smallholding and crofting estates. This embraced the agricultural research establishments, of which Scotland should be justly proud; the MLURI and the Scottish Crop Research Institute, which have since merged; the Scottish Agricultural Colleges; the Hannah; the Rowett; and others. In my last two years in the job, my master was The Scottish Office's Estates Department, with my client departments including the National Roads Directorate.

The 1990s were a busy time for highway development, with major schemes to upgrade the M74, for example, and, of course, the construction of major new bridges in the Highlands, including the Skye Bridge.

By the time I arrived in post the Skye Bridge had been built and wrangling about the tolls was well under way. When land is acquired under compulsory purchase legislative powers, whether they are invoked or otherwise, there is a convention in the UK that any land that is not used during the construction and is deemed to be surplus to requirements at the end of the project must be offered back to the person from whom it was acquired, or their 'heir in title'. The convention is called the Crichel Down Rule.

So it was with Eilean Ban, the island on which the Skye Bridge is supported. The land had previously belonged to Sir Tom Farmer, who sold it to The Scottish Office. He was approached about buying it back at the current market value but he declined. The policy then was to offer the land for sale for the best price. I briefed the selling agent. Most unusually for Scotland, it was being auctioned publicly, by the same agent who had successfully sold numerous properties along the route of the new M74.

At that time the anti-tolls campaigner Robbie the Pict (of whom more later) was being particularly vociferous. Secretary of State for Scotland Michael Forsyth was increasingly perturbed that Robbie was again going to make his life difficult and he had a meltdown when he learned that the Eilean Ban land was being auctioned that very afternoon. Just as I was about to set off to drive from Edinburgh for the auction in Glasgow I received an urgent call from Mr Forsyth's private secretary saying that the sale must not conclude. With scarcely a moment to spare before the auctioneer brought down his gavel, I finally managed to get through to the auction house and instructed the lot be withdrawn. There then followed more than a year of negotiations until the Born Free Foundation secured the land as part of its otter reserve.

The impact of improvements in road transport is clear to see in the many magnificent bridges that now criss-cross the country, but perhaps rather surprisingly Scotland also played an important part in the development of the motorised transport that would use them.

Sir William Arrol always had an eye to the future and diversified his business interests when he saw a potential opportunity. He set up Mo-car Syndicate Limited in Glasgow in 1895, from which grew the Arrol/Johnston plant producing cars at Paisley and latterly in Dumfries, until it closed in 1929. Argyll Motors, founded in 1899, had a prestigious factory in Alexandria on Loch Lomond and ran a sophisticated marketing campaign, selling lavish cars in Canada, the USA, Japan and New Zealand. Production was second only to Ford in Detroit but, like another car company set up by a Scot in the USA, David Dunbar Buick (1854-1929), whose parents had emigrated from Arbroath when he was two years old, the costs outweighed the sales income and, after a series of incarnations, Argyll Motors closed in 1930.

The Albion Motor Car Company was also founded in 1899 and, after an initial foray into car production at a factory in Scotstoun, it concentrated on commercial vehicles, particularly lorries. It was acquired by Leyland in the 1950s and sold trucks and buses across the globe, built in Bathgate. As its slogan 'Sure as the sunrise' celebrates, the company survives, now part of American Axle & Manufacturing, doing exactly what it says on the tin – manufacturing axles, together with chassis systems and crankshafts.

In 1907, Scottish car production was responsible for 11% of the UK's output. Scottish ingenuity also helped take road vehicle production to new horizons in 1916 with the widespread adoption of the pneumatic tyre, a significant improvement from the solid tyres of yesteryear. Developed in 1887 by Ayrshire-born John Boyd Dunlop (1840-1921), who thought up the idea of the tyre for his son's tricycle while practising as a veterinary surgeon in Ireland. Although the name Dunlop is synonymous with rubber tyres, there were problems with the patent rights when it emerged that the invention had originally been that of another Scot, Robert William Thomson from Stonehaven, as early as 1847.

Described as a somewhat diffident man by his partner, John sold up his share in the tyre business in 1895 to concentrate on a draper's business in Dublin. He certainly didn't make a fortune from tyres.

Scottish car production did have somewhat of a revival in the 1960s, with the production of the rear-engined Hillman Imp by the Rootes Group at Linwood. Significant Government funding went into the state-of-the-art production factory, which was seen as the saviour for the declining shipbuilding industry on the River Clyde.

The Imp pioneered the use of an aluminium engine in mass production when it was launched in 1963 and, although initially successful, sales dropped and Rootes was subsumed within the American-owned Chrysler Group. The Imp struggled through until 1976, and a further model, the Chrysler Sunbeam, was produced until final closure in 1981. The second car I owned, or rather had the use of, as it was a company car provided by the firm of surveyors and land agents I worked for in Forfar between 1976 and 1981, was a Chrysler Sunbeam. It was a very smart bright red hatchback and it took me many miles around the estates of Angus, Perthshire and Aberdeenshire where I learned my profession as a rural chartered surveyor.

I drove huge mileages in those days, regularly exceeding 35,000 miles per year, but it helped me to explore Scotland, visiting places to which I would not otherwise have gained access and meeting some very interesting characters. There is probably another book to be written about these adventures and experiences!

For car enthusiasts, I should mention that Argyll Motors had a resurgence, too, or nearly, in 1976. There were grand plans for an Argyll GT, a mid-engined sports car, to be built in Lochgilphead. Two things just did not add up, however. The first was that it was described as a real hybrid of modest 1970s motoring, with the hexagonal tail-lights from the Datsun Cherry, the dashboard from a Volvo, the steering wheel from the Triumph Dolomite and the door handles from the Morris Marina. The second was the price. At between £25,000 and £30,000, it equated to the price for a contemporary Ferrari 308 GTB!

This tale of brazen plagiarism in the automobile industry always reminds me of Johnny Cash's sideways take on life with his song about a Detroit car worker, *One Piece at a Time*, but at least all his ended up as Cadillacs, albeit from different years!

In 1900 there were 8,000 cars in Britain. This rose to 100,000 by 1910, to 1,056,214 in 1930, to 14 million by 1971, and to 25 million by 1999. In 2016 there were 37.1 million vehicles registered for use in the UK.

The development of the road network to meet the increasing demands engendered by the rise in the number of more reliable and powerful vehicles brought with it the need for new and improved road bridges. The first wave of significant public expenditure on the new highway network came in the late 1920s and 1930s, when the Government pumped money into building new infrastructure to provide for a burgeoning, largely urbanised, population.

The new road programme paralleled the development of raw materials used in the construction industry, most notably the progressive use of reinforced concrete.

Crossing the 'watter'

The problems encountered with crossing the Clyde in Glasgow continued in the 20th century. **King's Bridge**, a five-span bridge, just over 302 feet long and 50 feet wide, was completed in 1901. Floods in 1903 caused serious damage to the foundations and a weight restriction of 10 tons was imposed in 1919 – not a good start to the new century. The bridge was reconstructed between 1930 and 1933, at more than 10 times its cost 30 years earlier. The 1930s version was 70 feet wide between parapets, to a design by the City Engineer, **Thomas P. M. Somers**, and constructed by Sir William Arrol & Company. A footbridge built at Polmadie in 1901 also had an unpromising start as it had to be rebuilt after a bad fire in 1921, but it has survived until the present, albeit in a modified form.

The Roaring Twenties

Consent for a new bridge across the Clyde was granted in 1914, but the First World War intervened and the **George V Bridge** finally opened in 1928 at a cost of £171,557. Considered to be one of the strongest bridges ever built, it was a reinforced concrete structure of three spans, again designed by the City Engineer, Thomas Somers. As described previously, although this bridge appears to be an arched structure it is a continuous beam structure resting on cast-iron roller bearings to prevent excessive pressure on the foundations.

In 1923 Sir William Arrol built a Scherzer Roller Bascule Bridge across the White Cart River at **Inchinnan**, south of the Clyde, to replace a swing bridge and widen the crossing to 90 feet to facilitate access to the shipyards upstream. This is a remarkable piece of engineering. Fully restored by Renfrewshire Council in 2004, it is the only surviving rolling lift bridge in Scotland. It has an interesting pedigree, too…

American engineer William Donald Scherzer (1858-93) designed a bascule bridge that improved upon the technique used at Tower Bridge in London. Arrol had been one of four principal contractors on that project in the 1880s. A bascule bridge is a moving bridge with an extended span at one end counterbalanced with a heavy weight at the other. This counterbalancing technique means that very little energy and time is expended in lifting to the bridge to a near-vertical position. Instead of having a fixed pivot point taking the weight of the bridge, Scherzer's rolling bridge has a large-radius roller that moves on a track, and as it does so the centre of gravity shifts to the point of contact with the track. The Inchinnan Bridge is a draw for both the engineering enthusiast and the general public, and Doors Open Days have become a popular tradition.

Another tradition that formed part of my early life was Scottish fiddle and accordion music, exemplified by Aly Bain and Phil Cunningham, and the bothy ballads of Buchan. Scottish country dancing was part of the 'gym' class at Stirling High School in the weeks preceding the school dance. I liked the music, albeit that my dancing demonstrated no particular skills. My sister's German pen pal visited us in Stirling and we took her along to a local ceilidh to give her an insight into Scottish customs. Afterwards, Katarina announced, 'Bruce, he dances with much activity!'

I mentioned that Craigellachie Bridge had inspired a Strathspey tune. So did **Kinclaven Bridge**, crossing the Tay near its confluence with the River Isla, on the unclassified road between Ballathie and the famous Meiklelour beech hedge. Built in 1905 by public prescription and a large contribution from the Marquis of Lansdowne, this six-span masonry bridge, which replaced a ferry, is 462 feet long and provides an excellent vantage point from which to view the salmon fishers in this illustrious river.

There have been some brave attempts to find an economic solution to hardship in the Western Isles. Not least among these was the purchase by Lord Leverhulme of the Isle of Lewis at the end of the First World War, spending the next five years investing in infrastructure and projects to generate economic wealth. There is a reinforced concrete bridge at Tolsta, with three arched ribs and cantilevered extensions, which was built to provide vehicular access to Ness on the north-east coast. But the money ran out – as does the road some few yards beyond the bridge – hence its gaining the sobriquet of 'The Bridge to Nowhere'.

Crossing the River Spey had always presented challenges. Two

Kinclaven Bridge. *Iain Matheson*

Cromdale Bridge. *Mike W. Lowson*

bridges at **Cromdale** had succumbed to the devastating effects of flooding – Harper's bridge of 1881 was swept away in 1894 only to be replaced by another that met the same fate. In 1921 Dorman Long built a robust iron bridge. Not the prettiest of bridges – the comment about 'the Irn Bru bridge – made in Scotland from girders' comes to mind, but it at least survives to date. It cost £6,889, paid for from a 'War Surplus' Fund.

In 1924/25 a new bridge at **Inverurie** replaced an earlier, and by then outmoded, bridge across the River Don, which had been built by the Banff mason **James Robertson** in 1791. Of reinforced concrete with a carborundum finish, the structure is carried on the piers and abutments of the original bridge. It is a three-span bridge, 202 feet long, designed and constructed by Messrs **Tawse & Allan** of Aberdeen.

St Michael's Bridge across the River Nith at Dumfries complemented the town's other, earlier, bridges when it was completed in 1927 to ease traffic congestion. It is 233 feet long, comprising four spans, three of which have segmental arches and the fourth a semi-circular arch over a roadway. It was designed by **J. B. Brodie** and has sandstone facings and triangular cutwaters.

Sir Owen Williams (1890-1969) was responsible for a significant number of the bridge designs in this period, bringing a distinctively inter-war flavour to the use of concrete, cast in situ, as a building material. His work on Clydebank's **Duntocher Burn Bridge** is a good

example from the 1920s, also demonstrating the workmanship of the contractor, **Sir Robert McAlpine & Sons Ltd**.

The same combination of designer and contractor was responsible for the massive **Findhorn Bridge** on the old A9 at Tomatin, completed in 1924 and incorporating truss spans of the Vierendeel type. The spans are each 97ft 6in and the central pier is 14 feet wide. It is not the prettiest bridge you will encounter, but it certainly makes a statement in Strathdearn.

Williams also designed the Spey Bridge at **Newtonmore** in 1926. The south bank is slightly higher than the north bank, so the bridge level climbs on a gradient of 4% from north to south across its 260 feet, the three mass concrete arches being of different spans and widths, with curved spandrels. This bridge was also part of the A9 upgrade in the 1920s, but now forms part of the B9150.

Sir Owen Williams's contribution to bridge-building in Scotland was considerable. In addition to those above, he was responsible for bridges with segmental and faceted arches at **Lochy** (Fort William); across the River Truim on the B9152 at **Crubenmore**; at **Loch Alvie**; **Dalnamein** (skewed with splayed columns, replaced on the A9 since the 1970s); **Brora** (alongside the bridge from 1801); and Carrbridge (since demolished).

At **Montrose Basin** he built his largest and most prestigious bridge in Scotland between 1927 and 1930 to replace Brown's Chain Bridge carrying the A92 across the River South Esk. It was partly supported by

Sir Owen Williams's Findhorn Road Bridge *L. Bruce Keith (main picture)/Lewis Matheson*

a system of concrete chords akin to a steel suspension style, but structurally it was a double cantilever. The Montrose bridge was demolished in 2004.

In many of these projects he was joined by Scottish architect **Maxwell Ayrton** (1874-1960), and both also combined their professional talents on the old Wembley Stadium and the British Empire Exhibition Building in London in 1924/25. Owen went on to design Britain's M1 motorway in the 1950s. Although he died before it opened in 1972, his firm designed the most famous motorway interchange in the UK, the M6's Gravelly Hill Interchange, better known as 'Spaghetti Junction'.

According to author L. T. C. Rolt, who also wrote a biography of Telford, Owen was 'a great character with an impish sense of humour'. Rolt recounts the occasion when Owen went to examine James Dredge's suspension bridge at Lochy in Fort William, accompanied by his faithful dog. As Owen walked onto the bridge the dog refused to follow him and lay on his belly in the approach road, whining piteously. 'And when I examined the bridge,' said Sir Owen, 'by God, the dog was right!'

The story must have gone the rounds locally, for when the replacement concrete bridge was opened in 1928 by Cameron of Lochiel, escorted by a detachment of pipers, Lochiel's speech emphasised how delighted he was that Sir Owen had been able to be present, then added that the engineer had wisely left his dog at home. This bridge, traditionally known as Victoria Bridge, was replaced in the 1960s.

The 1930s: economic depression and the advent of Art Deco

Messrs **Blyth & Blyth** were also prominent bridge designers in the inter-war era, and their **New Dunglass Bridge**, which carried the A1 across the ravine at Cockburnspath, is a significant reinforced concrete structure from 1932. Finished with a coloured cement to match the freestone parapet, this 266-foot-long bridge is proudly juxtaposed beside the 1840s railway bridge and the old stone road bridge, the latter dating from 1798 and which, at 130 feet high, was the highest bridge in the world when it was constructed. There is now a new bridge carrying the realigned A1. An even older Dunglass Bridge, dating from the early 17th century, was itself bypassed by the 1798 bridge.

Blyth & Blyth designed several interesting bridges on the Glasgow to Inverness via Fort William road (A82) in the early 1930s when it was being much upgraded and improved. Across the **River Kiachnish**, close to North Ballachulish, their three-span reinforced concrete bridge is of the beam and cantilever type, built on a skew, with the shape of the

soffits giving the visual impression of Gothic arches. It replaces Telford's bridge, built in about 1810 when he was improving the road south of Fort William, but the old bridge still accesses Chiochnish House.

Across the River Nevis, Blyth & Blyth's 220-foot-long bridge is a vault arch structure with the reinforced concrete faced with pink granite rubble masonry. There are also new road bridges dating from that road improvement project, at **Oich**, **Invergarry** and **Righ**.

` The last-named bridge, Righ, is a couple of miles south of the Corran-Ardgour ferry. There is no bridge at Corran yet, and those who miss the last ferry face a 60-mile detour via Fort William and Loch Eil, as I can personally vouch for on two occasions while working at Ardtornish Estate on Morvern as a student in 1975. It was a very long way round late on a Sunday evening in the estate's blue Austin A55 van, despite its well-sprung seats and column gear-change.

A very fine example of Blyth & Blyth's elegant work in concrete is the **New Spey Bridge** at Grantown-on-Spey, built in 1931. It has a clear span of 232 feet and a rise of 27ft 6in, and there are four reinforced concrete ribs.

At **Etive Bridge**, between Tyndrum and Ballachulish, William Tawse Ltd built a 99-foot single-span bridge in 1932 to the design of McGregor, Sutherland & Hunt. It is a single bowed-truss reinforced concrete structure, with massive arched upper members and eight suspenders, and a slab deck with eight transverse stiffening ribs. It is one of a pair of such structures built on the A82.

The **Glen Bridge** across the Tower Burn in Dunfermline, built to relieve traffic congestion in the town as early as 1932, is a magnificent structure comprising one main span of more than 185 feet flanked on each side by three approach spans to give a total length of 530 feet across a deep glen. It was the brainchild of the Burgh Engineer, **D. H. Shaw**, working with **F. A. MacDonald & Partners**, Consulting Engineers, and incorporates many Art Deco features, including two pairs of lamp standards at either side of the main span, and swept wings.

Between 1932 and 1936 the first road crossing of the River Forth downstream of Stirling was constructed at **Kincardine-on-Forth**. The design was by Sir Alexander Gibb & Partners as consulting engineers, with **Donald Watson** as architect. It was a lattice steel multi-spanned viaduct on concrete piers and incorporated a swinging central section to allow shipping passage to the port of Alloa. When constructed it was the longest swing bridge in Europe and remained in use until 1988. The bridge has been largely superseded by the new Clackmannanshire Crossing, a short distance upstream.

Above The New Spey Bridge, Grantown. *Mike W. Lowson*

Below An old postcard view of the Glen Bridge, Dunfermline.

THE NEW GLEN BRIDGE,
DUNFERMLINE

It is, however, an understatement to claim that the Kincardine Bridge played a major role in developing industry in Central Scotland following the Second World War. Its strategic location ensured a transport network between Fife and the north and Scotland's industrial heartland, improved still further with the motorway system between Edinburgh and Stirling and the link to Glasgow in the 1970s. It is Listed Category A.

Sir Alexander Gibb (1872-1958), born in Broughty Ferry, was a giant among engineers – and what a pedigree. His great-grandfather, John Gibb (1776-1850) was a deputy to Thomas Telford and his father was Alexander Gibb, known as Easton, who designed the Bridge of Carron on Speyside. Sir Alexander was articled to Sir John Wolfe Barry and Marc Brunel, second son of Isambard Kingdom Brunel. After an impressive career as Civil Engineer-in-Chief in the Admiralty and Director-General of Civil Engineering with the newly created Ministry of Transport in 1919, Sir Alexander founded his civil engineering practice in 1922, which became the largest in the UK. It is often said that if you want something done, ask a busy man. Between business commitments, Sir Alexander also found time to write *The Story of Telford – the Rise of Civil Engineering*.

The bridge at Kincardine-on-Forth. *Iain Matheson*

The Second World War

The Second World War called for some innovative civil engineering to overcome the logistical challenges of transporting men and equipment to foreign shores. As early as 1942 Sir Winston Churchill was commissioning work on the design of 'piers for use on beaches. They must float up and down on the tide… Let me have the best solution worked out.'

The result was the floating roadway, an integral component of the Mulberry harbours used during the 1944 Normandy landings. It was designed by Allan Beckett (1914-2005), working to Lt Col W. T. Everall, and was tested under severe weather conditions at Cairn Head in Galloway. The War Office commissioned six bridge spans on pontoons, and they saw active service in France.

The Northern Isles

Other products of the war are still being used to good effect today. Churchill's motive in ordering the construction of what became known as the **Churchill Barriers** between several islands in the Orcadian archipelago surrounding Scapa Flow was strictly strategic from a military viewpoint. Their purpose was to prevent access by the German fleet, particularly submarines, to this major British naval harbour. The causeways, constructed by the labours of Italian prisoners of war, stand today as key road communication links between Mainland and Lamb Holm, Glimps Holm, Burray and South Ronaldsay.

The Italians argued that the use of their labour in this task contravened the Geneva Convention as it placed them at risk of enemy fire, and they certainly had a point. The war was over before the task was completed, but the beautiful chapel the Italians created out of two Nissen huts, concrete and bits of scrap metal at their camp at Lamb Holm has become a major tourist attraction.

While in Orkney, it is worth looking at the Brig o' Waithe, a three-arched stone bridge, some 2 miles north-east of Stromness. On Saturday 16 March 1940, during an abortive air raid on Scapa Flow and the Fleet Air Arm aerodrome at Hatston, a Ju 88 from Goering's Luftwaffe dropped its bombs on a number of small cottages beside the bridge. The Germans might have mistaken the fields next to Stenness as an aerodrome, as they had been used as an airstrip during peacetime. A young farm labourer, James Isbister, was killed by a piece of flying

Brig o' Waithe. *Deborah M. Keith*

shrapnel as he ran to help a neighbour, becoming the first civilian killed on British soil during that war. The raid killed five Orcadians and, of the 32 German bombs dropped at Brig o' Waithe that evening, eight failed to explode. Willie Farquhar, who was injured in the same attack, repaired his cottage and opened it as a watering hole for the British servicemen stationed in Orkney. It became known as the 'Golden Slipper' and proved highly popular as nearby Stromness was 'dry' at the time.

The Northern Isles of Orkney and Shetland do not have many bridges of particular note, although there are many small crossings of burns. Except for the Churchill Barriers, most of the links to the plethora of islands that make up the archipelagos are by roll-on roll-off ferries, or indeed the island 'hopper', including the world's shortest scheduled air service between Westray and Papa Westray in Orkney, a mere 2 minutes' flight time, or 1 minute if there's a tailwind!

In Shetland, the Trondra improvement scheme in the early 1970s provided bridges between **Trondra** and East and West Burra to encourage repopulation. It has been a great success. There are now 1,000 people living in the group of Scalloway islands, compared with only 20 at the 1961 census. The new residents have introduced a variety of activities, such as the annual 'Da Peerie Neep' ('the wee turnip') event at Trondra Community Hall, which involves numerous competitions including 'Toss the Neep'. It hasn't qualified as an Olympic sport, yet!

Government-assisted schemes are not a new idea. In 1849 a major incentive to construct roads and bridges was introduced in Shetland to promote economic growth, a significant need created by failures of the potato and corn crops and population growth in the first half of the 19th century. The work on the so-called 'meal roads' was carried out by the locals, paid a peck of meal for a 10-hour day (more if they had a horse and cart to contribute), supervised by the Royal Engineers.

On the Mainland peninsula, to the north of Scalloway, they constructed the **Brig o' Walls**, or 'da Brig o Waas' to give it its local pronunciation, in effect a causeway with culverts that provides vehicular access to Walls, a relatively rich pastoral area of Shetland. This bridge dates from 1850 and is understood to be the fourth bridge to provide a route into the extreme west of Mainland; it was widened in the 1880s by the Lordships, the community council of its day. Low parapet walls were added in the 1920s and railings in the 1960s, removed as recently as 2016 as the land around the bridge is now fenced.

One of the Trondra bridges. *Deborah M. Keith*

One of the earlier bridges to cross the Voe of Browland lay seaward of the Brig o' Walls, but could only be used at low tide. A semi-retired local resident, Norman George Hobbin, whom I met during a visit in 2016, recalled from his childhood seeing where it had been, although most of the top stones had been robbed for the later 1850 bridge. Was this an early example of reuse and recycling?

In 2014 the Shetland Amenity Trust renovated an old bridge between the Brig o' Walls and Brouster, or 'bridge farm'. It is basically a culvert bridge with the traditional clapper-style stones atop the old bridge, itself probably a replacement in the early 1870s of a yet earlier structure, having fallen into disuse by 1900.

We are getting a little ahead of ourselves chronologically but, on the theme of bridge restoration, 2014 was an impressive year. With funding from the Scottish Government, the Crown Estate, Dame Judi Dench and other benefactors, major renovation works were completed on the Jubilee Bridge at Appin, in Argyll. The original bridge, built to celebrate Queen Victoria's Diamond Jubilee in 1897, linking the Free Church at Kilmoluag with the Episcopal Church at Portnacroish (Holy Cross), was substantially rebuilt; a wooden bridge, it provides a pedestrian and cycle route over the tidal marshes of Loch Laich, offering stunning views of the hereditary home of the Stewarts of Appin, Castle Stalker, with its tower house dating from 1540.

Post-war years and austerity before the boom

There was little new bridge activity during the days of food rationing following the war. What was happening in the late 1940s and 1950s, however, on a massive scale, was the investment in the hydro-electric schemes across much of the Highlands. This required significant infrastructure, including the roads and bridges to build the system of hydro dams, pumping stations and aqueducts.

One example is on the Garry scheme. In the mid-1950s a high-tensile steel bridge was constructed in **Glen Quoich** for the North of Scotland Hydro Electric Board. The bridge is some 550 feet long in three spans, the two outer spans being 165 feet each and the central span 220 feet. This central span is composed of two cantilever arms each 44 feet long and a simply supported centre section of 132 feet. The steelwork was designed and built by **Sir William Arrol & Company**.

Innovation was alive, however. In 1953 the first pre-stressed concrete bridge in Europe was constructed at Callanish, near the megalithic standing stones. Great Bernera is linked with the Isle of Lewis by three

108-foot U-shaped beams, each of which was made by post-tensioning together eight pre-cast concrete units.

Baptie Shaw & Morton was a Glasgow-based civil engineering consultancy, much of whose work in the 1950s involved improving Scotland's bridge infrastructure. In 1958 the firm was responsible for the Ecclefechan Bridge on the A74 and the crossing of the River Carron near Grangemouth. The following year, the A73 improvements incorporated Cartland Bridge, and there was a railway crossing of the West Coast Mainline near Crawford.

The war delayed many infrastructure projects. A contract had been let in 1939 for the replacement of Rendel's bridge in Inverness, but it was not until 1959 that demolition took place and construction started on the present bridge, with its distinctive three semi-elliptical spans of pale pink concrete. Opened in 1961, my father would have been heavily involved with this project, working with the client council alongside the consulting engineers, Sir Murdoch MacDonald & Partners and the contractors, Duncan Logan (Contractors) Ltd.

It was shame that Sir Murdoch (1866-1957) did not live to see this new bridge in his native Inverness. Continuing the tradition of Scots who held the honour of being President of the Institution of Civil Engineers, he held this office in 1932. He worked for much of his career in Egypt on the Aswan Dam, and founded his own firm, which merged with Motts in 1989 to become one of the largest civil engineering consultancies in the world. Sir Murdoch was a character – he was convinced that there existed a Loch Ness Monster (as do I, in case you ever wondered) and persuaded the Secretary of State for Scotland to issue an order to protect it.

Since 1987, the principal road bridge across the River Ness has been Friars Bridge, a three-span pre-stressed concrete structure carrying the A82 downstream of the congested city centre.

The 1960s: a new era in bridge construction

The 1960s saw another dramatic stride forward in the development of Scotland's road-bridge infrastructure with the opening in 1964 of the **Forth Road Bridge**, the longest suspension road bridge outside America. Located a very short distance upstream from the Forth Rail Bridge, with her modernity and slender lines complementing yet contrasting with the engineering prowess of the viaduct, this is a suspension bridge of significance.

Thoughts of a road crossing of the Forth near Edinburgh had been around for several decades. **Mott, Hay & Anderson** was commissioned

A Duncan Logan lorry with a section of the structural steelwork for the Ness Bridge. *Don Fraser, Highland Council*

in 1926 to survey a route and they recommended a site close to the railway bridge as the most technically and economically feasible. Arguments raged about finance, especially the lack of it during the 1920s and '30s, then war intervened. It took until 1947 for a Joint Board to be reconstituted and the engineers reappointed. Alternative proposals, which included a tunnel, a tube lying on the bed of the firth and what might kindly be described as an inspired suggestion to thread a roadway through the steel skeleton of the railway bridge, were all rejected in favour of a new bridge. So, after decades of debate, construction at last started on 1 September 1958.

Based on the 1937 design of the Golden Gate Suspension Bridge in San Francisco, the scale of the project and the new technology used to form the majestic lines of the Forth Road Bridge relied on a consortium of engineers and contractors, under the banner of the **ACD Bridge Company**. The consortium brought together three of the world's foremost bridge builders: **Sir William Arrol & Company Ltd**, **the Cleveland Bridge & Engineering Co Ltd**, and **Dorman Long (Bridge & Engineering) Ltd**. The consulting engineers were seasoned engineers at Mott, Hay & Anderson, though presumably not the same team members, in association with Freeman, Fox & Partners. The structural calculations were all carried out using seven-figure logarithm tables. No computers in those days!

With a central span of 3,300 feet, side spans of 1,340 feet, a total length of 5,980 feet, and cables sweeping to the top of the 512-foot-high towers, the bridge incorporates a stiffened girder structure to counter the effects of wind causing vibration on the bridge's suspended deck, termed 'aero-elastic flutter', which had caused the catastrophic failure of the Tacoma Narrows suspension bridge in the USA in 1940.

The initial stages of construction involved the placement of huge cofferdams in the river where the two main towers would stand, with experienced divers engaged to carry out the dangerous work of pumping out the river water and pumping in the concrete. The foundations are embedded 100 feet into the river bed.

The light steel bridge deck is suspended from 11,618 high-tensile galvanised steel wires, each 0.196in in diameter, forming each of the two cables of 23.25-inch diameter; these were spun back and forth (excuse the pun) across the river, and secured at each end by two concrete anchorages, embedded in tunnels some 180 feet deep. This cable spinning was carried out using a wheel that effectively travelled more than 30,000 miles – that's one and a quarter times round the world – at considerable height above the water, often in high-wind conditions. The wheel was a new civil engineering technique and the work was carried out in a round-the-clock operation, whenever possible, lasting nine months.

Conditions were severe at times during the construction period. In February 1962 the gales, with wind speeds setting records at 123mph, wreaked havoc on the cables, and four weeks were lost from the programme in untangling the resulting 'knitting'. The winter of 1962/63 was notoriously bad, but work continued through the snow and biting cold.

The bridge construction employed 250 men and claimed the lives of seven of them, four of whom were on the bridge structure itself. The other three men died in the project's worst accident, on 22 June 1962, when an approach viaduct collapsed.

133

The Forth Road Bridge. *Deborah M. Keith*

The link between the north and south was made in 1963 as the box-girder sections of the superstructure were welded in place. The bridge construction used 29,000 tons of steel, of which 2,800 tons are in each tower, 16,000 tons in the roadway and other decks, and 7,400 tons in the high-tensile wires. The two road carriageways, each 24 feet wide and 10 feet apart, are carried on cross-girders, which have cantilevered extensions to support the footways and cycle tracks. When completed it was the fourth biggest suspension bridge in the world, the longest outside the USA, and the longest suspension bridge in Europe, a title it held for two years.

Her Majesty the Queen opened the bridge on 4 September 1964, which dawned as a real 'pea-souper'. However, this Scottish haar cleared as the Queen was driven across the bridge, allowing this landmark event in both engineering history and Scotland's transport heritage to be properly marked. The public response was overwhelming. There were traffic jams stretching 25 miles to cross the new bridge. The two ferries, *Mary Queen of Scots* and *Robert the Bruce*, which had served the motorist and road haulier well for so many years, stopped the day the bridge opened, but in a fitting way, which speaks volumes for 'joined-up thinking', the ferrymen started work that very afternoon as toll collectors on the bridge. The charge per car in 1964 was 2s 6d (12½p). The bridge, with associated approaches, had cost £19.5 million to construct.

The bridge reached its half-century in 2014, and to mark the occasion the excellent film footage of each stage of the construction from 1958, documented by local amateur film-maker Jim Hendry, was shown publicly for the first time. Entitled *The Long Span*, this film is part of Scotland's archive heritage and brought delight to many, including those who worked on the bridge, now all enjoying retirement, not to mention Jim himself, then aged 88.

Since 1964 time and heavy usage have taken their toll – by 2000 the bridge was carrying more than 24 million vehicles a year, 50% more than the design load. There has always been a rigorous maintenance programme on the whole bridge, with some £259 million having been spent since it opened. The ageing components most at risk are the joints, and some 700 have been replaced.

The main problem, however, has been with corrosion of the cables, and since 2004 the technique of blowing dry air through the cable ducts, a dehumidification process, has helped reduce the rate of corrosion, but not to attenuate it. Some context is worth considering here, though. Only 22 out of 11,618 high-tensile wires in the main cable actually broke.

The deterioration was one of the principal factors in reaching the decision in 2007 that a new crossing was required across the Forth, now called the Queensferry Crossing. Not that the iconic statement that the 1964 bridge makes on the Scottish landscape will be lost, or that the bridge will be mothballed. From 2017 it provides the main public transport corridor linking Fife and the Lothians.

While the problem with the corroded steel wires was being managed and closely monitored, another issue came to light during an inspection in December 2015. A crack of about 20mm was detected in the load-bearing inner support beam that links to the truss in the north-east tower. Engineers calculated that should a similar fracture occur on the opposite side, the road deck might fall by a minimum of 150mm. The bridge was being used by more than 60,000 vehicles every day, so the risks posed by this structural failure were too great to allow it to remain open to traffic until the issue had been satisfactorily remedied.

The cause was attributed to fatigue and overloading during the bridge's 51-year lifespan, but the closure, which actually lasted only 20 days, was exacerbated by media hype. The rerouting of the traffic for 33 miles via the Kincardine Bridge by taking the bridge out of commission certainly emphasised the point that we take so many things in life for granted and do not really appreciate their value until we are deprived of them. It is also a stark reminder that ongoing maintenance and repair – what in property parlance is termed asset maintenance planning – is an essential prerequisite to longevity.

The 1964 bridge's transition from principal actor in Scotland's transport network to its doyen may not have been as seamless as anyone with a sense of passion and pride in Scotland's heritage would have wished, but its sheer splendour, coupled with a continuing role, will, I am convinced, allow the bridge to grow old gracefully.

Gladly the angst was short-lived and the disingenuous December newspaper headlines became January's chip-wrappers. In October 2016 the Saltire Society properly recognised contractor Amey's valiant efforts in dealing with the engineering issue with its Greatest Contribution to Scotland Award. Accepting the award, Amey's major bridges director, Ewan Angus, commented that it had been 'a unique opportunity to showcase civil engineering to the nation'. The award plaque is secured to the north-east main tower.

The next link in the chain of upgrading the public road network on Scotland's east coast lay to the north, across the Kingdom of Fife. It again replaced a ferry service, this time the one carrying vehicles over the River Tay between Newport-on-Tay in Fife and the city of Dundee, the service affectionately known as 'the Fifie'. That was an affectionate moniker, as a Fifie was traditionally a sailing boat used for herring fishing on the east coast of Scotland from about the 1850s until well into the 20th century.

The **Tay Road Bridge** is a very different animal from the Forth Road Bridge, though. It crosses another great river, the Tay, which is the longest river in Scotland at 117 miles, and the largest in the UK by dint of volume of discharge.

The bridge design is functional rather than spectacular, but at 7,365 feet (1.4 miles) this 42-span box-girder design on concrete piers is one of the longest road bridges in Europe. The designer was **William A. Fairhurst**'s team and the contractor was a firm from Muir of Ord in

Below Beneath the Tay Road Bridge. *Lewis Matheson*

Below right Willie Logan's gravestone in Fodderty Cemetery, shaped like of a section of the Tay Road Bridge. *Mike W. Lowson*

Easter Ross, **Duncan Logan Construction Ltd**, which had made significant advances since the 1950s building the dams and related infrastructure for Scotland's hydro-electric schemes. The firm was headed by Duncan's son, Willie, a flamboyant character who had also established an airline business, Loganair, servicing Scotland's Highlands and Islands. Willie Logan was tragically killed piloting his own plane into Inverness just six months before the Tay Road Bridge project was completed, and his gravestone in Fodderty Cemetery is in the shape of a section of the bridge.

Test bores were drilled in 1958 as the precursor for the construction of a temporary bridge, which, in turn, facilitated the digging of cofferdams for the bridge's pillars in 1963. The bridge was opened by HM the Queen Mother on 18 August 1966. With the approach roads, it had cost £6 million and claimed the lives of five construction workers. The

opening was celebrated with a first day cover postage stamp and a 7-inch single record by local teenagers, Peter and Alison. I believe it turned out to be their only recording.

The ground level at the Fife end of the bridge is some 93 feet higher than at the northern end, so the bridge surface is on a gradient of 1:81. A competition in 2002 by Dundee-based radio station Tay FM to come up with an appropriate slogan to promote the bridge was abruptly cancelled when it became clear that the frontrunner was 'It's all downhill to Dundee'!

Speaking on the occasion of the bridge's Golden Jubilee in August 2016, Bridge Manager Alan Hutchison stated quite correctly that the bridge 'is a major piece of Scottish heritage transport infrastructure. It's been incredibly important when you consider the links it has created.'

The original viewing platforms, together with the redundant toll boxes, have now been removed. The road bridge carries 26,000 vehicles per day, more than five times the traffic usage anticipated in 1966, and has been strengthened to accommodate the additional loading from 44-tonne articulated lorries. The most unusual user of the bridge, however – or at least the one that raised the most eyebrows – was Bertie the runaway bull. Nicknamed 'Houdini', as he had escaped over a 6-foot wall at a Dundee abattoir, Bertie made it the whole way across to Fife one summer's day in 2000.

As part of the massive regeneration of Dundee, the City of Discovery, which includes the Victoria & Albert Museum on the waterfront, a mural has been painted beneath the bridge approach road, incorporating a portrait of William Fairhurst. A fitting tribute to the designer, it is the work of two Dundee College of Art graduates, Fraser Gray and Martin McGuinness.

In 1968 a new bridge was constructed across the **River Garry** on the road to the Queen's View, leading to Loch Tummel and Rannoch. A splendid structure comprising three spans of steel girders, supported on two pairs of tall concrete piers, the bridge replaced a Wade bridge from the 1720s and a bridge of 1833, the stonework of which survives on the riverbank. However, it's what lies below the new bridge that draws the crowds: the Highland Fling Bungee Jump, the first purpose-built permanent bungee jump platform from a bridge in Britain.

The 1970s: two more Clyde crossings

The comprehensive redevelopment of the central commercial core of Glasgow and its surrounding industrial and housing areas in the late 1960s brought with it the construction of more than 3 miles of elevated

The Garry Bridge's Highland Fling Bungee Jump. *Iain Matheson*

roadway, three road bridges and two footbridges. Carrying the new Inner Ring Road across the River Clyde, the massive **Kingston Bridge**, a twin three-span structure, was state-of-the-art when opened in 1970 by HM the Queen Mother.

Designed by **W. A. Fairhurst & Partners**, it took three years to build and cost £11 million. Reckoned to be the busiest bridge in Europe, the

Glasgow's Kingston Bridge. *Patrick MacKenzie*

five traffic lanes in each direction carry about 180,000 vehicles per day. With continued heavy loading, the structure is continually monitored to pick up early indications of the need for repairs. In 1999 the closure of the bridge for two weekends to raise the 50,000-tonne bridge deck by 15mm and move it 50mm to the south was the largest single traffic-management operation ever undertaken by Strathclyde Police. This £31.5 million project required 128 hydraulic jacks, making it the biggest-ever bridge lift, qualifying it for the *Guinness Book of Records*.

Constructed of in-situ pre-stressed concrete, the bridge consists of two independent structures, built by the free-cantilever method to avoid obstruction of vessels on the Clyde beneath. Due to the variable ground conditions in this wide river valley, the foundation piles are believed to be the heaviest steel pile sections used anywhere in the UK. The superstructure for each carriageway is carried by a 53-foot-wide three-cell box girder, but the design manages to convey elegance rather than massive proportion, with the use of dark aggregates to minimise the effect of staining in an urban location and with particular care afforded to the landscape. The network of approach roads is integral to the overall design of the bridge itself, with its 470-foot central span flanked by side spans each of 205 feet.

There is a chilling urban myth surrounding the Kingston Bridge. There were several notorious bank robberies in Glasgow in the late 1960s, and the getaway driver from the £20,000 robbery of the British Linen Bank in Williamwood in 1969, one Archibald McGeachie, is rumoured to be buried in one of the bridge's pillars, the victim of a 'disagreement' within the gang.

Some 8 miles downstream from the Kingston Bridge lies the majestic arch of the **Erskine Bridge**, designed by **Dr William Brown** of **Freeman, Fox & Partners**, bringing traffic from the south to Dumbarton, Loch Lomond and beyond. A high-level crossing of the Clyde at Erskine was first discussed in 1934, but the Erskine Bridge Joint Committee was not established until March 1963. Completed in 1971, the modern box-girder bridge of cable-stay design replaces a much earlier ferry service and is the most downstream of all the bridges across the River Clyde. It has a steel superstructure and is the only Scottish bridge with single cables over central towers above the main piers. When it was built it was the longest bridge of its type in the world and a precursor of the Millau Viaduct in France.

The two main spans are each of 1,720 feet, not including the two approach spans, each of 224 feet. The masts are 125 feet high and the steelwork weighs approximately 11,000 tonnes. The total cost of construction, including approaches, was £7 million. In 1996 the bridge was closed for several weeks after an oil rig being towed down the Clyde collided with the deck. The resulting damage cost £3.6 million to repair.

As a schoolboy in 1971 I accompanied my father, who was Chair of the Scottish Branch of the Institute of Highway Engineers, to the pre-opening inspection of the bridge. We met the bridge's supervising engineer, **Oleg Kerensky**, one of the leading bridge-builders of his age. As a young engineer he had worked on Sydney Harbour Bridge and designed the original Medway Bridge in Kent, which, when it opened in 1963, was the longest concrete span in the world.

Oleg was the son of Alexander Kerensky, who, as Russian Prime Minister, was deposed by the Bolsheviks in October 1917. Oleg's motto for life, quoted in his Presidential address to the Institution of Structural Engineers in 1970, was 'Work to the utmost of your ability; accept success or failure with equal humility.'

I rank my early encounters with bridges as a privilege that has served me well, as has trying to live by Oleg's maxim.

Glasgow hosted the International Garden Festival in 1988. A showpiece for the art and science of gardening in its broadest sense, these events proved very popular with the public, and were certainly

The Erskine Bridge. *Paddlesteamers.info*

instrumental in spearheading urban regeneration in Glasgow, Liverpool, Stoke-on-Trent and Gateshead, all four of which staged the show. They were included in many family days out when these festivals were in vogue in the 1980s and early '90s. I recall careering around Glasgow's site with my daughter, Lauren, in a pushchair, my footweary condition rewarded with a cool pint of McEwan's lager when we met up with our friends Tim and Marcia from New Jersey, pushing their toddler Shona on a similar jaunt.

As part of the modern high-tech infrastructure, Glasgow got a new bridge over the Clyde, the world's largest pedestrian swing bridge. Known as **Bells Bridge**, after the sponsor, Bell's Whisky, two of its spans are cantilevered and supported on cable-stays, allowing them to rotate through 90-degrees to provided passage for river traffic. Although the bridge was designed as a demountable structure, it has now become permanent. In engineering terms, it has a life expectancy of 100 years.

Much further north, Telford's cast-iron span bridge with masonry arches over the Kyle of Sutherland at Bonar Bridge, such a magnificent structure in 1812, was destroyed by floods in 1891. It was replaced two years later by a steel bridge, by **Crouch & Hogg** and Sir William Arrol, built to carry a single traction engine weighing 25 tons. By the 1970s,

Bells Bridge, Glasgow. *Iain Matheson*

aunt, Isobel Sinclair, whose aim was to see her son created Earl. He was not the brightest star in the clan, however, as her son drank the potion too, leaving Isobel to commit suicide rather than face the gallows.

The 1970s also saw a new bridge across the Tweed. Opened in 1975, the **Galafoot Bridge**, comprising four massive steel beams supported on concrete piers, carries the Melrose bypass, which reduces traffic congestion in the historic town.

On the west coast, the ferry at **Ballachulish** was replaced by a three-span continuous steel girder bridge across narrows between Loch Leven and Loch Linnhe. The end spans are propped cantilevers extending to the shoreline from the two piers. I was one of the last passengers on the Ballachulish ferry in 1975, making my way back to the Ardtornish Estate after the Spring Lamb Sales at Thomas Corson's West Highland Auction Mart in Oban. We raised a toast to the new bridge with a dram in the hotel as we awaited the ferry.

Opening up the North in the 1980s

however, the requirement for trunk-road bridges was that they should be able to carry single vehicles of 180 tons, so Crouch & Hogg recommended a new bridge. The 1973 **Bonar Bridge** is a tied bowstring steel arch with a 350-foot span, the first of its kind in Scotland.

The rollers at the west end allow the steelwork to expand or contract, and each can carry a load of 500 tons. The radial curved arch ribs, towering 67 feet above the roadway, form the main supporting members of the bridge, and the cross-bracing between the arch ribs allows wind resistance up to 140mph. The bridge cost £450,000. Upon completion, the 1893 bridge was dismantled.

On the eastern coastal route to Wick, **Baptie Shaw & Morton** provided a new bridge on the A9 at **Helmsdale** in 1972, which bypassed Telford's stone bridge. Constructed in concrete supported on steel trapezoid girders, the new bridge resulted in the removal of Helmsdale Castle. Dating from 1488, the castle had been a ruin since the 1800s. In 1567 it had witnessed the poisoning of the 11th Earl of Sutherland by his

Between 1979 and 1991 three significant bridges were constructed north of Inverness, which eased the access and travel time from Golspie, Brora, Dornoch, Tain, Invergordon and Dingwall to the capital of the Highlands, and in part contributed to the very substantial growth of the city. Known collectively as 'the Crossing of the Three Firths', the first, and longest, structure was the **Cromarty Bridge**, across the firth of the same name. At 4,803 feet, this pre-stressed concrete beam bridge, comprising 68 spans, was opened in 1979 and cost £5 million. It replaced several ferries (only Nigg to Cromarty is still in operation, and only in the summer) and, more importantly for the traveller or haulier, saved nearly 10 miles on a round trip by road via Conon Bridge.

In 1982 the Beauly Firth, an inlet of the Moray Firth, was spanned by the **Kessock Bridge**, linking Inverness to the rich agricultural lands of the Black Isle. This is a cable-stayed bridge, at the time of its

Bonar Bridge. *Deborah M. Keith (main picture)/Lewis Matheson*

Galafoot Bridge, Melrose. *Colin L. Shearer*

construction the longest in Europe, and the first in the UK with a harp, rather than fan, configuration. Designed by the German engineer **Dr Ing Helmut Homberg**, and built by **Cleveland Bridge**, it cost £33 million. The joint engineers were **Crouch & Hogg** and **Ove Arup & Partners**. There are 64 cables of spiral-strand steel suspended from two pairs of hollow steel towers rising 130 feet above the deck. The bridge incorporates seismic buffers to absorb any geological shock waves, as it is situated on the Great Glen fault line, and the steel piles were driven to depths of nearly 200 feet below seabed level. At 3,465 feet in length, it is an impressive sight and has become a favoured location for photographing dolphins in the firth below, and, sadly, also for suicides.

Birds can often be a problem on bridges, with their droppings. On Kessock Bridge, however, a peregrine falcon, which regularly perched on the north end, ensured that the only pigeons on the bridge were those it brought in from Inverness for its lunch.

The third bridge in this linkage, the **Dornoch Bridge**, did not open until 1991, but it offset a 26-mile round road trip via Bonar Bridge, so was an important landmark. Designed by **Ove Arup** and **Crouch Hogg Waterman** of Glasgow and built by **Christiani & Neilsen** as a 2,929-foot-long pre-stressed box-girder structure with 21 spans on inclined leg portals, it was at the time of its construction one of the longest bridges in Europe to be built by the 'cast and push' method, or incremental launch. The bridge deck was built in a temporary factory nearby,

Kessock Bridge. *Lewis Matheson*

Kessock Bridge. *Mike W. Lowson*

The Kylesku Bridge. *Don Fraser*

with each section, weighing approximately 14,000 tonnes, being pushed with 600 tonnes of hydraulic force over bearings placed on the top of the bridge supports. The bearings required to be as non-resistant as possible, so the engineers designed them in a material called polytetrafluoroethylene (PTFE), which is more familiar in the home as Teflon on non-stick pans. This innovative construction process won the Dornoch Bridge a Saltire Award for 'advancing the art of civil engineering in Scotland'.

In north-west Scotland, the A894 Ullapool to Tongue road, along the indented coastline, was significantly improved in the last quarter of the

20th century, including the replacement of the Kylesku ferry with a splendid road bridge stretching 902 feet across the Caolas Cumhann narrows at the mouth of Loch a Chairn Bhain. With its 433-foot main span carried on V-shaped inclined piers, and the road deck 78 feet above the water, the **Kylesku Bridge** was designed by **Ove Arup & Partners** and was opened by HM the Queen in 1984. A bridge of beauty within its wild topography, it has won awards from the Saltire Society, the Civic Trust, the Association for the Protection of Rural Scotland and the Concrete Society, all richly deserved as it is a magnificent piece of engineering in a dramatic landscape.

Along the northern coastline lies the glorious **Kyle of Tongue**, an area I first encountered during a camping trip to Coldbackie with some schoolfriends from Stirling in 1972, the year I passed my driving test. It was the year after the causeway and bridge crossing, designed by **Sir Alexander Gibb & Partners**, had opened to provide a road link across the Kyle, taking full advantage of the scenic vistas afforded of both seascapes and mountain hinterland. Such a link had been ventured as far back as the 1830s; indeed, a ferry had operated until 1956, but it was 1971 before the detour around the head of the loch was rendered unnecessary. The bridge element of the crossing was refurbished in 2011 to ensure its longevity, although motorists can still enjoy the experience of a single-track road with passing places further west as the A838 leisurely winds its way round the majestic Loch Eriboll, which has so far escaped the bridge-builders' attempts to hasten journey times.

The causeway and bridge at Kyle of Tongue. *Deborah M. Keith*

The Skye Bridge. *Lewis Matheson*

The 1990s: a new bridge across the Atlantic

Providing a physical link between mainland Scotland and the largest of the Inner Hebrides, the Isle of Skye, is the **Skye Bridge**, opened in 1995 to replace the Kyle of Lochalsh to Kyleakin ferry, which had operated for nearly 400 years and since 1935 had been run by Caledonian MacBrayne. The Clachan Bridge in Argyll had long claimed to be the 'Bridge over the Atlantic', but here was a second, and on a much grander scale. Shepherd & Wedderburn, solicitors for the Skye Bridge Company, ran an advertisement proclaiming: 'For the first time since the Ice Age, the Isle of Skye is linked to the mainland.'

The bridge itself is eye-catching, but also draws the eye to the frame it forms around the distant Cuillin Mountains when approaching from the east along Loch Alsh. There are, in fact, two bridges – the main cantilevered span plus the smaller Carrich Viaduct, the structure that connects the mainland with the island of Eilean Ban. It was on Eilean Ban that Gavin Maxwell and his family of otters made their home in the 1960s, immortalised in the book and film *Ring of Bright Water*. Eilean Ban also boasts a Stevenson lighthouse, with a clockwise internal staircase, which is contra-traditional design; most circular staircases are anti-clockwise, facilitating ease of access to draw a sword when such was the means of defence to ward off hostile intruders.

Lighthouses are impressive structures, very often in prominent positions to maximise their functionality in guiding those at sea and warning of hazards. Most are now largely redundant, having been superseded by modern GPS navigation systems even in the most basic of vessels. There is a certain irony, therefore, in the events of 10 October 2010 when one of the Royal Navy's flagship submarines, HMS *Astute*, ran aground on a shingle bank in Loch Alsh, close to the bridge. The official inquiry report concluded that the submarine's officer on watch that night was not using the correct radar and did not have a maritime chart. Enough said.

But the Skye Bridge, or Drochaid an Eilein Sgitheanaich to give it its Gaelic translation, has another story to tell, with consequences for several other landmark bridges in Scotland and those who drive across them. The bridge was the first major capital project in Scotland funded by the Private Finance Initiative (PFI), a means of securing infrastructure investments and subsequent maintenance and management from private investors rather than the traditional Government funding for such large-scale projects. In 1989 the Conservative minister at The Scottish Office, Lord James Douglas-Hamilton, announced a bidding round, inviting tenders to construct the bridge (the approach roads were paid for by the Government). The

contract was awarded to **Miller-Dywidag**, a Scottish-German consortium, with a financial partner in the Bank of America. **Arup** collaborated on the design of the bridge.

When the bridge opened in 1995, the ferry ceased and the consortium's licence to operate the bridge kicked in. The consortium's rationale for building it, at a cost estimated at approximately £25 million, was that tolls would be charged, but rather than the 'somewhat less than £1' envisaged by the local council, the initial toll for a round trip was £9, which rose steeply to £11.40 by 1999. This was 14 times the round-trip price charged by the Forth Road Bridge, which was more than twice the length, making the Skye Bridge, in the words of protestors, 'the most expensive road in Europe'.

These protestors, under the banner of Skye and Kyle Against Tolls (SKAT), were ably led by a colourful character and veteran campaigner, Brian Robertson, aka Robbie the Pict. There were mass protests and a vigorous non-payment campaign – 'can pay, won't pay' – with some 500 people arrested, 130 of whom were subsequently convicted. Only Andy Anderson, the SKAT secretary, was imprisoned, albeit briefly.

The whole tolls saga became a hotly political and legally contentious issue, with Robbie the Pict running, unsuccessfully, for election as an MSP on an anti-toll platform. His rationale included the claim that King William the Lion of Scotland had granted two Royal Charters to Inverness in 1180 that prohibited the tolling of people in Inverness-shire or Moray. Robbie claimed that such Royal Charters are protected in the Claim of Right of 1689 under which the Scottish Parliament accepted William and Mary of Orange and the subsequent Hanoverian Succession. This interesting hypothesis did not get as far as being tested in a 20th-century court, however.

With the creation of the Scottish Parliament, a public buy-out of the bridge was orchestrated for approximately £27 million in 2004, and toll collection ceased with immediate effect. With more than that amount having been collected from drivers since 1995, the protestors' argument that it had already paid for itself was certainly valid.

This was a landmark decision by the newly formed Parliament and heralded the beginning of the end to all bridge tolls in Scotland. The Erskine Bridge tolls ended in 2006, followed by the Forth and Tay road bridges in 2008, under the Abolition of Bridge Tolls (Scotland) Act.

Venturing west from Skye to the archipelago of the Outer Hebrides, we encounter a string of islands, some of which are linked by causeways. Only two islands, however, are linked by bridge, a recent structure across the **Kyles of Scalpay**, linking the island of Scalpay to the much larger island of North Harris.

Above and above right The bridge across the Kyles of Scalpay under construction and completed. *BAM Steel Structures/Western Isles Council*

Above far right The Baillieston Interchange. *W. F. Millar, Geographweb*

The depth of the channel, at 100 feet, the strength of the current and the need to maintain navigation made a causeway here impractical, so engineers **Halcrow** designed a structural steel tapered box-girder bridge with raking legs. The main span is 561 feet, making it the eighth longest in Scotland, and the total length is 961 feet. Given the low traffic flows, the bridge deck is a single lane, making the structure very narrow in relation to its span. It also carries the island's water supply, and the deck is on a rising gradient between Harris and Scalpay. The bridge was opened by Prime Minister Tony Blair in August 1998, accompanied by the oldest resident on Scalpay, Mrs Kirsty Morrison, aged 103. The structure was part funded by a grant from the European Commission and has won a Saltire Award for Design & Construction and the Institution of Structural Engineers' Special Award Commendation.

Bridges within modern transport highways

The modern highway network across Scotland has spawned complex intersections with their myriad of flyovers and underpasses. Particularly impressive is the M8/M73/A8/A89 **Baillieston Interchange** to the east of Glasgow, with its veritable web of bridges criss-crossing in all directions. A current major upgrade and improvements, incorporating motorway extensions and a new railway bridge to carry the Rutherglen and Coatbridge line beyond the existing Cutty Sark Bridge (so named for the whisky advertisement that adorned

it for many years), will ensure that the Interchange meets the transport needs well into the 21st century. Due to be completed in 2017, such landmark infrastructure projects should be viewed, from an aesthetic perspective, for the overall visual impact of the connected structures, rather than as isolated features designed as independent structures in the landscape.

The Scottish Government's Transport Scotland, formerly the National Roads Directorate, grasped this concept in its 'Family of Structures' approach to landscape design for major infrastructure projects, developed in the late 1990s by Professor Andy MacMillan (1928-2014), Emeritus Professor of Architecture at Glasgow University and Scotland's leading Modernist architect.

Rather than making individual judgements on each component, this approach took a holistic view of the composite effect of the roads, bridges, overpasses, underpasses and footbridges. Aesthetics will often be a matter of personal preference – indeed, the word has its roots in the Greek for 'sensitivity' – so personal perceptions do play a large part in any judgement. I struggle, however, to understand why anyone would fail to find some satisfaction from the harmony of movement created by these modern civil engineering projects.

To make the point with an even more striking example, given the considerable civil engineering involved, consider the M90/M9 Interchange to the south-east of Perth, where the network of bridges and cuttings carries roads to the north, south and west. The major road network was created by blasting into the rock face so that sweeping curves could safely be fashioned to guide the travellers along their journeys. As well as a major construction project, it also created opportunities to incorporate new technology. The road to the north is carried over the River Tay by the **Friarton Bridge**, completed in 1978 at

Friarton Bridge. *Deborah M. Keith*

a cost of £8 million and the first lightweight concrete bridge in Europe.

The box girders on which the deck rests are supported on eight pairs of reinforced concrete pillars, and the total span, high above the River Tay, is 570 feet. The consulting engineers were **Freeman Fox & Partners**, with the design team led by Dr Oleg Kerensky, and the principal contractor was the **Cleveland Bridge & Engineering Company**.

Bridges for recreation

Footbridges can open up access for the walker to many beautiful areas, often in remote locations. **Athnamulloch Bridge** forms part of the trail from Glen Affric towards Kintail, through exceptional scenery. Probably dating from the 1920s, it is an example of a prefabricated-type structure that would have been delivered to the site and erected by estate workers. It is a welcome sight for those approaching the Youth Hostel at Alltbeithe after a day's walking. The suspension footbridges in Glen Cassley in Sutherland were provided by the estate to cross the river as it cuts through the rocky gorge and across open moorland.

In 1953 a native of Peebles, John S. Fotheringham, who had earned his fortune in South Africa and had been Mayor of Johannesburg, bequeathed funds for the building of a pedestrian bridge across the Tweed in the Hay Lodge Park. Ramps were added in 2006 to facilitate disabled access. As there is now a loop comprising the **Fotheringham Bridge**, the arched road bridge and **Priorsford Bridge** downstream, locals stage a charity fundraising 'Three Bridges Race' each May.

Aberfeldy Golf Course boasts the world's first bridge constructed entirely from composites – plastics reinforced with glass and cables of Kevlar aramid fibre in a polyethylene coating. Designed by **Maunsell Structural Plastics** in association with **Dundee University** as an impressively light structure, this cable-stayed footbridge spans the 207 feet across the River Tay, allowing access to the extended course, and was opened in time for the club's centenary celebrations in 1995. Perhaps this bridge points to the road ahead for innovative construction that spans the divide between sustainability and functionality.

Linn Gardens, the botanical gardens in Dunbartonshire, contain an elliptical arched stone bridge that was the inspiration of the owner, Scottish designer **Jim Taggart**. He was so keen to build his own bridge that he took two Open University courses in mathematics to learn the algebra, whereupon he set about building the 17-foot-long bridge into the bedrock. Visitors to the gardens can see the algebraic equation carved into a rock, which he called the Destiny Stone, beside the bridge.

But one footbridge has been photographed, painted and televised worldwide perhaps more than any other – that providing a crossing point over the **Swilken** Burn for golfers playing up the famous 18th hole on the Old Course at St Andrews. This bridge has witnessed the closing short-iron shots of many international championships, most notably the Open Championship and the Dunhill Masters, as well as those of countless thousands who have sought the honour and pleasure of a round at the Home of Golf.

I have been fortunate to attend two Open Championships at St Andrews, in 1970 and again in 1984. On that first occasion my father took me when I was 15. I had taken up the game a couple of years previously, and that year the Open lived up to its reputation as a

The Fotheringham footbridge at Peebles. *Colin L. Shearer*

Aberfeldy Golf Course – recycling at play. *Iain Matheson*

cliff-hanger. Doug Sanders had a short putt to win the famous Claret Jug on the 18th green. He missed, and subsequently lost in an 18-hole play-off to the Golden Bear, Jack Nicklaus.

Famously, Sanders later said: 'They still ask me if I ever think about that putt I missed to lose the 1970 Open at St Andrews. I tell them that sometimes it doesn't cross my mind for a full five minutes.'

Despite the permanent damage caused to my legs by that terrible car crash back in 1981, I still manage to play golf today, although usually now with the aid of a golf buggy. It has to be said, however, that the accident did little to hamper any chances I might have had of striding over the world-famous Swilken Bridge while leading the final round of the Open. Those chances were non-existent then, and are no better now!

The Swilken Bridge at the Old Course, St Andrews. *Lewis Matheson*

11. Bridges of the New Millennium

From Finnieston to the future

Turning 40 is a milestone in anyone's life. I'd reached that age in 1995 and, as many folks do, I decided on a plan. I had more than 20 years' experience and two professional qualifications to my name: RICS chartered surveyor and CIWEM chartered environmentalist. I'd been in private practice and central government. With a new millennium on its way, what I needed was a fresh challenge that melded the experience I'd secured thus far.

When I saw the advertisement for the post of Chief Surveyor at English Nature, I knew this was the type of job I wanted … but in Scotland. If I applied and was granted an interview, that would be wonderful experience for when my ideal job came up in Scotland.

I applied, was interviewed and was offered the post. It meant relocation to English Nature's head office in Peterborough. Sadly, I'm still waiting for the job I planned for in Scotland to come along!

Not that being 'down south' meant I couldn't continue to admire Scottish bridge engineering. I had an England-wide remit and, with a rich and diverse National Nature Reserve estate of 66,000 hectares and 15 area offices, I had the opportunity, indeed privilege, not only to see some of the most magnificent landscape and wildlife the country had to offer, but also to work with some engaging and enthusiastic colleagues.

Some of the scientists were world experts on aspects of fauna and flora, to whom I could only look on in wonder. In my travels I came across many bridges and other massive civil engineering structures such as harbours and canals, the legacy of Scottish engineers plying their profession in England, such as Thomas Telford and also the Rennies, Robert Mylne, Louis Harper, Alexander Stevens and Sir William Arrol.

I developed a better understanding of the countryside of England and Wales through another jaunt – an annual reunion of usually five but, when we're lucky, six very good friends who assemble each May under the banner of the 'Boys' Walking Weekend'. Ostensibly a country walk in a different part of the UK on each occasion, it's a fraternity of guys who all trained together as British Rail Management Trainees in the era before privatisation. So what am I doing there?

It's a long story, and definitely for another day, but Colin Shearer and Mike Hogg, in particular, should be held to account, and I am much the richer for all their friendships over nearly 40 years. On such weekends

we've crossed and paused to marvel at Telford's Pontcysyllte Aqueduct on the Llangollen Canal, and his Waterloo Bridge at Betwys-y-coed, and enjoyed canal strolls along many waterways, now offering recreation for walkers as well as boating enthusiasts, which owe much to the engineering legacy of Scots engineers.

The two decades since the Millennium have seen some significant new ventures into bridge-building activity, not least in Scotland. The year 2000 was a landmark that people wanted to record in a tangible way, and there are countless memorials round the world to testify to the new century.

Yet further regeneration in Glasgow

Glasgow, facing a significant regeneration challenge on the Clyde, grasped the opportunity to incorporate strategic traffic and pedestrian

The Clyde Arc – the 'Squinty Bridge'. *Iain Matheson*

Bridges of the New Millennium
Key to bridges mentioned in the text

1	Millennium	NS 591 647
2	Clyde Arc	NS 571 650
3	Tradeston	NS 583 648
4	Garrion, Wishaw	NS 793 512
5	Port Eglinton Viaduct	NS 585 638
6	Clackmannanshire	NS 920 878
7	Forthside, Stirling	NS 797 936
8	Bracklinn Falls	NN 644 084
9	Diamond Bridge, Aberdeen	NJ 940 102
10	Gelly, Bankfoot (proposed)	NO 067 354

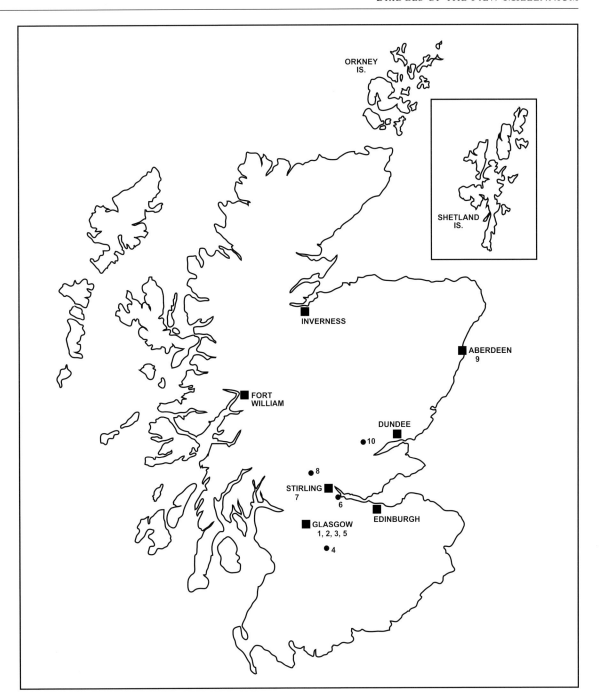

movements in a series of bridges opened in the first decade of the new Millennium. For example, **Millennium Bridge** itself, the lower of two bridges connecting the Scottish Exhibition & Conference Centre (the 'Armadillo') with Pacific Quay, was opened in 2002 as part of the Glasgow Science Centre development. This pedestrian and cycle bridge has a tubular steel framework, with the middle spans split into two bascules that can be lifted by radio-controlled hydraulic cylinders to allow river traffic to pass.

The Finnieston Bridge, or **Clyde Arc**, is a vehicular bridge opened in 2006, and is more frequently referred to by its moniker the 'Squinty Bridge', as its main span features a bowstring asymmetrical tied steel arch; viewing this impressive road bridge at night shows this off to best effect. Designed by the **Halcrow Group** and built by Kilsyth-based civil engineers **Edmund Nuttall**, the bridge cost £20.3 million, but is designed to last for 120 years. The Arc won the Saltire Award for Civil Engineering in 2007, ascribing it as 'an elegant addition to the skyline'.

Tradeston Bridge – the 'Squiggly Bridge'. *Iain Matheson*

Inset Port Eglinton Viaduct. *Alec MacKinnon*

The third impressive new bridge is the **Tradeston Bridge**, which features a sinuous double curve, like a wave, to create a landmark waterfront structure. The Glaswegians, in characteristic humour, have nicknamed this the 'Squiggly Bridge' to complement its sister structure a short distance downstream. Again designed by the **Halcrow Group**, this time in partnership with Scandinavian architects **Dissing & Weitling**, the bridge was built by **BAM Nuttall** and completed in 2009 at a cost of £7 million.

Further upstream, the new **Garrion Bridge** crosses the Clyde near Wishaw and incorporates the older single-carriageway bridge, dating from 1817, in a new roundabout layout to ease what had become a notorious traffic bottleneck. The reinforced concrete bridge was opened in 2002.

The largest civil engineering project in the new Millennium in Glasgow, however, has the been the long-awaited M74 link to the M8, south-west of the Kingston Bridge. The project, which cost approximately £692 million but came in about £15 million under budget, was run by Interlink M74, a joint venture between Balfour Beatty, Morgan Est, Morrison Construction and Sir Robert McAlpine. Heralding its opening in 2011, the leader of Glasgow City Council, Councillor Gordon Matheson, described the completion of the new road as

'…a momentous day for Glasgow and for Scotland. Its completion will bring opportunities for thousands of individuals and businesses, support east end regeneration, and help us deliver the best possible Glasgow 2014 Commonwealth Games.'

It had been a long hard fight to secure the planning permission, with much made of increased pollution by the environmental lobby, but the evidence to date suggests otherwise. Indeed, as at 2017 Scotland's record on delivering carbon targets for reducing greenhouse gas emissions is impressive, with the country showing leadership in contributing to the international climate change targets.

No one can argue that the 2014 Commonwealth Games turned out to be anything other than a triumph for Glasgow, both in terms of sporting achievement and for the hospitality for which the city is renowned. The project has also brought in its wake several key urban regeneration schemes that have, in turn, improved the economic, social and environmental qualities of parts of Glasgow. For me, that holistic approach to seeking positive outcomes for all lies at the very heart of that oft-misunderstood and misinterpreted phrase 'sustainable development'.

One section of the M74 Extension has particular resonance for bridge enthusiasts. June 2011 saw the completion of the **Port Eglinton Viaduct** carrying the six lanes of the new motorway across the West Coast Main Line railway, Salkeld Street, Eglinton Street and Devon Street. The two three-lane carriageways are structurally separate, each supported by a pair of open-top box girders, curved both in plan and in elevation, and with a composite reinforced concrete deck slab. Each carriageway is 200 metres long and weighs more than 4,000 tonnes.

Rather than being placed by conventional crane lifts, the length dictated that each section of the viaduct be winched into place, moved by back-to-back 418-tonne-capacity pulling and restraining strand jacks operating on a continuous cable running from one end of the launched structure to the other. The contractor was Cleveland Bridge and the extremely clever computer-controlled operation the responsibility of Dorman Long Technology. It had to carried out at night while no trains were operating, so Glaswegians awoke to a slightly different view of the new structure each morning!

A new bridge across the Forth, and the rise of 'people power'

November 2008 saw the opening of the **Clackmannanshire Bridge**, situated upstream from the Kincardine Bridge, which by then was

Clackmannanshire Bridge. *Yee Associates*

subject to heavy traffic pressure. The designers, **W. A. Fairhurst & Partners**, and contractor **Morgan Vinci** used the continuous deck launch method of construction, making it the second largest bridge in the world to be built by this method. It has 25 concrete piers with decking weighing 5,000 tonnes, is three-quarters of a mile long, and cost £120 million. At the opening, First Minister Alex Salmond described the bridge as 'a world-class infrastructure project'.

Significant environmental mitigation measures were introduced to provide alternative roosting and feeding areas for wintering birds by creating additional mudflats and saltmarsh habitats along the river. The naming of the bridge caused some controversy, which was resolved through the ballot box: the name Clackmannanshire Bridge topped the poll.

As oft-times before, the bridge inspired poetry. Tom Murray, playwright and poet, put pen to paper with 'On the Opening of the Clackmannanshire Bridge':

'Like a child stretching to maturity
Before our eyes
It now stands strong and proud
As if it has always been.

The current of change wraps itself around its limbs.
A fresh wind brushes against its concrete skin.
Soon it will sing the song of others
Dance to the rhythm of journeys unfolding.

In the distance the Ochils nod their ancient
Heads in approval of the newcomer.

People power named this bridge
Gave direction to their hopes and dreams
Gave notice for the maps to be rewritten.
Signed the welcome book for visitors.

People power named this bridge.
Created their future in the present.'

Motorway service stations don't usually conjure up images of inspired architecture, but let me introduce you to Harthill Services on the M8 between Glasgow and Edinburgh. In 2008 the services were given a facelift with a footbridge of nearly 290 feet, incorporating 12 helical tubes that wind round and enclosed the structure in a criss-cross mesh – quite unexpected and refreshing.

Part of the major regeneration of Stirling in the first decade of the new Millennium included **Forthside Pedestrian Bridge**, linking the city centre with the new Forthside development across the railway tracks. Completed in 2009, architects **Wilkinson Eyre** and structural engineers **Gifford & Partners** (a collaboration that was also responsible for Newcastle's award-winning Gateshead Millennium Bridge) designed a visually light structure comprising triangulated inverted Fink trusses, which change size to create a twisting form and with parapet panels of toughened laminated glass. These appear to glow at night, creating a 'glass ribbon' of colour along the 371-foot length of the bridge. Much applauded as an inspired piece of engineering, the bridge has sadly been

Forthside Pedestrian Bridge, Stirling. *Iain Matheson*

The Bracklinn Falls footbridge. *Malcolm Strong*

subjected to several incidents of vandalism. Another inspired idea, again emphasising public engagement on these occasions, was to invite six William Wallaces from across Scotland to participate in the opening ceremony.

A spectacular new footbridge at the **Bracklinn Falls**, near Callander, was constructed in 2010 to replace the original cast-iron bridge, built for a visit by Queen Victoria, which had been swept away by a flood of Biblical proportions in 2004. The Falls are in a gorge that is inaccessible to large plant, so the bridge needed to be built and installed using hand tools only – and, given its beautiful location and its popularity with visitors, its appearance required to be iconic.

Designed and built by **Malcolm Strong** of **Strong Bridges** for the Loch Lomond & Trossachs National Park Authority, it is a trussed pinned arch with a curved deck, all built out of Scottish-grown timber. It comprises four 12-foot-long Douglas fir trunks forming an A-shaped truss with a copper sheeted roof canopy. The bridge was built on the bank and winched into position using a temporary twin-railed structure. Most appropriate for this location, with the Falls as a backdrop, the bridge deserved its highly-commended placing in the International Footbridge Awards in Poland in 2011.

In 2016 the largest modern bridge constructed in Aberdeen for 30 years was opened. Crossing the River Don between Bridge of Don and Tillydrone, a ballot of local schoolchildren voted that it be called the **Diamond Bridge**, honouring the Queen's Diamond Jubilee and also the city's affiliation with the Royal Navy destroyer HMS *Diamond*.

Bridges are 'linkages' for more than just transport and people. Several years ago I saw an impressive bridge in the Netherlands, provided to act as a wildlife corridor across a major highway that had severed a nature reserve. I have seen other examples on the Icefield Parkway, a truly stunning drive between Banff and Jasper in Alberta, Canada.

Now there are plans in place to create 'green bridges' in Scotland. The Central Scotland Green Network, whose aim includes facilitating collaborative work on environmental improvements, ran a competition in 2013 to design a green bridge across the M73 to create an effective link for the Seven Lochs Wetland Park in Lanarkshire. A local architect, **Euan Maharg**, won the competition and is working on his proposal with the partners involved.

Proposed improvements to the A9 north of Perth include at least one wildlife bridge near Bankfoot. The new structure, the **Gelly Bridge**, which will incorporate one lane of scrub vegetation with mammal tunnels beneath, is an effort to encourage pine martens, otters, deer and red squirrels to cross the busy highway, which dissects a large area of forest.

The advent of wildlife bridges is an encouraging development, integrating functionality with landscape and the wider environment. This is surely sustainable development at work, securing the much-needed improvements in our highway networks to facilitate economic growth and societal benefits, while safeguarding and enhancing the environment so critical for society's well-being.

So what does the future hold? There will be many new bridges, some to meet the needs of a growing economy and service new development, others to replace existing bridges that have reached the end of their economic life or structural capacity.

Construction of the Aberdeen Western Peripheral route, the city's long-awaited bypass, involves a number of new bridges including a major new one over the River Dee at Maryculter. A proposed wind farm development near Tweedsmuir provides for a new bridge beside Carlow's Bridge, on the minor public road that gives access to the Talla and Megget reservoirs. There are plans already approved for a new Cross Tay Link Road, incorporating a bridge to bypass Perth to the west and link to the existing road network north of Scone. Will there ever be a bridge linking Bute to the mainland? Or a new bridge to cross the Tweed at Peebles? Or a bridge across Loch Eriboll?

Wherever they are, the bridges of tomorrow will demonstrate new thinking in terms of design, incorporate innovative materials in their construction and improve the communication links throughout the country. They will continue to make a statement about the landscape in which they are set and, indeed, open new vistas on Scotland to the communities who use them, be they local residents, travelling salesmen, commercial hauliers, transient visitors or just those who enjoy a good walk or cycle ride across these key components of our communication heritage.

And why stop at Scotland? A causeway between the Stewartry and Cumbria, creating a new link across the Solway? Perhaps a tidal barrier that generates electricity from underwater turbines, while on the surface there's a fast transport link to the South. Or a bridge to Ireland? In 2007 a think tank known as the Centre for Cross Border Studies proposed a bridge to provide an international rail link between Stranraer in Scotland and Belfast in Northern Ireland. It's a distance of 21 miles. It sounds improbable, but when you consider that the world record for the longest bridge crossing a sea is the 26.4 miles of the Jiaozhou Bay Bridge in China, then anything is possible!

12. SCOTLAND'S WORLDWIDE LEGACY
From local roots to continental routes

Turning 50 is yet another milestone in one's life. By 2005 the Haskins Report had concluded that my then employer, English Nature, should amalgamate with parts of the Countryside Agency and Defra to form Natural England. It was, at heart, a rationalisation exercise and I was hugely busy integrating about 66 different offices from the legacy bodies into a 'smarter way of working'.

It was actually very good fun and the team was up for the challenge. We all had to apply for the new posts created and I was successful in being appointed Head of Property, which again was a fascinating job for a surveyor, embracing as it did both our rural and commercial office estate and the multitude of different management agreements we had with landowners and key stakeholders on Sites of Special Scientific Interest (SSSIs), which cover 7% of England's land area.

Once the excitement of the challenge of creating a new organisation had ebbed a bit, I got to wondering 'what next?'. I was in my very early 50s and was up for at least one last career challenge. I spotted an advertisement for the role of Head of Property at Scottish & Southern Energy plc, which sounded interesting. Here was a Scottish company, a FTSE 30 energy company, with interests across the UK and Ireland and the leading light (forgive the pun) in renewable energy. Its pedigree was grounded on the North of Scotland Hydro-Electric Board with its extensive estate of hydro dams.

The parent company had recently acquired Airtricity in Ireland, bringing it a significant wind farm estate, which it had ambitious plans to expand in Scotland, too. It also owned Southern Electric in England and SWALEC in Wales, and a diverse range of contracting businesses. Property was a key resource, so this job would present a major challenge, but one I was up for. As a chartered environmentalist, I've had a long-held belief that renewable energy is a critical component of sustainable development.

Over a round of golf at Oundle, Northamptonshire, I asked my friend and colleague Mark Felton what he thought of my idea. 'Go for it,' was his advice, and his thinking, too, was that I needed a fresh challenge.

It was good advice and I definitely made the correct decision. I had teams based in Perth, Edinburgh and Reading, with a chartered surveyor, the very affable but professionally shrewd Peter Houlihan, in Dublin. The decision to stay in Peterborough seemed sensible. Deborah and her family lived here and the 'commute' was very doable, especially by train. Over the following seven years I'd get to know the East Coast Main Line, Paddington to Reading and the airport and Luas tram line in Dublin like long-time friends.

My daughter Lauren went to study Geography at Edinburgh University and I was thrilled that she had inherited my love for that subject. She helped me with fact-finding for the bridges, particularly on early researches while driving through the Scottish Borders. I hope she enjoys reading this book!

Projects at SSE took me back to some of my old haunts in Scotland and some new ones, too, particularly on the new wind farm sites being developed. These are normally held on 25-year leases from the landowners, with my property team negotiating access rights and the provision, maintenance and repair of the infrastructure, including roads and bridges.

In most cases the agreement requires SSE to reinstate the land and access roads at the end of the lease term. I always thought that this was a missed opportunity to leave proper access routes into often very remote locations, which could be of long-lasting public benefit to walkers, ramblers, cyclists and birdwatchers, as well as the estate itself for commercial activities, such as sporting and forestry.

Others might complain about 'scars on the landscape', but the roads and bridges created by such investments in renewable energy are actually the signs of economic activity, just as the remains of settlements high above the shores of Loch Tay have become valued as an integral part of the heritage of today. These roads and bridges are functional and it seems such a waste to destroy them rather than put them to good purpose in promoting multiple land use as they continue to provide access, and a window on the world, to our remote countryside.

So here was I, a Scot to my core, based in England but working across the UK and Ireland. It was a route that many had taken before me. The contributions and influence of Scots across the world is out of all proportion to the size of their native land.

Scotland is a small country with, traditionally, a relatively small population, but her influence in terms of contribution to the world's

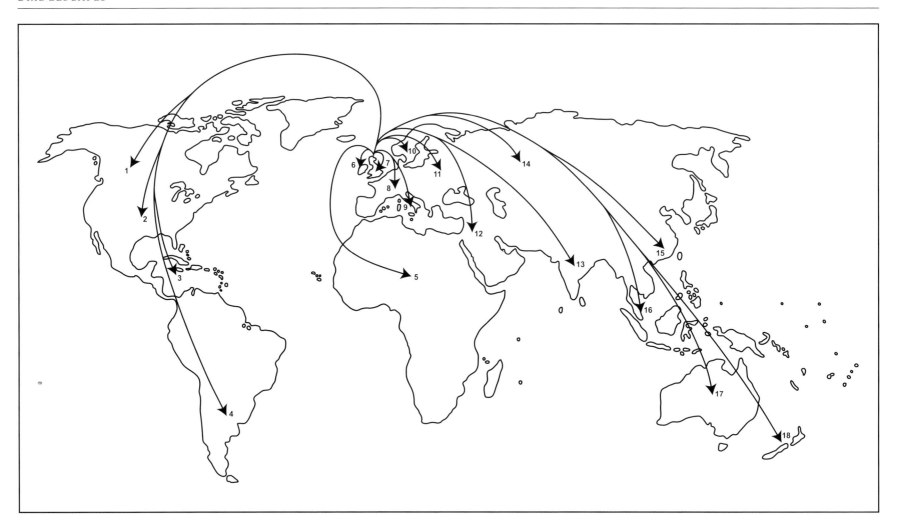

Beyond Scotland

1 Canada (Quebec, East/West
   Coasts
2 USA (Missouri, Pennsylvania,
   New England)
3 Jamaica
4 Argentina
5 Africa:
   Egypt (Cairo)

Lesotho
Nigeria
South Africa
Sudan
Uganda
6 Ireland (Dublin, Cork,
   Waterford)
7 England (East Anglia, London,
   Lancaster, Shropshire)
   Wales (Menai, Llangollen)

8 Prussia
   Hungary
9 Italy (Naples)
10 Denmark
   Sweden
11 Estonia
12 Iraq
13 India (Lucknow, Calcutta,
   Bombay, Ganges)
   Nepal

14 Russia (Kiev, St Petersburg)
15 China
   Taiwan
16 Singapore
17 Australia (Sydney)
18 New Zealand (North and
   South Islands)

great explorers, scientists, both pure and applied, philosophers, politicians, soldiers, writers, inventors and engineers goes well beyond any expectation as a nation. Perhaps it is that solid pedigree of a Scottish education that has fashioned the minds of so many young Scots across the generations to develop keen and inquisitive natures and apply these to new endeavours. Linked to that must also be the economic opportunities that appeared attractive in seeking to make one's way in new and emerging countries where aptitude and perseverance could find expression. Whatever the motivation, the record ably demonstrates that trait as having borne ample fruit.

Many things are hailed as inventions of the Scots to which they can improperly lay claim. Among these are the bagpipes, which originated in the Middle East and Ancient Greece and may have been brought to Scotland by the Romans. Haggis is also a dish the Romans may have introduced, although it could equally as well have come from Scandinavia. It is alleged that Lancastrians in the north of England ate something akin to haggis and even that one of them, a Quaker named Thomas Rawlinson, invented the 'short kilt' in the 1720s. As for porridge, they were eating oats in a sort of soup in Egypt when the Pharaohs were around, and any self-respecting Northern European or Russian has seen the advantage of this human central heating for many a century.

That admission made, it is indisputable that the Scots have discovered or invented a multitude of products that have made the world a better place, or at least made it more comfortable. To name but a few of the more obvious: penicillin (Sir Alexander Fleming); anaesthetics (Sir James Young Simpson); pneumatic tyre (Robert William Thomson, but mostly credited to John Boyd Dunlop); condensing steam engine (James Watt); pedal bicycle (Kirkpatrick Macmillan); coal-gas lighting (William Murdoch); making cast steel from wrought iron (David Mushet); wire rope (Robert Stirling Newall); adhesive postage stamps (James Chalmers); telephone (Alexander Graham Bell); television (John Logie Baird – well, in the case of both Bell and Baird, with a little help from their colleagues); radar (Robert Watson-Watt), the process for extracting paraffin from coal (James Young); the raincoat (Charles Macintosh); macadamised roads (the basis for, but not specifically, tarmac – John Loudon McAdam); logarithms (John Napier); modern economics (Adam Smith); and from Captain Brown's old friend, Sir David Brewster, the kaleidoscope.

That tradition not only lives on but is thriving. In 2016 two more Scottish innovators were inducted to the Scottish Engineering Hall of Fame. James Goodfellow, born in Paisley in 1937, invented the automated cash machine (ATM), which has revolutionised banking for the customer. His genius in linking an encrypted plastic card to a personal identifier, the PIN, benefited James financially to the tune of £10, a bonus from his employer.

Another Scot born in 1937, Sir Duncan Michael, hails from Beauly, but transformed Ove Arup & Partners into a global consultancy and was the lead structural engineer on the Sydney Opera House. As Gordon Masterton, chair of the judging panel at the Institution of Engineers and Shipbuilders in Scotland, aptly remarked:

'Scotland can rightly claim to have provided the educational base for many of the world's greatest engineers who have gone on to lead great companies and make world changing inventions. Duncan Michael and James Goodfellow are living proof that this tradition is alive and well.'

As in the fields of other applied sciences, so with civil engineering, and especially bridge-building, Scotland has produced innovators of exceptional capability and energy whose legacy is of paramount significance. Throughout this book the Scottish bridges of **John Rennie** and his son, also **John**, and those of **Thomas Telford** and **Robert Mylne** have featured strongly. The contribution to the advancement of bridge-building made by these engineers extends well beyond their native land. Indeed, in many cases their greatest legacy lies beyond Scotland.

A book celebrating Scottish bridges would be incomplete if it did not acknowledge the contribution Scottish bridge engineers have made, notably in England and Wales, but also in other parts of the world. John Rennie, Thomas Telford and William Arrol are among an elite band of engineers honoured in the Scottish Engineering Hall of Fame, established in 2011. The first three Presidents of the Institution of Civil Engineers were Scots – Thomas Telford, James Walker and Sir John Rennie – and these founding fathers of the profession have left many fine examples in their works as a testimony to both applied science and creative design, or, in the words of its Royal Charter, the 'art of directing the great sources of power in nature for the use and convenience of man'.

And there are many who can claim to have contributed significantly to this endeavour, in many parts of the globe.

The Carron Iron Works, near Falkirk, has a long history of producing iron for industrial, domestic and military uses, but it also spawned engineers who, learning their trade there, emigrated with their skills and ideas. Both **John Baildon** (1772-1846) and **Charles Baird** (1766-1843) were apprentices at Carron in the 1780s when they decided to go east, John to Prussia and Charles to Russia. John was employed by Frederick the Great's successor, Frederick William II, to design the first blast furnace specifically to use coke, and also built the first cast-iron bridge in Prussia. Charles built up one of the largest engineering works in St Petersburg and built the first Russian steamship. His cast-iron arch bridge at Chugunny, crossing the canal adjacent to his works, completed in 1805, was the first of its kind in Russia. His works also supplied the chain for the suspension bridges in St Petersburg.

Another Scot operating in St Petersburg in the same era was **William Hastie** (1755-1832), whose design for constructing cast-iron bridges was first used to replace the existing timber Polizeiska bridge across the River Moika, opened in 1806. Hastie was principally an architect and town planner whose legacy includes the development of the Russian towns of Kiev and Omsk, and the Romanov Tsars' summer palace near St Petersburg, Tsarskoe Selo.

Among this noble band of Scottish expatriates who did sterling work in foreign parts, there were a few somewhat eccentric characters. One such was **John MacTaggart** (1791-1830), described as a civil engineer and author, one of 11 children born of Galloway farming stock in Kirkcudbrightshire. Moving to London in the 1820s, he established a newspaper entitled 'The London Scotchman' and then his Scottish Gallovidian Encyclopaedia. Describing Scottish culture, antiquities and nature, it was rapidly withdrawn from circulation until the 1870s, due to 'local sensitivities'.

His principal engineering endeavours lay ahead, however, and for reasons not recorded John Rennie Jnr recommended MacTaggart for appointment by the Board of Ordnance as clerk of works on the construction of the Rideau Canal in Upper Canada. This involved the design and supervision of a series of seven bridges across the Ottawa River, the largest being a 212-foot wooden triple-arch truss across a very deep and fast-flowing channel.

He may have been an engineer of some repute, but his interpersonal skills appear to have left something to be desired as he was reprimanded on several occasions for insubordination and drunkenness; the final straw was offending the Lieutenant-Governor of Nova Scotia, for which he was dismissed.

It was **Nicol Hugh Baird**, lately arrived from Scotland via working with his uncle, Charles Baird, in Russia who succeeded MacTaggart, and made an altogether better impression.

The Mylne Family, whose engineering origins lay in stonemasonry in Scotland – they were master masons from the reign of King Charles I in the 17th century – were responsible for many royal castles, including Holyrood House in Edinburgh. **Robert Mylne** FRS (1733-1811) was an architect and engineer of considerable international acclaim, both he and his brother, William, having trained in Rome. In 1758 Robert was the first Briton to be awarded first prize in the concourse of the Academy of St Luke. This wider European education, so much a part of the Enlightenment period, brought a wealth of experience on the brothers' return to British soil, which manifests itself in the designs they inspired.

Robert Mylne's early successes included a design of exceptional quality to win the competition for London's Blackfriars Bridge, built in the 1760s. Dr Samuel Johnson loudly voiced his protests, as he wanted local talent. Boswell, however, patriotically supported Mylne and expressed delight that a descendent of a family of master masons should be awarded the contract.

Completed in 1769, the bridge had nine semi-elliptical arches, the first such design in a large bridge in Britain, but the scouring effect of the Thames and the susceptibility to frost damage took their toll on the Portland Stone masonry and, within 100 years, Blackfriars had been demolished and replaced.

Robert Mylne also designed and built the London water supply; Tonbridge Great Bridge across the River Medway in Kent; Ridley Hall Bridge in Northumbria; and the Middle Bridge across Hampshire's River Test at Romsey, which was demolished in 1930. His later work in Scotland included the Aray Bridge and Dubh Loch Bridge for the Duke of Argyll, and the Clachan Bridge at Seil Island in Argyll, a high arch over the tidal channel between the island and the mainland, with its somewhat pretentious sobriquet of being the 'Bridge over the Atlantic'. At Clachan Mylne's involvement was in revising and improving the design of John Stevenson of Oban, who was also commissioned by the Earl of Breadalbane as the contractor. The blind oculus in each spandrel add decoration to this bridge from 1791.

Another family steeped in the civil engineering heritage of both Scotland and beyond is the Rennies, originating from the Phantassie Estate at Linton in East Lothian. **John Rennie (Senior)** (1761-1821) was the fourth son of a farmer who died when John was five years old. John was educated at Dunbar High School and, when his mathematics teacher was appointed rector of Perth Academy, he recommended John as his successor, a job he did for six weeks!

John studied scientific subjects at Edinburgh University under Dr John Robison (1739-1805), the professor of natural philosophy who was interested in the application of science to engineering works. Robison

The 'Bridge over the Atlantic' at Clachan. *Jane Morris*

also invented the siren, but although his teachings may well have inspired Rennie to pursue an engineering career, they lacked sufficient breadth to merit his student being awarded a degree.

Rennie, undaunted, headed for London and in 1783 was appointed by James Watt to supervise the building of Albion Mills in Blackfriars. This led to commissions back in Edinburgh to design flour mills at Leith, and at Cadiz in Spain and Nantes in France. Standing 6ft 4in tall, Rennie was a giant in stature as well as engineering prowess. His son described him as being 'naturally of a quick irritable disposition', which could be suppressed so as to display only 'cool, steady and determined behaviour'.

A modest man, and very practical in his abilities and outlook, his hobby was collecting old books. Evidently his friends used to collect books for him from all over Europe during their travels and bring them back to London.

His masterpiece in architectural and engineering design was London's Waterloo Bridge, completed in 1817, on the model used for his earlier Kelso Bridge over the Tweed. Waterloo Bridge comprised nine semi-elliptical arches of 120-foot span, beautifully proportioned with

refuges supported over each pier in twin columns. The Italian sculptor Canovo declared it 'the noblest bridge in the world, worth a visit from the remotest corners of the earth'. The Prince Regent changed the name of the bridge from its original, Strand Bridge, on the second anniversary of the Battle of Waterloo.

Rennie's use of stone and cast iron to produce bridges with exceptionally wide arches was again evidenced in Southwark Bridge, completed in 1819. This was the largest cast-iron arch to be built in Britain and stood until 1913. The Prince Regent wished to confer a knighthood on Rennie but he declined the honour. It remained for his second son to accept the title Sir John Rennie, at the official opening of London Bridge. Rather fittingly, Sir John was appointed engineer for that bridge following the Select Committee's decision to adopt his late father's design.

The products of John Snr, who died in 1821, are also evidenced in bridges he designed for the King of Naples in Italy and as part of the imperial expansion of India at Lucknow.

His expertise was renowned well beyond bridge design, however: he was responsible for canals at Lancaster and the Kennet & Avon; the docks at Leith, Port of London and East India; and the Sheerness naval dockyards in Kent, which was the largest work in terms of single project

John Rennie Senior (1761-1821). *Courtesy of the Institution of Civil Engineers*

Sir John Rennie Junior followed in his father's footsteps as a prodigious engineer with a wide spectrum of expertise. His work concentrated on harbours, such as Donaghadee in Ireland, but it is London Bridge that perhaps attracts the most attention from tourists these days, not in its original setting but as a feature of Lake Havasu City in Arizona, some three hours' drive from Phoenix. It was to this theme park resort in the desert that entrepreneur Robert McCulloch shipped the granite facings of the stone arches when he purchased London Bridge at auction in 1968 for £2.49 million. At 928 feet long, this Rennie bridge is almost certainly the largest antique ever sold. I believe there is some truth in the rumour that the American thought he was purchasing Tower Bridge!

William Adam, born in 1689 and educated at Kirkcaldy High School, was the patriarchal head of a family that came to architectural prominence in the 18th century. Three of his four sons became architects. William's legacy includes Wade's bridge at Aberfeldy and some fine Gothic designs on the Duke of Argyll's estate at Inveraray. His son, **John Adam** (1721-92), succeeded him in his lucrative appointment as mason to the Board of Ordnance in North Britain and introduced elliptical arches as an innovative design feature for the Avenue Bridge at Dumfries House, near Cumnock.

Another son, **Robert Adam** (1728-92), inspired by his well-funded Grand Tour of Europe, is best remembered for his landscape paintings, both real and imaginary, borrowing designs or motifs from Palladio Piranesi, conceiving bridges as features in the landscape. These studies were carried through to his architectural practice and, as well as Scottish examples such as the winding 'antique' viaduct at the National Trust for Scotland's Culzean Castle and Montagu Bridge at Dalkeith House, the legacy of estate bridges includes Derbyshire's Kedleston Hall and Audley End in Essex. Although much altered in later years, his design for the impressive Pulteney Bridge in Bath, with three-segmented arches, was a fine example of a bridge lined on both sides by shops.

The most famous Scottish civil engineer of all was undoubtedly **Thomas Telford** (1757-1834), a founding father of the profession, whose contribution marked the era of pioneering innovation in the design and construction of roads, bridges, canals, harbours and docks. This infrastructure, representing an enormous investment by both the public and private sectors, was to create the transport networks that made Britain an industrial nation.

Telford was born at Westerkirk in Eskdale on 19 August 1757 of humble beginnings. His father, a shepherd on Glendinning Farm, having waited until middle age before marrying, died a few months

costs before 1830. His work on the Lincolnshire Fens, especially in the Eau Brink Cut, near King's Lynn, brought major improvements to the drainage of this rich agricultural area. He also collaborated with other pioneering engineers, as with Stevenson on the Bell Rock lighthouse and with Joseph Whidbey on the Plymouth Breakwater, a massive engineering undertaking. John is buried in St Paul's Cathedral.

after the birth of his only child. Young Thomas had a good village school education and was known among his friends in his youth as 'Laughing Tam', being a warm and jovial companion.

He was an apprentice mason engaged in the building of the Langholm Bridge, some 7 miles from Westerkirk (opened 1775), and later on the construction of the New Town of Edinburgh. Aged just 23, he rode to London on a borrowed horse, itself an impressive feat, and worked for two years on the building of Somerset House. He was then employed in the County of Salop (Shropshire) as mason to William Pulteney, one of the Johnstones of Westerhill, who had changed his name upon marriage to the heiress of the Earl of Bath and become the richest commoner in England. This may sound like patronage, but according to Telford, 'We quarrel like tinkers.' It did, however, provide a foothold on his road to success.

As Surveyor of Public Works for Salop, Telford's career took off. He started building bridges at Montford and Longbridge to meet the needs of the heartland of the Industrial Revolution. In 1793 he was appointed 'General Agent, Surveyor, Engineer, Architect and Overlooker' to the Ellesmere Canal project, which led to commissions for the Shrewsbury Canal in 1795 and many more consultancies. He built the second-ever cast-iron bridge, after Coalbrookdale, at Buildwas in 1796, and set up home and head office in London to manage his burgeoning professional practice.

As the Buildwas project was completed, Telford embarked on aqueducts, most notably Pontcysyllte, its 19 spans carrying the Llangollen Canal over the Dee Valley, making it the longest and highest aqueduct in Britain. Opened in 1805, it was designated as a World Heritage Site by UNESCO in 2009. Sir Walter Scott said it was the most impressive work of art he had ever seen. At Telford's own request, it appears in the background of the official portrait of him by Samuel Lane to commemorate his election as President of the Institution of Civil Engineers.

Telford also designed and built Hythe Bridge over the River Severn at Tewkesbury, and Holt Fleet and Bewdley bridges in Worcestershire, the latter still standing today as one of the most elegant bridges in England. Telford had his own Waterloo Bridge, but across the Conway River at Betwys-y-coed. This bridge, completed in 1815 of course, incorporates a rose, a thistle, a shamrock and a leek, each painted in the appropriate colours, in each of the spandrels.

Despite great achievements in Scotland with the Highland Roads and Bridges and the Caledonian Canal, his greatest legacy was arguably in England and Wales. He can be said to have provided the link between

Thomas Telford. *Courtesy of the Institution of Civil Engineers*

Scotland and England in the construction of the Glasgow to Carlisle road. South of the border, the roads between London and Holyhead and from Chester to Bangor opened up significant trading routes, the former incorporating the world's first large suspension bridge, the 580-foot span of the Menai Strait Suspension Bridge, completed in 1826.

Thomas Telford was founding President of the Institution of Civil Engineers and, under his aegis, a Royal Charter was granted in 1828. Among his other achievements were London's St Katherine's Dock and the rather interestingly named Over Bridge, over the Severn, near Gloucester. Opened in 1830, this was the lowest road bridge crossing on the river until the Severn Bridge was built in the 1960s.

The poet Robert Southey, a personal friend who accompanied Telford on his tour of Scotland in 1819 and wrote his biography, called him 'Pontifex Maximus' and 'the Colossus of Roads', the latter a play on the statue of Helios, one of the Seven Wonders of the Ancient World.

Despite his rightfully acclaimed engineering legacy, another of Telford's friends, Sir David Brewster, the Scottish physicist and mathematician who invented the kaleidoscope, claimed that he 'had a singular distaste for mathematic studies, and never even made himself acquainted with the elements of geometry'!

He did, however, read books in French and German and was, throughout his adult life, a benefactor to the poor in Eskdale. Suffering from deafness in his later years, Telford was determined to occupy his time in constructive fashion, arranging his engineering papers for publication. He is buried in Westminster Abbey. Perhaps the most fitting character reference was provided by his Deputy in the Highlands, Joseph Mitchell:

'Thomas Telford was the soul of cheerfulness, and used to keep his guests in a river of laughter. His ordinary manner to a stranger was that of a happy, cheerful, clear-headed upright man; but any attempt to impose on him, or any exhibition of meanness or unfair dealing, called forth expressions of stern indignation and severe invective.'

Is that not as wonderful an epitaph as any man could wish? And what a legacy!

Others achieved records, too. **Alexander Stevens**, from East Lothian, who had major success with his bridges at Hyndford, Drygrange and Ancrum, also won commissions south of the border. With his son he built the Lune Aqueduct on the Lancaster Canal in 1798 to a design by John Rennie. This aqueduct, comprising five arches each of 70-foot span, is the largest all-masonry aqueduct ever built in Britain. He was also responsible for Sarah's Bridge across the River Liffey at Islandbridge near Dublin, completed in 1793.

The greatest contribution to Ireland's bridge heritage by a Scot, however, came from a designer who undertook no training as an architect or engineer, but was a brilliant classic academic and scientist. He was **Alexander Nimmo**, born in Cupar in 1783, who was Rector of Inverness Academy at the age of 22. During the school holidays he was employed by Thomas Telford to carry out surveys of county boundaries and new roads. He enjoyed this work so much that he resigned from his rectorship, although Joseph Mitchell claimed that the school governors had removed him and censured him for failing to attend church with the boys. In any event, Telford recommended him for appointment as an engineer in Ireland, where he was engaged by the Irish Bogs Commission on surveys. Together with considerable harbour development works, Nimmo went on to design the Wellesley Bridge, now the Sarsfield Bridge, across the River Shannon in Limerick, and the two bridges at Poulaphouca between Wicklow and Kildare.

The development of the Indian subcontinent, spearheaded by the British Empire, involved significant civil engineering feats. In 1850 **George Turnbull**, born in Luncarty in Perthshire, was appointed Chief Engineer of the East Indian Railway and set about building the first railway line in India, the 541-mile route from Calcutta to Benares. He surveyed the largest tributary of the River Ganges, the monsoon-ravaged River Sone, in 1851; this presented a mighty challenge to bridge, and it was 11 years later, following the import of thousands of tons of iron from England, that he was able to inspect the completed structure and accompany another Scot, Lord Elgin, Governor General of India, to the inauguration. The magnificent 4,726-foot Koilwar Bridge, now called the Abdul Bari Bridge, was the second-largest bridge in the world at the time, and is the steel rail/road bridge featured in the film *Gandhi*.

Lord Elgin had a bridge named after him; the Elgin Bridge is a 3,695-foot-long railway viaduct across the Ghaghra River in Barabanki district. It has the unusual pedigree of having been constructed over dry land, then the river was diverted under it! I wonder if my father ever thought of that one?

Turnbull left his native Perthshire in 1820 to train under Thomas Telford, building St Katherine's Dock in London. He became Telford's clerk, and was involved in his burial in Westminster Abbey, later gaining a reputation as an innovative civil engineer leading to his major work in India. He died in 1889.

In Singapore there is yet another Elgin Bridge, again named after James Bruce, the 8th Earl of Elgin. The original dated from 1862 but was replaced by a concrete bridge in 1926.

Another Scottish colonial, **Sir John Anderson** (1858-1918), born in Gartly in Aberdeenshire, and Governor of the Straits Settlement and High Commissioner for the Federated Malay States from 1904 to 1911, gave his name to Anderson Bridge in Singapore. During the Japanese Occupation (1942-45) the severed heads of criminals were hung from the bridge to deter the citizens from law-breaking. The bridge now has a more glamorous role as part of the Formula 1 circuit for the Singapore Grand Prix.

The oldest surviving bridge across the Singapore River is the Cavenagh Bridge, dating from 1869. Originally to be named Edinburgh Bridge, it was built in Glasgow by **R. & W. Maclellan** and shipped out to Singapore to be assembled by Indian convicts. A suspension bridge, it was restored and strengthened in 1987. The Read Bridge also has Scottish roots. It was the initiative of Scottish businessman **William Henry Macleod Read** (1819-1909), who emigrated to Singapore in 1841 and owned a cardamom spice plantation on the site of today's Istana, the official residence and office of the President of Singapore.

One of New Zealand's most successful civil engineers was **Peter Seton Hay**, a Scot born in Glasgow in 1852/53, who emigrated with his parents aboard the Storm Cloud in 1860. Educated at Dunedin University, he was renowned for his ability for solving prodigious mental calculations without the use of logarithmic tables. He mistakenly left his tables at camp one day but, rather than waiting until he returned that evening, he sat down in the bush and worked out the tangent calculations from first principles.

Gaining rapid promotion in the Public Works Department in Wellington, Hay designed many bridges, including six significant viaducts on the North Island's Main Trunk Line, which traverses heavy bush and gorge country. The Makohine Viaduct, at 750 feet long and spanning a 250-foot-deep gully, was completed in 1902.

In 1905 the completion of the entire Trunk Line became dependent on the Makatote Viaduct, bridging the stream that rises on the western slopes of the volcanic Mount Ruapehu. It took J. & A. Anderson of Christchurch three years to construct and was at the time the largest engineering project of its kind in New Zealand to be carried out by private enterprise. Although not the highest viaduct in the country, Roy Sinclair describes it in his book *Journeying the Railways in New Zealand* as 'a dizzy steel structure, spanning an entire valley' and as 'one that commands considerable awe – perhaps more than any other New Zealand structure.' The Makatote Viaduct is 825 feet long and 259 feet high, and continues to carry passengers across the densely forested gorge.

The steel viaducts at Hapuawhenua, Taonui, Mangaweka and Manganui-a-te-ao are also impressive engineering feats. The Hapuawhenua Viaduct was one of two curved structures on this line. Built in 1907 to Hay's designs, it was subsequently replaced in the late 1980s with a separate curved viaduct. The Mangaweka Viaduct, started in 1902 and spanning 950 feet, was erected in just 12 months. The North Island Main Trunk Line remains the stuff of legend, commemorated in poem, song and prose. It's the classic railway journey for thousands of Kiwis.

On the South Island, Hay designed the double-decker combined road and rail bridge across the Awatere River near Seddon, which opened in 1902. In 1906 he became Engineer-in-Chief, but died prematurely the following year, aged 54. He did not live to see many of his greatest engineering designs come to fruition, such as the 5-mile railway tunnel through the Southern Alps, from Otira to Arthur's Pass, the longest tunnel in the Southern Hemisphere at that time, nor New Zealand's hydro-electric power schemes.

The most iconic bridge in the Antipodes must be Sydney Harbour Bridge, and Scots were major players in its construction. On 23 February 1926 a party of 76, including 21 stonemasons, five quarrymen and two toolsmiths, left Aberdeen Joint Station on a journey via Tilbury Docks in London, where they would board the Australia-bound P&O liner *Barrabool*. The Aberdeen-based *Press and Journal* reported that they were being sent 'to assist the building of a bridge in Sydney.' The newspaper commented: 'The men who are going are the cream of their craft. The local granite trade will be severely hit by the departure of so many skilled workers.'

The principal task was to build the bridge's granite-faced pylons. The Chief Engineer, Dr John Bridfield, argued that these structures would 'add to the architectural adornment of the structure, which would otherwise be utilitarian.' The pylons would also add 20% to the cost, but he was surely correct in his insistence.

The bridge's construction was overseen by Scottish-born engineer

Sydney Harbour Bridge, Australia. *Deborah M. Keith*

Lawrence Ennis. The granite was sourced from Moruya Quarry, some 200 miles south of Sydney, but this part of the exercise was very much a Scottish affair. Ennis appointed a Kemnay man, **John Gilmore**, as manager, who in turn took another two Aberdeenshire men, **Archie Davidson** and **Bill Morrison**, to be foremen at the quarry face and in the stone-dressing sheds. Many more Scots were recruited and emigrated on the Assisted Passage Scheme. One little girl, aged three, was reported as saying, 'It's a lang way to go to build a brig.'

It may have been a long way, but another young girl saw it as a career opportunity. **Dorothy Donaldson Buchanan** (1899-1985) was born in

Sir William Arrol. *Courtesy of the Institution of Civil Engineers*

Langholm and studied civil engineering at Edinburgh University. She went out to Australia as one of Dorman Long's design team, working with Sir Ralph Freeman on the Harbour Bridge. The experience served her well, as she became the first female member of the Institution of Civil Engineers, in 1927, and on her return to Britain designed the George V Bridge in Newcastle, better known as the Tyne Bridge, and a Sydney lookalike. She also designed London's Lambeth Bridge.

Another bridge, close to Sydney, which owes its pedigree to Scottish engineering is at Hawkesbury. **Sir William Arrol** (1839-1913), whose legacy includes the Forth Rail Bridge, also built the original bridge over this Australian river in 1889. The original piers remain beside the 1946 replacement.

Sir William established his famous structural engineering company in the early 1870s when Glasgow was fast becoming the 'Workshop of the British Empire'. Based at Dalmarnock Iron Works, his impressive portfolio of structures across the globe includes the Bombay Rolling-Lift Bridge (1900); the Barrow and Suir bridges in Waterford, Ireland (1905 and 1906); the Cairo Bridge over the River Nile (1906); the Howra Bridge in Kolkata (1911); and, in the firm that bears his name, the steel bridge across the Benue River in Nigeria (1932) and the Samawa Suspension Bridge across the River Euphrates in Iraq (1958). The list is substantial – and that's just the bridges. There are further examples in Argentina, Ghana, South Africa, Sudan, Uganda, Lesotho, India, Nepal, Singapore, Jamaica, Denmark and China.

Another bridge-builder, whose family owned a foundry in Aberdeen, was **Louis Harper**. His legacy of light wire suspension bridges appeared in Nepal (Chundra [Chovar Gorge], Tursoli River, Tadi, Sundari and Mangaltar); India (Bombay, Baroda and Jumna); Estonia (Narva); and South Africa (Tsomo), among others. Closer to home, he also designed and supplied bridges at Sellack Boat (near Ross-on-Wye), Bandon (County Cork, Ireland), and three bridges in Grimsby.

The development of Canada into a thriving economy owes much to Scottish endeavour, with prime ministers, traders, lawyers and scientists among them. In the 1920s almost a quarter of Canadian industrial leaders had been born in Scotland and another quarter had Scottish-born fathers. Nova Scotia, after all, is the Latin for New Scotland.

Civil engineering played a huge part in opening up Canada as settlement expanded westwards. As Chief Engineer on the Northern Railway of Canada, then the Canadian Pacific Railway, **Sir Sandford Fleming** (1827-1915) was Canada's foremost railway construction engineer, being an ardent advocate of linking the Atlantic with the Pacific by a transcontinental railway as a means of spearheading the growth of Canada. Born and raised in Kirkcaldy, Fleming emigrated to Halifax, Nova Scotia, when he was 18 and, following significant surveying expeditions to find a passage through the Rockies, was instrumental in initiating Canada's biggest public works project of the 19th century.

Although viewed as unnecessarily expensive when built, Fleming's insistence that the bridges be constructed on masonry piers with wrought-iron spans was to prove an astute move, given the number of timber truss bridges lost to forest fires in the early settlement days. Now replaced by a modern bridge, the original stone piers of the multi-span bridge across the Miramichi River in New Brunswick remain as a testimony to resilience. It is not for his railway endeavours alone that Fleming is remembered, however. He also designed Canada's first postage stamp, the Threepenny Beaver, and proposed a single global 24-hour clock, thus inventing the concept of international standard time.

One of Canada's most successful businessmen was the contractor on the transcontinental railway, **Sir Robert Gillespie Reid** (1842-1908), who, through a contract to build the Newfoundland Railway, became one of the largest landed proprietors in the world.

Born in Coupar Angus, Reid emigrated first to Australia in 1865, where he met his wife and built stone viaducts through the Blue Mountains in New South Wales. By 1871 he was in Ontario in partnership with James Isbister, building bridges, principally for railways, but moved to California in the late 1870s; there he established an unparalleled reputation as a bridge-builder in difficult terrain on western sections of the American transcontinental railway. His major achievements in America include building an international railway bridge across the Rio Grande and a bridge crossing the Delaware Gap.

Back in Canada, his company, Isbister & Reid, was contracted from 1883 on the Canadian Pacific Railway and built an international railway bridge over the Niagara River and the Lachine Bridge over the St Lawrence. In 1887 Reid started construction of the foundations of the Grand Narrows Bridge, linking Cape Breton to mainland Nova Scotia, a significant challenge as the strait is some 92 feet deep at this point and not solid bedrock. The currents are strong and erratic and the break-up of the ice in the spring was also a hazard. It took three years to complete the railway bridge, a massive structure with a swing span to allow passage of shipping, but this contract on the Intercolonial Railway gave him his stake in Newfoundland.

The mighty challenge for the Canadian Pacific Railway was building the track through the Precambrian Shield that divides the North American continent, otherwise known as the Rocky Mountains. In the late 1850s the Chief Factor of the Hudson Bay Company, **Sir James Douglas** (1803-77), had the Great North Road constructed as the primary route along the Fraser and Thompson rivers to service the Cariboo Gold Rush. Douglas, whose father was Scottish, was educated at Lanark and at 16 emigrated to join the North West Company, becoming the Governor of Vancouver Island and the 'Father of British Columbia'.

Such was the success of goldmining that Douglas improved the road in the early years of the 1860s, blasting footings on the steep-sided valleys and gullies to build bridges, allowing the road to reach Barkerville and provide a route for $6.5 million-worth of gold to be transported to the coast in a single year.

Although Douglas was the first politician to champion the construction of a national railway and highway, it was the vision and perseverance of three other Scots, and the engineering tenacity of a fourth, that would bring the project to completion.

Canada's first Prime Minister, **Sir John Alexander MacDonald** (1815-1891), was born in Glasgow and emigrated with his parents to Kingston, Ontario, in 1820. During his first term in office he secured the accession of British Columbia as part of the Canadian Confederation on the promise that a new Trans-Canada railway would be completed by 1883.

In his second term, which started in 1880, the final push was made. The Canadian Pacific Railway Company (CPR) was incorporated in 1881 with **George Stephen**, later 1st Baron Mount Stephen (1829-1921) as President and his cousin, **Donald Alexander Smith**, later Lord Strathcona (1820-1914), as his associate. Both men hailed from Morayshire, Stephen from Dufftown and Smith from Forres. They appointed an acclaimed American rail manager, William Cornelius Van Horne, as General Manager, but it was the Cromarty-born and Inverness Royal Academy-educated civil engineer **James Leveson Ross** (1848-1913) who they entrusted with the challenge of forging a railway line through the Rocky and Selkirk mountain ranges, building high timber bridges spanning the Stoney, Mountain, Surprise and Cascade creeks across the Columbia and Beaver rivers.

The highest timber bridge ever built was the original Stoney Creek truss bridge, built in 1885 across a deep gully in Rogers Pass through what is now Glacier National Park. Although subsequently replaced by steel trestles, the wooden structures at Mountain Creek and Surprise Creek were the second and third highest timber bridges on the CPR main line. There is no excuse made for using modern Canadian-speak to describe these engineering marvels as 'awesome'.

The spot chosen for the final joining of the rails between east and west was in Eagle Pass, at Craigellachie, named after the village on Scotland's River Spey near George Stephen's childhood home. Donald Smith hammered home the final spike on 7 November 1885.

On the western seaboard, Scots were making their mark too. The Capilano Suspension Bridge in North Vancouver is a major tourist attraction dating from the 1950s. The original suspension bridge across this deep ravine was built in 1889 of hemp ropes with a deck of cedar planks by **George Grant Mackay** (1827-93). He was a native of Inverness and had a substantial career as a landowner, owning the Glengloy Estate near Spean Bridge, before emigrating to British Columbia aged 61 and becoming the 'Laird of Capilano'.

Scottish engineers were also heavily involved in the railroad ventures in the United States of America, many of which were funded by Dunfermline-born steel baron and Scots emigrant Andrew Carnegie.

Among the 19th-century colonists were two friends from Edinburgh – **James Pugh Kirkwood** (1807-77) and **James Laurie** (1811-75). Kirkwood had been apprenticed to Thomas Grainger working on Scottish viaducts

Capilano Suspension Bridge, Vancouver. *Deborah M. Keith*

for 10 years when, in 1832, the pair decided to emigrate to work for William McNeill, who had designed the Carrolton Viaduct some two years previously.

Kirkwood embarked on a career on railroad construction, principally in the New England states, but was also the Construction Superintendent on the stone-arch Starrucca Viaduct in Pennsylvania, reputedly the most expensive railroad bridge, relatively speaking, in the world, and was Chief Engineer on the Missouri Pacific Railroad. On his return to New York in 1855 his career pursued a public health agenda. He was instrumental in the development of water treatment systems, most notably water filtration techniques, in many North American cities, and was one of the pioneers of river pollution control. He wrote a defining textbook on his techniques and became known as the 'Father of Slow Sand Filtration'.

There is resonance here with my professional institution, the Chartered Institution of Water & Environmental Management (CIWEM), which also has its roots in the wastewater and public health issues of the late 19th century. While working at SSE I saw an advertisement for the role of Trustee at CIWEM, and my boss and mentor, Michelle Hynd, fully supported me in applying. It was my first appointment as a non-executive director and offered the opportunity to give something back to developing the organisation that had been a pillar in my career.

When I retired in 2014 I could offer more time to CIWEM. Jim Oatridge, Chair of the Trustee Board, invited me to establish and chair the International Task Group to raise the profile and enhance the reputation of the Institution globally, and thereby grow both its influence on water and environmental management issues and our membership.

It's been an exciting and rewarding experience, from developing the strategy to an engagement with a wide circle of fascinating people across the world. It's taken me as far as New Zealand, to Africa and to several parts of Europe, where we're building bridges of a different sort with our counterpart organisations in the wake of the fateful Brexit referendum.

In 2016 I became the Institution's President, a great honour and the opportunity to help others to develop and hone their professional skills and experience to meet the very challenging demands of the UN's Sustainable Development Goals (SDGs), agreed in September 2015, and set out in 'Transforming the World – the 2030 Agenda for Sustainable Development'.

'Water' has its own SDG, No 6, but of the 16 other SDGs we believe that 13 of them will only be achieved if the interdependencies with water are solved at the same time. All these challenges must be viewed in the context of worldwide climate change.

Travelling abroad during my CIWEM Presidency has given me further opportunity to appreciate the contribution of Scottish engineers across the globe as they sought to conquer the challenges of their day, just as we are facing up to the many challenges of our contemporary world.

In North America, James Laurie prospered, as had his friend James Pugh Kirkwood. Laurie designed the major lattice riveted wrought-iron bridge across the Connecticut River, one of the first of its kind in the USA. He also oversaw construction of the Lyman Viaduct and the Eads Bridge in St Louis, Missouri. His prime legacy, however, is that of founding father and first President, in 1852, of the American Society of Civil Engineers (ASCE). For a Scot to be the first President of one international professional institution is one thing, but to have both global engineering learned societies founded by Scots is quite a testimony to Scottish engineering prowess. A fitting footnote here is to add that Kirkwood succeeded Laurie as the Second President of the ASCE.

One of Europe's most famous bridges, the Szechenyi Lanschid, or Chain Bridge, across the Danube in Budapest was designed by an Englishman, William Tierney Clark, but it was a Scotsman with the same surname, **Adam Clark** (1811-66), who, as Chief Engineer, supervised its construction. Opened in 1849, it was the first permanent bridge across the Danube, linking Buda and Pest and, at 1,230 feet, was considered one of the modern world's engineering wonders.

Today Scottish civil engineers continue to make their mark on bridges across the globe. **Don Fraser** MBE, brought up in Clachnaharry in Inverness and Head Boy at Inverness High School, was involved in the Kessock, Cromarty, Kylesku and Skye bridges in Scotland. Moreover, internationally he contributed professional expertise on the Øresund Bridge (25,738 feet), linking Denmark and Sweden, and was Deputy Director for Lloyds Register team on 250km of bridges and viaducts within the Taiwan High Speed Railway Project, costing £3.6 billion. In 2010 Don was the Senior Technical Advisor for Halcrow on the construction of South Korea's largest infrastructure project, the Busan Geoje Fixed Link, an 8.2km four-lane highway comprising two cable-stayed bridges and the world's deepest immersed road tunnel.

Don's most recent engagement has been on the new Queensferry Crossing, set to continue centuries of spectacular success and innovation in Scottish bridge-building.

Bruce as CIWEM President at the Environment Agency Flood and Coastal Conference at Telford in 2017. *Courtesy of CIWEM*

The Chain Bridge, Budapest. *Deborah M. Keith*

13. QUEENSFERRY CROSSING: THE NEW FORTH BRIDGE

From cantilever to cable-stay

When faced with a few moments of inactivity during a long rail journey, or perhaps reclining, replete, after a fine feast, it can be fun to spend the time organising a fantasy dinner party. You know the kind of thing – invite a dozen guests from history and spend time over the meal listening to them and discussing with them their contributions to times past.

There are many variations on the theme. Perhaps it is great golfers of the past you would invite, or great footballers, or great musicians, or great politicians, or glamorous movie stars, or great humanitarians, or a mixture of them all.

If I were to be inviting great bridge-builders to dinner, some of the celebrated names of the past such as Telford, Arrol, Rennie or Adam would be shoo-ins, but three others who are, as yet, less well known outside the engineering community would surely be guaranteed a seat at the table. How they came to be working together on Scotland's biggest bridge-building project of the present century thus far is part skill, part circumstance and part luck. They might never have ended up in the same office looking out across the Forth but for the relatively rapid deterioration of the vital Forth Road Bridge.

Issues of rusting cables and continual carriageway resurfacing work on the 1964 bridge, coupled with a significant rise in traffic volume, meant that Scotland urgently needed to invest in a new crossing of the Forth, and sooner rather than later. It was calculated that the suspension cables were suffering from an estimated 8-10% loss of strength as a result of corrosion.

The road bridge, which had been designed to carry up to 11 million vehicles per year, and carried 4 million when it opened, was carrying 23 million vehicles by 2006. In February 2007 Scottish ministers decided that the new crossing would be either a bridge or a tunnel, so the cost/benefit analysis of each option began. Tavish Scott, the then Scottish Transport Minister, announced at the time that '…doing nothing is not an option, given the importance of this crossing to the Scottish economy and the people of Fife.' Finance Secretary John Swinney later declared that it would be 'the largest construction project in a generation in Scotland'.

The debate over what form that crossing should take ranged from those promoting a conventional bridge to those wanting a tunnel and those who believed that the opportunity to create a tidal barrage, which would generate energy as well as act as a transport conduit, should not be missed. There was considerable environmental debate, captured and appraised in the Environmental Impact Assessment report, published in November 2009.

Finally, the Forth Crossing Act received Royal Assent in January 2011, and construction began that September.

It wasn't a moment too soon. On 4 December 2015 the Forth Road Bridge was temporarily closed to all traffic because of structural faults. The inevitable traffic chaos that resulted in the especially busy pre-Christmas period saw Transport Scotland lay on extra trains and buses, and even consider reintroducing a ferry service across the river to cope with the pressure.

Following repair work the bridge reopened to cars on 23 December, but not to HGVs until the following March. By now the urgent need for a new bridge was widely appreciated.

Scotland has a strong sense of democracy; witness the first national referendum on independence in September 2014, when 84.6% of those on the Scottish Electoral Roll, including for the first time 16- and 17-year-olds, voted. Likewise with naming important structures, especially a new bridge across the River Forth, it was apt to invite the public to suggest suitable monikers.

From a long list of 7,600 suggested names, a shortlist of five was selected by a panel and the public were invited to choose between Queensferry Crossing; Caledonia Bridge; Firth of Forth Crossing; Saltire Crossing; and St Margaret's Crossing. From 37,000 votes cast, the Queensferry Crossing polled 12,039 votes to emerge as winner. The runner-up was Caledonia Bridge with 10,573 votes. The winning name was announced by then First Minister Alex Salmond on 26 June 2013.

By then my three invited fantasy dinner party guests were fully occupied by creating the iconic structure that now spans the river. Construction Project Director Michael Martin, Senior Designer's Site Representative Don Fraser MBE, and the Commission Director for Jacobs-Arup Joint Venture (JV), Iain Murray, are key figures in the massive scheme and each has strong Scottish roots, Iain being a

Glaswegian and Don a Highlander. Michael, although born in Carlisle to a Scottish father and English mother, describes himself as 'a Borderer by birth and a Highlander by adoption'.

The client on the project was Transport Scotland, The Scottish Government's transport agency. The Client's Advisors were a Jacobs-Arup Joint Venture. Both firms have a keen pedigree in Scottish bridges, as the Baptie Group and Ove Arup respectively, the former acquired by the Jacobs Engineering Group in 2004. The contractor appointed on a competitive tender basis was Forth Crossing Bridge Constructors (FCBC), comprising Hochtief, American Bridge, Dragados and Morrison Construction. FCBC appointed a design joint venture between Ramboll, Leonhardt Andra & Partners and Sweco to carry out the detailed design. As with any such major project, there is much more than just the bridge. The total scheme includes 13 miles of new approach roads and an Intelligent Transport System, a traffic management system built into the M90 and M9 motorways on either side of the bridge, enabling variable speed restrictions and lane closures to be displayed on overhead gantries.

It was at the FCBC offices overlooking the construction site that I met this distinguished trio in February 2017, just a few months before the bridge's planned opening, to discuss their careers and their work on the Queensferry Crossing.

Don Fraser is one of the most respected bridge-builders of his generation, perhaps of many generations. A product of Inverness High School, as outlined in the previous chapter his portfolio now covers some of the most beautiful and most important structures not only in Scotland but also internationally. At the Queensferry Crossing, his main purpose is to help the contractor turn the design into reality.

'FCBC has overall responsibility for the design and construction of the new bridge, while the Design JV is responsible for design. My role is to monitor the work and make sure we are in a position where we can certify that it has been built in accordance with the design. At the end of the day there will be final construction certificates with Michael's name on the top and mine down below.'

He perhaps thought his career might be winding down before the new bridge came along, but once a bridge-builder, always a bridge-builder.

'My wife said to me that there was no way I could ever settle at home knowing that this project was going on a few miles down the road. She was right.'

Ironically, he never intended to spend so much of his life in bridge construction.

'My father was a forester so, as a 16-year-old, I was always going to and from crofts and driving old Fergie tractors to earn a few pounds.

I did think about becoming a vet but heard that it took seven years to qualify so I thought stuff that! I never wanted to be stuck in an office in the city, I always wanted to be outside.'

Don started his career with Baptie Shaw & Morton – now Jacobs – in Glasgow.

'I did some work with the Peterhead Harbour Development and then, in 1974, I joined Crouch & Hogg for the A9 works around Inverness. The way the new road was developed created the need for many new bridges. That year I found myself on the Cromarty causeways and that led to my involvement in the Cromarty Bridge, which, in turn, led me to the Kessock Bridge, in a joint venture with Arup.'

Next, Arup was looking for a Resident Engineer (RE) on the Kylesku Bridge, and it seemed that few wanted to go there because it was 'too far north of Watford'.

'I ended up there as RE. I was a young guy so it was a huge challenge. We moved there as a family for what turned out to be two wonderful years.

Looking back, I did seven Highland bridges, two in Korea, and other mega projects, but the real wow project for me, and the toughest challenge, was Kylesku. We were there, living in the community, registered on the electoral roll, my oldest lassie went to primary school there and we loved it.

Michael and I worked together there as a team, long before modern team-building techniques were fashionable. It just happened naturally because we had the right people on the job with the right approach.

That said, the structure was hugely challenging and I had a lot of sleepless nights. I lost a lot of weight and was totally exhausted afterwards. It ended up as the perfect picture-postcard bridge, though.'

Michael agreed: 'If ever I was ever going to have a nervous breakdown it would have been on Kylesku Bridge,' he says, smiling through the clearly painful memories. 'It was a magnificent project to be involved in – but a hard one, too.'

Michael's own bridge-building pedigree is mightily impressive, despite modest beginnings.

'When I was younger I wasn't particularly academic so I actually left school at 16. My ideal career then would have been teaching PE, woodwork and metalwork, but I was good at maths so I went to a technical college, incidentally one where my mother taught, so I knew all the lecturers.

One was a civil engineer, probably more of a clerk of works actually, but I remember going to his house for dinner with Mum and Dad and there I saw back copies of the New Civil Engineer journal with loads of jobs advertised in fantastic places, such as Africa. So I decided to become a civil engineer and see the world.'

It didn't quite work out that way, however.

'After graduating from Leeds University with a BSc (Hons) in Civil Engineering, I joined Ove Arup as a graduate engineer working in London, but my wife Mary and I soon decided we would emigrate to Canada, as we both hated big cities.

Just then my supervising civil engineer told me I was due to go out on site as part of my career development. He said he could get me on a site out of the city. "How about Inverness?" he asked.'

Michael knew the Highlands well, having spent many a childhood camping holiday there and having worked on a croft at Inverasdale as a 16-year-old, so it was a no-brainer. He went. 'That's where I met Don, working on the Kessock Bridge.'

Two years later, the Martins decided that they really liked Inverness, so decided to settle there. He took a job with a then small, but ambitious, company called Morrison Construction.

'Morrison were only working in the Highlands at that time so I did some jobs at Invershin, Aviemore and Grantown-on-Spey. At that time they were good at building roads but less strong at building structures, which is why they recruited me, because I came from a design background.'

Morrison bid for the Kylesku Bridge contract despite never having previously built a bridge other than one that you could spit over. They won it.

'It was a massive leap for Morrison, almost one too far, but we got there. One of the reasons we did was relationships. I knew Don extremely well as Resident Engineer, I was Chief Engineer and Ove Arup & Partners was the designer, so in spite of all of the difficulties we worked really well together.'

Morrison then grew rapidly and Michael went on to become the company's Chief Engineer and Engineering Director.

'We did Dornoch Bridge as a design and construct project where Don was RE and I was Chief Engineer. Sadly, we didn't win the Skye Bridge contract, despite spending a year bidding for it.'

Don chipped in: 'They proposed a cable-stay bridge, which I think would have been much more elegant than the solution eventually adopted.' All in the room sagely nodded their agreement.

Michael joined the main board of Morrison, by then a publically listed company, but a couple of years afterwards the business was sold.

'It was a difficult time. I worked on with Anglian Water Group (AWG) for five years and eventually had to move south to England. Then they decided to sell their non-core businesses.

At the time I was 53, financially secure, and had always kept the house in Inverness. My boys, who had been taught at Inverness Royal Academy, were now through university and Mary, who had run a very successful pre-school nursery, had moved south with me. The pull of the Highlands was strong so, in 2005, I decided to retire back to Inverness and get out the golf clubs and the salmon rods.'

His planned retirement didn't last long, though. Less than a year later, and after a short spell giving project management advice to Atkins, one of the UK's largest engineering consultancies, Michael was asked to become Chief Operating Officer at Scottish Water Solutions, the biggest public/private partnership in Scotland with a massive £2.4 billion programme of investment works in the pipeline.

After six successful years there, he finally decided to retire for good. But he'd barely fixed the reels to the salmon rods once more when his best-laid plans were again shelved.

'Many of my former Morrison colleagues were by then working with new parent company Galliford Try, and when they were successful bidding for work on the new Forth Replacement Crossing, I was asked if I would be prepared to represent them on the Joint Venture's Supervisory Board. I was delighted to accept.

I couldn't say no. To be asked as a retired person in my 60s seemed an ideal opportunity to be associated with a unique project without actually carrying the burden of being responsible for it.'

Michael sat on the Supervisory Board for 18 months before the then Project Director moved on to another post overseas.

'It was immediately clear I was going to be asked to take over. It was a difficult decision, but it was eased by the fact that there was something special about this job and there were so many people that I knew here.

I knew that I would probably wake up every morning for the next few years regretting that I had agreed to do it, but I also knew that I would regret it for the rest of my life if I didn't do it.'

By this time Iain Murray was already well into his demanding role as Commission Director for the Jacobs-Arup Joint Venture. Joining the project in 2010, his role was to develop, from the initial work that had been done, all the route selection, promote it through the parliamentary bill, prepare all the tender documentation, run the tender process in conjunction with the client, and from then on work with the client on site as part of an integrated Employers' Delivery Team to deliver the project. 'In simple terms, we have to ensure that the client gets what they asked for,' he says.

Iain, too, has an impressive CV for his current role. His father was an electrical engineer who worked mainly on hydro-electric schemes.

'When I was eight we moved to Tongland, near Kirkcudbright, where Dad worked at the power station there. Subconsciously, that probably kindled my interest in engineering.'

Iain graduated from Paisley College of Technology, now the University of West Scotland, in 1986 and joined Baptie Shaw & Morton, with whom he had worked on the Gatehouse bypass in the summers of 1984 and '85. His first job was on the Dunblane bypass, then he worked on part of the new A90 dual carriageway near Stonehaven. Next he was appointed Deputy Project Manager on the new M74 section from Kirkpatrick

Fleming to Gretna. 'I can still remember the tender price for that job. It was £34,567,890,' he says, relishing an engineer's love of detail.

A spell at the then National Roads Directorate, part of The Scottish Office, saw him looking after junctions on the A90 Perth-Dundee road, including Longforgan and Inchmichael, and others between Aberdeen and Stonehaven.

A number of major public/private partnership (PPP) road projects followed, including the Waterford bypass in Ireland, the A92 Dundee-Arbroath dualling, the M74 extension, which included Port Eglinton viaduct, and the Clackmannanshire Bridge.

Jacobs-Arup initially started work on the Forth Replacement Crossing project in 2008. What does Iain see as the major challenges he has faced?

'Probably the foundations of the towers. The construction solution using caissons was a good one but had considerable uncertainty as they had to be sunk to the rock some 40 metres down and you are never sure what you will find when excavating, or how many boulders you will hit.

The Forth Bridge used a similar solution, but back then in the 1890s they had men inside the caissons digging down. We never put anyone in our caissons apart from divers carrying out regular checks. The whole way it was done was excellent.'

As the job progressed, other challenges began to increase.

'There was a period in the early days when construction teams in the various separate parts of the project were able to work pretty much in isolation, such as on the foundations or approach viaducts, so the networks were working away on their own. As we approached the end, however, all the disciplines had to come together. The logistics now of figuring out what you can do, and when, are massive.

The weather plays a big part for the contractor as some works are impacted by temperature and others by wind. Sometimes schedules have to be worked out on a daily basis. Wind speed has been the biggest challenge as it limits when the high tower cranes can operate.

Like an orchestra, everyone starts rehearsing in separate rooms but then gradually all must come together to perform the finished work together.'

Everyone did come together, and now the bridge is complete. The Queensferry Crossing was opened on 30 August 2017 and, despite some

Left Queensferry Crossing: the final piece of the jigsaw. *Forth Crossing Bridge Constructors, David Watt*

Right The view from the tower. *Forth Crossing Bridge Constructors, David Watt*

terrible weather during construction, it was finished largely on time and below budget.

Marking the official opening by Her Majesty the Queen on 4 September, exactly 53 years since she opened the Forth Road Bridge, Nicola Sturgeon said, 'The Queensferry Crossing is a symbol of a confident, forward-looking Scotland and – as well as providing a vital transport connection for many years to come – it is a truly iconic structure and a feat of modern engineering.' The Chief Executive of Visit Scotland, Malcolm Roughead, commented that, 'At this unique moment, the country will become the world's first destination to have three bridges spanning three centuries in one stunning location… People are fascinated worldwide by bridges, whether it's for their beauty, grandeur or breathtaking engineering prowess. The addition of the Queensferry Crossing consolidates the Forth Bridges as global icons of Scotland and we look forward to showcasing all three awe-inspiring structures to the world for many years to come.'

As with its siblings the Forth Rail Bridge and the Forth Road Bridge, it is immediately in the record books. It is the longest three-tower cable-stayed bridge in the world and, by some considerable margin, the largest to feature cables that cross mid-span. The 30,000 tonnes of steel and approximately 150,000 cubic metres of concrete provide a bridge 2,700 metres long. The towers – at up to 210.6 metres – are the tallest of any bridge in the UK. In 2016 the cantilevers on either side of the central tower were recognised by Guinness World Records as the longest pair of

free-standing balanced cantilevers ever built anywhere in the world. And the South Tower foundation caisson saw the biggest, continuous, underwater concrete pour ever carried out.

The central tower rests on Beamer Rock, an islet in the Forth, something of which Don Fraser approves.

'I think the three-tower concept is absolutely right for this site and the Beamer Rock in the middle was just asking for a central tower.

To be honest, though, I never dreamt another bridge across the Forth would actually happen.

I went to Heriot-Watt University and our structures lecturer there was a former Royal Engineers Colonel who had been seconded to the contractor for the foundations of the Forth Road Bridge. I remember being so impressed by his lectures on it that I thought it would be great to get involved in something like that. Never thought I actually would.'

The new bridge certainly is an impressive structure, and beautiful. How did the team manage to balance elegance with economy? Don explains:

'In the design and construct system, the method of procurement is that the contractor appoints the designer, they talk together and decide what design to go forward with. This can lead to some bridges looking a bit utilitarian. I think Kessock is like that.

On the Queensferry Crossing, however, Transport Scotland appointed Jacobs-Arup as their advisors and they decided the external shape of the crossing and came up with what they wanted. They took that scheme through all the approval process and then went out to tender, so the finished job has to look like what the client envisaged. The detailed design is what we do but the overall appearance was set beforehand.

It was the same with Øresund and with Stonecutter's in Hong Kong – you not only get a great bridge using this approach but you get something beautiful to look at, too. An iconic structure showcasing 21st-century civil engineering at its best.

It really complements the railway bridge. I now live in Dunfermline, just a couple of miles from the bridge, and what we hear locally is that everyone says what a wonderful bridge it is.'

The new bridge's 'wow factor' was not always immediately apparent to those who have suffered the agonies of building it, however. Don adds:

'I was out on the bridge this morning. Instead of wondering about the wow factor, all I remember was that it was bloody cold and there's a lot of work to do. A case of being too close to the concrete to see the bridge! The wow factor will doubtless come with time.'

Iain Murray:

'I think you can still have something of a wow factor, but when you are involved day-to-day you don't appreciate the progress you are making.

We are all conscious that we are working in an area where you have a 19th-, a 20th- and a 21st-century bridge. If there is anything that was iconic, it's that there have been generations before us doing exactly the same thing. Everyone appreciates they are working on a once-in-a-generation project.'

Inevitably, the finished product and the passage of time will hide many of the massive challenges involved in building it. Michael:

'Ultimately, the building of the bridge will be forgotten. It will become a world famous bridge, so eventually the challenges of its construction will be history and it will speak for itself. And everyone involved in its construction will be proud of what we have achieved together.

But on a day-to-day basis, it is an exceptionally difficult project. It was very competitively bid, it is a joint venture of four companies, not only of four different nationalities but they have never worked together previously. In order to build it, we have had to bring people from all over the world. Although my background is technical, as Project Director it is really all about managing the people.

There is a particular skill to managing a joint venture. You have to be a politician and find a way of making all your partners feel you are appropriately representing their interests, while at the same time doing what you think is right, which actually might not be what they think is in their interests.'

Don agrees:

'We are in an international joint venture. We are very aware of the daily pressures we face but my colleagues in Southampton, Stuttgart or Copenhagen are all working on other projects now so it can be challenging to get immediate answers to problems.'

Michael adds:

'People are a lot harder than engineering, because they are emotional. Things are not black and white.

Being publically funded, this job is politically sensitive, which can be an unwelcome additional burden. I appreciate political sensitivities, but this is a construction project being carried out on the boundaries of technology and in an extremely exposed location. Certainties that politicians would like to have are not necessarily certainties that I can deliver.

These days, the media tend to focus on the negative story when, with regards to this project, the focus should be on the fantastic achievement of successfully constructing this unique and ground-breaking bridge in an incredibly short period from inception to completion and in very hostile weather conditions.'

Suddenly there is a sense of indignation in the room that the many impressive engineering achievements and incredible technical challenges of the project have often been trivialised into political soundbites or cheap newspaper headlines. Clearly, these men really care passionately about what they are doing. But ever the professionals, they swiftly move on. Michael continues:

'When I took over, I knew I was going to be responsible for a workforce of up to 1,500 people on a major bridge project. It is hard to put into words how much of a responsibility that is.'

Of the more than 10,000 people employed by the project over the lifespan of the construction programme, more than 75% had a home address in Scotland. Despite the most rigorous health and safety regime in place, one was killed during construction. Michael describes the feeling:

'One of my biggest regrets is that one man was killed on our watch, even though it was nothing directly to do with building the bridge. It could have happened in any workshop anywhere. I feel an enormous sense of frustration that I can't turn the clock back.'

Iain adds:

'There were a number of fatalities building the other two bridges, so our mission at the start was to build it without any fatalities. We set out to work under a banner of "Bridging the Forth Safely" and we wanted everyone to come to work and go home again safe.

Sadly we are not going to achieve that. The biggest disappointment of the project was that day. It has left its mark on everybody involved in the project.'

So, as they approach the finishing line, is this characteristically modest trio of distinguished engineers aware of their starring role in the historical pantheon of Scottish bridge-building?

'I believe you have to do your best at all times,' says Don. 'People in the future might well associate us with these bridges but I don't really think about it.'

Michael, too, is pragmatic about his place in history:

'You are not thinking about that when you take on the role, but you are aware of the enormity of the job in hand. You know that when this bridge is finished, it will sit alongside a World Heritage bridge and will become part of a bigger World Heritage Site.

When the pain has gone, it will all be worth the three years of high pressure for me. I can still clearly remember the enormous sense of relief that I felt when I drove away from Kylesku after that job was done. It was like an enormous burden being lifted. I am sure I will feel the same here at the Queensferry Crossing.

A bridge when finished is an entity, but it is actually a combination of millions of individual operations, large and small, all put together by human hands. They have to come together in a very precise sequence over many years and the complexity of that is hard to explain to someone who isn't directly involved.'

My final question was to ask the trio what they would like people to think when they look at the new bridge. There was a long silent pause before Iain Murray hit the nail on the head.

'It is a feat of engineering,' he said. And he's completely correct.

It was a privilege to speak with Michael, Don and Iain, worthy successors to those who have gone before, and fine examples to those who will follow them

But there was another product of the construction project that few would have anticipated. While preparing for the new structure, archaeologists working on the south bank of the Forth unearthed an oval-shaped pit, some 23 feet long, which is estimated to date from the Mesolithic era, 8240BC, making it the oldest known dwelling house in Scotland, and by some margin. The Neolithic village of Skara Brae on Mainland Orkney dates from 3180BC. Stonehenge and the Great Pyramids of Egypt are modern developments by comparison!

That seems a fitting way to bring to an end my journey through Scotland's bridge heritage. In celebrating the opening of a truly magnificent structure in the new Queensferry Crossing, we find, as throughout our travels, that our appreciation of bridges opens many more horizons on the stories woven into Scotland's uniquely rich and dramatic economic, military, social and cultural history.

We'll never know if those Mesolithic people on the banks of what was then a very different and much larger River Forth looked across at land on the other side and considered it another world altogether. If they came back today, they would likely step back in frightened amazement at the three wonderful bridges built near their simple dwellings.

But no doubt they would have had dreams and ambitions, too, and progressively, over millennia, human imaginings of ever greater crossings would gradually become reality.

I wonder if our descendants will look back at the great bridges of today and wonder how we did it with what to us are cutting-edge technologies but what to them will seem to be primitive techniques?

History proves that bridge engineering never stands still. Nor have I. My journey from childhood on the shores of Loch Ness across almost every mile of this great country, and many places abroad, is far from over.

I still have many more bridges to cross.

14. CHALLENGES CONTINUE
From early days to new beginnings

As this particular part of my personal journey through history, celebrating Scotland's bridge heritage, draws to a close, I am once again taken back to those early days as a youngster on the shores of Loch Ness and those epic journeys accompanying my Dad on his various sojourns on bridge inspections across the Highlands and Islands.

I could never have then imagined the enormous impact such outings would have on my personal and professional life. It is probably true to say that those pioneering and innovative bridge-builders of our past could equally never have imagined the scale of the legacy they were creating, not only in terms of transport improvements but also in the wider context of landscape form and function.

My career has been varied, in both public and private sectors, and on both sides of the border, but it has always been fulfilling, fascinating and fun. In addition to my day-to-day jobs, I have taken a great interest in my two professional bodies. Involvement in both the environment and rural faculties in the RICS, while I was at English Nature, provided helpful networking opportunities, and I became Chair of the Rural Faculty in 2001.

I also became involved with CIWEM, particularly on the amenity, recreation and conservation panel, which was another useful opportunity to network with a wider fraternity of specialists, but with a shared believe in the relatively new concept of sustainable development.

I have actually been an active member of both those professional institutions for many years. I started by joining the Dundee and Angus Branch of the RICS's Scottish Junior Branch in 1977. The first event I organised was a car treasure hunt – that's what people did for a 'social programme' in those days! It took me several weekends to organise as I had to think up all the clues too. On reflection, it was too involved.

It started easily enough in Dundee's South Tay Street and was intended to conclude with a stovie supper in a Blairgowrie hotel, but it meandered round Arbroath, Forfar and Kirriemuir en route, which, to say the least, took several hours. 'Over-ambitious' was how the Branch Chairman described the event, expressing surprise that a young surveyor would not better appreciate distance and time, and their

relationship. He did, however, also remark that nine out of the ten cars had successfully completed the course, if not answered all the questions.

After nearly 40 years, the couple in the tenth car, a Ford Capri, remain unaccounted for. The Chairman was kind enough to tell me afterwards that he didn't think they had been particularly interested in the car treasure hunt anyway and might well have been sidelined to some other activity while driving round the back roads of Angus. Perhaps they were bridge enthusiasts, too, seeking sight of the simple or spectacular, although on reflection it is somewhat more likely that their passions were of a more common nature than for the voussoirs, spandrels, arches and spans of our incomparably rich bridge heritage.

My wife Deborah and I always seek out a bridge when we're on our travels. In 2005 we walked across the arch of the Sydney Harbour Bridge – 'The Coathanger' – just as the sun set over the city, the opera house and the harbour. In Budapest we walked across the Chain Bridge. In North Vancouver we crossed the Capilano Suspension Bridge.

All these bridges have strong Scottish connections, as related in this book. I have failed to find a Scottish connection with another of our 'trophies', the Brooklyn Bridge, linking Manhattan and Brooklyn, but I am sure that there is almost certain to have been a New Yorker of Scottish descent engaged in its design or construction.

Crossing the iconic Forth Rail Bridge on a mild May morning, heading to Edinburgh, my spine still tingles at the unfailingly impressive sight of the three Forth crossings so close together. There is no evidence today, as the sun bathes the river in a benign morning glow, of the storm-lashed waters of the Forth that put the fear of God into early travellers and similar apprehension into those who faced the nauseous crossing by small boat. Nowadays we have confidence that when the storms return and the gales vent their fury on these shores once again, the bridges will remain, defiant and magnificent, to do their job properly.

Perhaps the highly stressed and overworked commuters flooding to and from Edinburgh each day have other things on their minds, but it would do no harm for them to reflect on the native Scots talent that allowed them to make their journey in the first place.

It is easy to forget today the scale of the challenge that Scottish bridge-builders faced, not only here but across the globe, to create structures of all shapes, styles and sizes that have stood the test of time and continue to serve splendidly their original purpose. That so many men and women of extraordinary skill and vision achieved so much from the crucible of so small a country is indeed a remarkable story.

We can learn important lessons from looking at the successes of the past. As this book relates, the great Scottish bridge engineers made an enormous contribution to solving the population, urbanisation, transport and communication issues that faced our world in the Industrial Revolution, and since. What a legacy! They did it through ingenuity, endeavour and innovation, and these same traits are as relevant now as then if we are to create a positive outcome. Today, more than ever, we desperately need our Telfords, Adams, Rennies and Arrols, and a host of equally creative talent with their innovative approaches to problem-solving.

We do still have it in bridge-building. The new Queensferry Crossing, as seen from the window of my ScotRail train gliding smoothly southwards across an earlier worldwide icon, is testimony to that.

My inherent and lifelong positivity gives me the confidence to believe that Mankind has it within its power to rise to the challenges and to make that essential difference, before it really is too late.

GLOSSARY

Abutment — The structure supporting a bridge at either end and resisting the horizontal forces.

Bascule — A counter-balancing mechanism where the deck rotates about a pivot to allow the bridge to open.

Box girder — A hollow beam.

Cable-stay — One of a number of independent high-tensile wires extending from the tower to support the bridge deck.

Cantilever — A projecting beam supported at one end only.

Caisson / cofferdam — A pressurised watertight and airtight chamber used in the construction of bridge foundations beneath water level.

Centring — The temporary wooden framework used to construct an arch, holding it up until it is self-supporting.

Crown — The uppermost point of an arch.

Cutwater — Additional masonry in a 'V' shape to protect or strengthen the lower part of the piers of a bridge by dividing the flow of water. Where the cutwater is a different shape it is referred to as a starling.

Keystone — The uppermost stone of an arch, which holds the voussoirs in place.

Obelisk — A square ornamental pillar tapering towards the top and ending in a pyramid.

Pier — The supporting structure between two or more arches or girders.

Pile — A long vertical section of concrete embedded in the ground as part of the foundations.

Pylon — A tower between which the chains or cables of a suspension bridge are slung.

Rib — A ridge of stonework projecting from the soffit of a bridge to strengthen it.

Segmental arch — A shallow type of arch formed by an arc of less than a semi-circle.

Skew — A bridge constructed so as to cross the river or road at an oblique angle, favoured by railway bridge engineers to avoid changing the direction of the railway line.

Soffit — The underside of an arch or beam.

Span — The distance between the supports of an arch or beam.

Spandrel — The triangular space between the springing and the crown of an arch.

Springing — The point at which an arch begins to curve upwards from its supports.

Truss — A beam consisting of a series of triangular sections that transmit the forces/loads.

Voussoirs — The wedge-shaped stones making up an arch.

BIBLIOGRAPHY

A Heritage of Bridges between Edinburgh, Kelso and Berwick (R. A. Paxton and E. Ruddock)

A History of Modern Scotland (Neil Oliver)

A History of the Scottish People (W. W. Knox)

A Span of Bridges (H. J. Hopkins)

An Encyclopaedia of Britain's Bridges (David McFetrich)

Arch Bridges and their Builders 1735-1835 (Ted Ruddock)

Batsford's Glasgow, Then and Now (Carol Foreman)

Biographical Dictionary of Civil Engineers in Great Britain and Ireland, Volume 1: 1500-1830, Volume 2: 1830-1890 (ICE)

Bridge – The Architecture of Connection (Lucy Blakstad)

Bridges – Heroic designs which changed the world (Dan Cruickshank)

Bridges – The science and art of the world's most inspiring structures (David Blockley)

Bridges of Britain (Eric de Mare)

Bridges of Glasgow (T. Kenneth Aitken)

Bridges – Three Thousand Years of Defying Nature (David J. Brown)

Cabrach Feerings (the late James Taylor JP, edited by Janet Anderson; Banff: The Banffshire Journal Limited, 1920)

Civil Engineering Heritage (2 Volumes) (Roland Paxton and James S. Shipway)

Echoes from the Border Hills (J. P. Hyslop)

Glasgow from the Air: 75 years of Aerial Photography (Carol Foreman with the RCAHMS)

High Peaks Engineering (Rocky Mountain Marvels) (L. D. Cross)

Highland Bridges (Gillian Nelson)

'Highland Road Bridges' (Paper to the Institute of Highway Engineers, J. Forbes Keith; Inverness, 1958)

History of Suspension Bridges (A. A. Jakkula, 1941)

How to Read Bridges (Edward Denison and Ian Stewart)

I Never Knew that about Scotland (Christopher Winn)

Journeying with Railways in New Zealand (Roy Sinclair, 1997)

Kessock Bridge – 20th Anniversary

Life in the Atholl Glens (John Kerr)

Lives of the Engineers (Samuel Smiles)

'Military Roads and Fortifications in the Highlands, with Bridges and Milestones' (Paper by Thomas Wallace to the Society of Antiquaries of Scotland, 1910/11)

New Ways through the Glens – Highland Road, Bridge and Canal Makers of the early 19th Century (A. R. B. Haldane)

On Tour with Thomas Telford (Chris Morris)

Rails Across New Zealand (Matthew Wright, 1962)

Scottish Life and Society, Volume 8: Transport and Communication (Ed Kenneth Veitch)

'The Ancient Bridges of Scotland' and 'Roads and Bridges in the Early History of Scotland' (Papers by Harry R. G. Inglis to the Society of Antiquaries of Scotland, 1911/12; National Museum of Scotland)

'The Architecture of Robert Adam – South Bridge' (Essay by Julian Small)

The Brig of Ayr and Something of its Story (James A. Morris)

The Conservation of Early Iron Suspension Bridges in Scotland: A Survey of Problems and Practice (P. A. Verity)

The Drove Roads of Scotland (A. R. B. Haldane)

The Evolution of Bridge Building in Scotland to 1900 (R. A. Paxton)

The Forth Bridge – A Pictorial History (Sheila Mackay)

The Forth Rail Bridge (Douglas G. McBeth)

The Forth Road Bridge – The Official Story (Forth Road Bridge Joint Board)

The Happy Pontist (website)

The High Girders (John Prebble)

The Highland Railway (H. A. Vallance)

The Military Roads in Scotland (William Taylor)

The National Trust Book of Bridges (J. M. Richards)

The River Clyde from the Source to the Sea (Keith Fergus and Ian R. Mitchell)

The Scottish Office, National Roads Directorate: 'Landscape Design and Management Policy' (Report by Professor Andy MacMillan, Emeritus Professor of Architecture at Glasgow University/Glasgow College of Art, November 1997)

The Sir William Arrol Collection (RCAHMS)

The Tay Bridge Disaster (John Perkins)

The West Highland Railway and its Viaducts and Bridges (M. Harris)

Thomas Telford (Rhoda M. Pearce)

Two Railway Bridges of an Era (Arnold Koerte)

Understanding the World's Greatest Structures (Stephen Ressler)

INDEX